Spices, Salt and Aromatics in the English Kitchen

Elizabeth David, whose cookery books have inspired and influenced a whole generation, developed a taste for good food and wine when she lived with a French family while studying French history and literature in Paris at the Sorbonne. A few years after her return to England, Mrs David made up her mind to teach herself to cook, in order to reproduce for herself and her friends some of the delicious food she had learned to appreciate in France. She found not only the practical side but also the literature of cookery of absorbing interest and has been studying it ever since. Mrs David has lived and kept house in France, Italy, Greece, Egypt and India, learning the local dishes and cooking them in her own kitchens. Her first book, *Mediterranean Food*, appeared in 1950. In 1951 she published *French Country Cooking* and in 1954, after a year of research in Italy, *Italian Food*, which became a Book Society recommendation. *Summer Cooking* was published in 1955 and *French Provincial Cooking* in 1960. In 1970 came *Spices, Salt and Aromatics in the English Kitchen*. *An Omelette and a Glass of Wine*, published in 1984, is a selection of her journalistic work originally written for a wide range of publications.

In 1973 Mrs David severed all connection with the business trading under her name. After this she concentrated on study and experiment for *English Bread and Yeast Cookery*, for which she won the 1977 Glenfiddich Writer of the Year Award. In 1976 she was awarded the O.B.E. and in 1977 was made a Chevalier du Mérite Agricole. In 1979 she was made an honorary doctor of the University of Essex and in 1982 she was elected Fellow of the Royal Society of Literature. Elizabeth David was awarded the C.B.E. in the New Years's Honours List of 1986.

Food writers and journalists frequently cite Elizabeth David as the person who did most to improve the quality of domestic life in the depressed post-war years. The *Sunday Times* has said 'Elizabeth David must have done more than anyone for British home cooking in the past twenty-five years', and Geoffrey Wheatcroft has called her 'the Englishwoman who has done most and best for this country in the last generation'. On the publication of *French Provincial Cooking*, *Queen* wrote 'this book will add a new depth of authority to your knowledge'.

ELIZABETH DAVID

Spices, Salt and Aromatics in the English Kitchen

***

PENGUIN BOOKS

For Renée

PENGUIN BOOKS

Published by the Penguin Group
Penguin Books Ltd, 27 Wrights Lane, London w8 5tz, England
Viking Penguin, a division of Penguin Books USA Inc.
375 Hudson Street, New York, New York 10014, USA
Penguin Books Australia Ltd, Ringwood, Victoria, Australia
Penguin Books Canada Ltd, 2801 John Street, Markham, Ontario, Canada l3r 1b4
Penguin Books (NZ) Ltd, 182–190 Wairau Road, Auckland 10, New Zealand

Penguin Books Ltd, Registered Offices: Harmondsworth, Middlesex, England

First published 1970
Reprinted 1971
Reprinted with revisions 1973, 1975
9 10 8

Copyright © Elizabeth David, 1970
All rights reserved

Printed in England by Clays Ltd, St Ives plc
Set in Monotype Poliphilus

* *

Contents

Contents

* *

Preface

FOR some two thousand years, English cookery has been extremely spice-conscious, not surprisingly to anyone in the least familiar with the history of the spice trade in Europe and the part played in it, successively, by the Phoenicians, the Romans, the Arab conquerors of Spain, the Norman crusaders, the merchants of Venice and Genoa, the religious orders which fostered the arts of healing, medicine and distillery, the Portuguese explorers who opened the sea route to the Indies, the Dutch empire-builders who wrested the spice trade from Portugal, the British East India Company whose merchants in their turn made London for two centuries the greatest spice mart in the world.

It is often believed that the lavish use of spices in old English cooking can be explained by the necessity to mask half-decayed food and to give zest to a monotonous diet of salt meat and boiled fish. To some extent, these deductions are no doubt correct. Surely, though, there are other reasons, one of them being quite simply that the English have a natural taste for highly seasoned food – as do most northern people – and since trade with the Near East and southern Europe brought us early in the evolution of our cookery considerable opportunities for indulging the taste, we took to spiced food with an enthusiasm which seems to have been almost equal to that shown by the Romans at the height of their preoccupation with the luxuries of living. A study of English recipes of the fifteenth century leaves one with the impression that to the cook the spices were a good deal more important than the food itself. One or two published manuscripts* of the period do, it is true, instruct that certain game birds – notably pheasant, quail, teal, plover, woodcock and snipe – should be served with 'no sauce but salt'. Boiled flounders and one or two other fish are given the same exemption from the spicing of ginger, pepper, mace, cloves, cinnamon and galingale† specified for ninety per cent of the meat and fish dishes. Those recipes calling for fewer spices make up for the lack in mustard and vinegar, herbs and wine and ale.

---

* *Two Fifteenth-century Cookery Books*, published by the Early English Text Society. (Bibliographical details on page 249.)

† A root or rhizome of the ginger family.

Dried fruits, such as dates, figs, raisins and currants, were imported from Greece, the Levant and Spain. Together with quantities of almonds and pine nuts – commonly used at that time – the dried fruits were freely mixed with meat and fish stews, pies and pasties. Vegetable colouring from herbs, roots and flowers – saffron was the most highly prized – were other auxiliary ingredients of much importance. Pomegranates were evidently familiar in European and English cooking in the fifteenth and sixteenth centuries, for the seeds were used for decoration – 'florsche it about with pomegarnett seeds' is a recurring instruction in these recipes. One late-sixteenth-century author, Sir Hugh Plat, describes a method of keeping 'pomgranats fresh til Whitsundtide'.

Cookery books and manuscripts should not, however, be taken as representing the whole picture of what any given people were eating at the period they were written. They are simply indications of the general character of the food and of the ingredients available to those who could afford them. It seems unlikely that dishes so extravagantly spiced, sweetened and coloured were eaten very often, even by those rich enough to buy such luxuries, for luxuries they were, and it has to be borne in mind that until the late-seventeenth century, recorded recipes, in England as elsewhere in Europe, were predominantly those of the royal households, of the nobility, the great land-owning barons, the princes of the Church, and the prosperous merchants whose prestige demanded a visible parade of wealth as much upon their tables as in the matter of personal adornment. In Europe, spices were the jewels and furs and brocades of the kitchen and the still-room. Medicine and pharmacy also were dependent upon tinctures and oils and elixirs extracted from roots and leaves, herb and spice plants, and their fruit and seeds. Pepper and cloves and juniper branches were burned to sweeten the air in the houses of the rich, lavender and rosemary were strewn on the floors, potent honey-based drinks such as mead, hydromel and metheglin were heavily spiced and scented with musk, ambergris, roses, violet leaves, marjoram, honeysuckle, cinnamon, ginger and sweet briar. It seems not to have occurred to anybody at this time that so many aromatics and flavourings ended in cancelling each other out.

It was mainly from the far Orient, overland via Arabia and the Red Sea, Egypt, and the ports of Venice and Genoa that spices reached England. Venetian merchants, strategically situated midway between the Levant and Western Europe, became the great middlemen of the spice trade. They sent their cargoes to Flanders and the Low Countries and to

England in galleys which, until the end of the fifteenth century, were a common sight in the ports of Southampton and Rochester.

Alas for Venice. The virtual monopoly of the European spice trade which had made the Serene Republic rich – who knows which palaces, now crumbling to their ruin on the Grand Canal, were indirectly subsidized by the spice-hungry English – was doomed. One day in May 1498 the Portuguese explorer Vasco da Gama anchored his ship off the port of Calcutta. The sea route to the Indies was discovered at last. Three months later da Gama set off on his return voyage to Lisbon, bearing news that the ruler of Calicut was prepared to barter cinnamon and cloves, ginger and pepper, in exchange for gold and silver and, curiously, scarlet cloth. No longer would Europe be dependent upon the compli-cated overland route from the East, no longer would the Arab traders, the Sultans of Egypt, the port officials of Alexandria, the dealers of Venice, be in a position to exact their heavy tolls and set their own price on the luxuries they had made necessary to European life.

Thirty years after Vasco da Gama's discovery of the sea route to India, although the galleys of Venice were still to be seen in English ports, their cargoes were no longer spices but 'glass and other things of no value'. The European spice trade had passed into the hands of the Portuguese, who held on to it – with difficulty – for a century, only to lose it to the Dutch, whose trade with Java and the Spice Islands, as the Moluccas came to be known, led to the formation in 1602 of the powerful Dutch East India Company. By the sixteen-eighties the Dutch had established almost total monopoly of the highly profitable trade in cloves and nutmegs, while the Portuguese retained a corner in the cinnamon business.

At this period, English cooking was still heavy with ginger and pepper, cinnamon, cloves, nutmeg and sugar. The food of Italy and Portugal, Flanders, France, Holland and Germany was similarly spiced and scented. It was not until towards the middle of the seventeenth century, when the British East India Company, originally formed by the mer-chants of London in 1600, had become a power to reckon with, that English cooking began to develop along lines which we can recognize today. Spices and sugar were more readily available and became rela-tively cheap, were therefore less prized and used with more discretion. More varieties of vegetables and fruit were grown, the urge to disguise every piece of fish, flesh or fowl as something else seems to have abated, at least temporarily, although spices were still very much used – as they are today – in the puddings, cakes, pickles and wines made in the houses of the gentry. Spiced drinks were a fashionable fad as well as remedies for all

minor ailments. Recipes for caudles and possets –the ancestors of milk
punches and egg nogs – spiced ale and cordials abound in the cookery
books of the period. The later Restoration playwrights found good copy
in this harmless mania. In *The Way of the World* (1700) Congreve takes
a dig at 'all auxiliaries to the tea-table, as orange brandy, all aniseed,
cinnamon, citron, and Barbadoes water';* Farquhar in *The Beaux
Stratagem* (1707) puts into the mouth of an innkeeper an envious description of a huge silver tankard 'near upon as big as me; it was a present to
the Squire from his Godmother and smells of nutmeg and toast like an
East India ship'. Congreve again, in *Love for Love* (1695) makes an
early mention† of the pocket nutmeg graters which became such a beautiful and practical fashion of eighteenth-century England; and the elegant
silver cinnamon casters or muffineers of the Georgian period were
another by-product of the fashion for sprinkling spices on food and into
drinks.

Those who could not afford spices, or did not like them, flavoured
their warming drinks with garden herbs, in the manner described by
Robert May‡ in a recipe for a Posset of Herbs: 'Take a fair scowred
skillet, put in some milk into it, and some rosemary, the rosemary being
well boiled in it, take it out and have some ale or beer in a pot, put it to the
milk and sugar. Thus of tyme, carduus,§ cammomile, mint, or marigold
flowers.'

From this period too stems the English interest in the Indian chutneys
and pickles brought home by the East India merchants. Housewives
made valiant attempts to copy these exotic products; in country-house
kitchens and still-rooms, cucumbers and melons were pickled to taste
like mangoes; elder shoots preserved in spiced vinegar were alleged to
taste like bamboo; recipes for lemon pickle hotted up with horseradish
and mustard flour, and for 'Indian pickle' of vegetables – the forerunners
of today's piccalilli – occur in most of the later eighteenth-century
cookery books. Evidence of the growing interest in these pickles is to be
found in the frequent copies or slightly modified versions of published
recipes which occur in the Ms receipt books of the period. Such fantasies
however were still known only to the privileged classes. To the poor, even
a jar of humble pickled onions or red cabbage would have been an

---

* A spirit-based cordial spiced with cloves and the zest of oranges and lemons.
† Quoted on page 247.
‡ *The Accomplisht Cook*, first published 1660, 5th edition 1685.
§ Probably *carduus benedictus*, the blessed thistle. An infusion of the leaves was
considered a remedy for colds and fevers.

occasional luxury. Farm and factory labourers, artisans and clerical workers, still lived on a very restricted diet; even had they had the where-withal to buy spices and large quantities of sugar and vinegar, their cooking facilities were so primitive and their equipment so scanty that only the most basic forms of cookery could be attempted. Fuel was expensive and could not be wasted on the lengthy processes involved in pickling and preserving.

Following the pickle and chutney implant into English cookery, and simultaneously with the establishment of curry dishes* as a part of our national cookery, came the relishes, the ketchups and sauces which were the forerunners of the bottled sauces of today. They too came to us via the East India Company and its traders, and like so many eighteenth- and nineteenth-century foods owe their development to the need for products which would stand up to long sea voyages and help to relieve the mono-tony of the food available both to the crews of ships and their passengers. The old 'store sauces' based on vinegar and horse-radish, soy and garlic, on pickled walnuts, oysters, cockles, mushrooms, lemons, anchovies, and onions gradually became known either as catsups† or by the name of some individual who was thought to have originated a particular blend. By the mid nineteenth century, hundreds of British families must have had their own – or what they thought was their own – formula for some such sauce. Some of these sauces were regarded as particular to fish, some to grilled meat, others to roast game, others again were hailed as 'universal sauces'. One such, which appears to have been commercialized in the late-eighteenth century was Harvey's. A recipe for this sauce, mentioned in cookery books and lists of necessary stores throughout the nineteenth century, is given in a cookery dictionary of 1832.‡ Ingredients were anchovies, walnut pickle, soy and shallots, plus a whole ounce of cayenne, three *heads* of garlic, a gallon of vinegar and cochineal for colouring. The whole lot was mixed together, stirred two or three times

*A fairly early recipe for 'a currey' appears in Hannah Glasse's *Art of Cookery*, 1747. It is a quite simple formula for a kind of fricassee of chicken spiced with turmeric, ginger and pepper 'beat very fine'. There was as yet no commercial ready-mixed curry powder on the English market. This seems not to have appeared until about seventy or eighty years later.

† These sauces seem to have derived from caveach, a spiced-vinegar pickle in which cooked fish was preserved. In different forms, such as scabeche, caviche, and so on, the term occurs throughout European cookery. *The Oxford Diction-ary of English Etymology* claims however that catsup is a word of Chinese origin.

‡ *The Cook's Dictionary* by Richard Dolby, late cook at the Thatched House Tavern, St James's St. New edition, 1832.

every day for a fortnight, strained through a jelly bag until perfectly clear, bottled and corked down. Harvey's, like its rival Worcestershire sauce commercially launched in 1838, was used as a condiment to flavour other less ferocious compounds. Eliza Acton published a much-copied formula called Christopher North's sauce, in which Harvey's was the vital ingredient. Quinn's sauce for fish, based on salt anchovies, was another much-printed recipe of the nineteenth century, Pontac ketchup was made from elderberry juice, vinegar, anchovies, shallots and spices, and among those commercial sauces of the eighteen-seventies and eighties which reflected the selling power of an Imperial association were Nabob's, Mandarin, Empress of India, and British Lion. Yorkshire Relish, Clarence sauce, Dr Kitchener's salad cream, Burgess' Anchovy Essence (the firm of Burgess had been established in 1760), and Elizabeth Lazenby's range of sauces (Harvey's was among them) were all popular in the late-Victorian era.

Silver-plated cruet stands fitted with glass sauce-bottles, wicker baskets with compartments for sauce-bottles, silver labels to hang round the necks of cut-glass sauce flagons all date from this period. Our meat and fish sauces or liquid seasonings, noted *Law's Grocer's Manual* (*circa* 1892) 'seem peculiar to England. In France next to none are made; they have been tried but would not sell.' Nobody could make such an assertion today. Ketchups and bottled sauces – Worcester is particularly popular – are to be seen in every other hotel dining-room in France, and indeed in Switzerland and even Italy.

The all-conquering tomato sauces and ketchups of today were little known before 1900. The first recipes had appeared in English cookery books during the first years of the nineteenth century. Seventy years later *Cassell's Dictionary of Cookery* quoted five methods of making tomato store sauce and three ways of making tomato ketchup. In varying quantities, all eight recipes specify cayenne pepper or chillies, plus other spices such as ginger, allspice, mace and black or white pepper. Some of the mixtures called for heavy doses of vinegar, and two further recipes– one specifying carrots, ale, spices and vinegar, the second apple pulp coloured with turmeric and flavoured with cayenne – are given under the heading of 'mock tomato sauce'. An unfamiliar world indeed, a world in which tomato sauces were rare enough for cookery writers to feel the need for such imitations. The need, if ever it really existed, was not a lasting one. The import from America of cheap canned tomatoes in bulk was soon to put commercial tomato ketchups upon the tables of thousands of households not in a position to make such relishes for themselves nor to buy them from classy provision merchants or those purveyors of imported produce known until 1914 as Italian warehousemen.

With the establishment of tomato ketchup as the most popular and the cheapest English condiment after vinegar and mustard, came commercial competitors such as the enormously popular H.P., O.K., Flag, and many others, more or less successful, and often simply known as 'sauce'. It is mainly through the medium of these sauces, ketchups and relishes that as a nation we consume, indirectly, such immense quantities of spices, pepper and vinegar, although the massive displays of spices and dried herbs now to be seen in giant supermarkets, department stores and self-service provision shops do seem to point to a popular revival of interest in the direct use of spices rather than through the medium of made-up sauces and ketchups.

It is difficult to determine whether it is the efficient distribution and display methods of the American and Canadian companies who pack and market the bulk of spices and aromatics on sale in the supermarkets which are responsible for this new surge of interest, whether it is the manifestation of a growing dissatisfaction with the monotony of mass-produced foodstuffs, their lack of character and savour, or whether it is simply part of the evergreen and ever-growing appeal of mixing something new and original in the cooking pots. One thing is certain: in the second half of the twentieth century we are finding that spices, aromatic herbs and flavourings have as much allure for us as ever they had for our ancestors of four hundred years ago. In terms of money, these oriental and Arabian and Mediterranean flavourings are no longer status symbols; they no longer possess the charm of the unattainable; and if we are buying them and using them more than ever before then it can only be because they fulfil a true need.

Very obviously, this book offers a sample only of the immense number of English spiced and aromatically flavoured dishes. My choice is an entirely personal one. There are, for example, very few fish recipes. This is because I think that with few exceptions the fish of our own seas and rivers, given that they are fresh, are best cooked very simply. Salt and lemon juice are ordinarily the only necessary seasonings, and fresh herb sauces the best accompaniments. If fish is not fresh, then, speaking for myself, I do not find it worthwhile, and although spices and wine, saffron and fennel and ginger may improve the taste of frozen fish, they cannot restore the lost texture or the fresh smell. So a chapter on the straight-forward cooking of fish will be included in a future volume of this series.

Preface

My recipes for vegetables are, in this book, as sparse as those for fish, and for very much the same reasons. These too, with green salads and fresh herbs, will be dealt with in another volume. Meanwhile, those interested will find many recipes for fresh English vegetables, salads, and fresh herb sauces in a little book called *Summer Cooking** written some fifteen years ago, mainly out of a wish to preserve some memory of the seasonal aspect of fruit and vegetables before everything green, that, as Kipling wrote 'grew out of the mould', disappeared straight into the packet, the dehydrating machine, and the deep freeze.

English bread, yeast and fruit cakes, creams, ices, syllabubs, trifles, and fresh fruit will form the subjects of other volumes in this series.

London. June, 1970.   ELIZABETH DAVID

*Museum Press, 1955, and Penguin Books, 1969.

* *

Introduction

HOUSE-BOUND after a temporarily incapacitating illness during the early nineteen-sixties I enjoyed my compulsory leisure re-reading old favourites in my cookery library. Some of the books had been my earliest kitchen companions and it was instructive to discover which had survived the passage of time and my own changes of taste, increased knowledge, experience of writing and publishing my own cookery books, and my travels in search of gastronomic information.

Among the authors who came out as sturdy survivors were, predictably, Marcel Boulestin and more surprisingly, Mrs Leyel of Culpeper House fame.

It was partly that Mrs Leyel's writing still appeared fresh and alluring even if her recipes struck me as sketchy in the extreme, more relevantly the growing realization, as I read through *The Gentle Art of Cookery*, that the book was yet another manifestation of the English love affair with Eastern food and Arabian Nights ingredients.

During the 1939 war years, circumstances had landed me in Alexandria and subsequently in Cairo. In my turn I fell under the spell of the beautiful food of the Levant – the warm flat bread, the freshly pressed tomato juice, the charcoal-grilled lamb, the oniony salads, the mint and yogurt sauces, the sesame seed paste, the pistachios and the pomegranates and the apricots, the rosewater and the scented sweetmeats, and everywhere the warm spicy smell of cumin. Because I had so often pored over Mrs Leyel's cookery book without quite realizing what she was putting into my head, the food of the Levant appeared more attractive than perhaps I should have found it without the background of that book. Come to that, I wonder if I would ever have learned to cook at all had I been given a routine Mrs Beeton to learn from instead of the romantic Mrs

15

Leyel, with her rather wild and imagination-catching recipes.

Below is the tribute to Hilda Leyel which came out of my re-reading of her books. It appeared in the *Spectator* in July 1963.

*

Although Hilda Leyel is better known as foundress of the Society of Herbalists and the Culpeper House herb shops, and as author of some half dozen books* on herbs and herbal medicine than as a cookery writer, *The Gentle Art of Cookery* is a book which should have its place as a small classic of English culinary literature. My own feelings towards *The Gentle Art,* one of the first cookery books I ever owned, are of affection and gratitude as well as of respect.

One of the fallacies about the passing of judgement on cookery books is the application to the recipes of what is believed to be the acid test implied in the question do they work? A question which always reminds me of the Glendower-Hotspur exchange in *Henry IV*:

> I can call spirits from the vasty deep.
> Why so can I, or so can any man.
> But will they come when you do call for them?

The question I should have wanted to ask Glendower would have been not so much whether he expected the spirits to turn up as whether he really wanted them to and what he intended doing about it if they did.

What one requires to know about recipes is not so much do they work as what do they produce if they do work? A cookery book which gives foolproof recipes for seed cake and pears bottled in crème de menthe and straw potato nests is a good cookery book only to those in whose lives seed cake, pears bottled in crème de menthe and straw potato nests play an important part. A book which tells you as Mrs Leyel's did that you can make a purée from fresh green peas and eat it cold and that a cold roast duck will go very nicely with the purée is not

* See p. 251.

necessarily a bad cookery book because it does not tell you for how long you must roast the duck nor how many pounds of peas you will need for the purée. I am not now speaking from the point of view of an experienced cook whose path has been crossed by a great many roasted ducks (and by no means all of them perfectly done, no matter how much one may know about timing, temperatures, basting, or not basting) and who with a modest effort of memory is able to recall that twelve ounces of shelled peas make just enough peas for two and that to get twelve ounces of shelled peas you must pick or buy one pound of peas in the pod, or perhaps two pounds if they are small or even three if they are very small. No. I am recalling rather the reactions to Mrs Leyel's book of a young woman quite ignorant of cooking techniques but easily, perhaps too easily, beguiled by the idea of food as unlike as could be to any produced by the conventional English cook of the time; and at this distance it is not difficult to perceive that Mrs Leyel's greatest asset was her ability to appeal to the imagination of the young.

Lack of technical instructions and vagueness as to quantities were faults – if faults they were – which didn't bother me because I did not know that they were faults, did not suspect what I was up against and would, I think, not have believed anybody who had tried to tell me.

Allowing for questions of temperament as well as of taste the young and totally inexperienced will usually prefer a book which provides stimulus to one which goes into technical details, makes strenuous efforts to keep the reader on the straight and keeps to the main roads of established cookery. At the age of nineteen one is better off having a stab at Mrs Leyel's 'marrons glacés in half an hour' than learning that the confection of professional *marrons glacés* involves no less than sixteen separate and distinct processes and that to make enough for two people is likely to mean a week's work.

Stimulus. That was the quality which Mrs Leyel's book provided, and in plenty, for she had the gift of making her recipes sound enticing. Re-reading *The Gentle Art* and some of those little books of Mrs Leyel's published by Routledge under the collective title of *The Lure of Cookery*, which includes *Meals on a Tray, Picnics for Motorists, The Complete Jam Cupboard* and *Green Salads and Fruit Salads*, it has to be admitted that Mrs Leyel suffered from incipient jellymania – the incidence of dishes set with gelatine and turned out of moulds is high even for an English cookery book – and here and there lost her head over a picturesque idea. A picnic dish of hollowed-out lemons stuffed with salmon mousse evokes an alluring freshness of sharp scent and cool flavour; how many dozen lemons I wonder would make enough containers for say four people and would the mousse still be in the lemons by the time you had driven the picnic basket from London to, say, the top of Firle Beacon? Small and carping criticisms, these, compared with the positive virtues of Mrs Leyel's attitude to cookery, the most attractive of which, I now see, was her love of fruit, vegetables and salad and her treatment of them almost as dishes to which meat and fish and poultry were little more than incidental accompaniments or scarcely necessary adjuncts of a meal. Indeed, *The Gentle Art* was notable for the way in which the recipes were classified. Appended to the vegetable chapter were two separate sections dealing with mushrooms and chestnuts respectively. How right of Mrs Leyel to emphasize the strangeness of these foods by separating them in the reader's mind from potatoes and sprouts and beans. The fruit chapter in *The Gentle Art* includes such rare recipes as a compote of pomegranates, an orange salad flavoured with sherry and lemon juice (a tablespoon of each to four oranges – she did give precise quantities when she knew that to overdo a flavouring would spoil the dish) and strewn with fresh mint leaves, a melon steeped in maraschino-flavoured syrup then filled with white grapes, white currants and pistachio nuts. In a five-page section devoted to recipes for almond creams, almond soups, almond puddings and almond pastes was a recipe for a rice cream to which ground almonds are added and 'when cool pour into a silver dish and sprinkle with powdered cinnamon and decorate with whole almonds'. When I first had Mrs

Leyel's book nothing and nobody on earth could have sold me
an English rice pudding, but a rice cream made with lemon and
almonds and served in a silver dish, well, that gave one something to think about, silver dish and all.

Evidently much beguiled by the idea of Eastern cooking
with its almonds and pistachio nuts, apricots and quinces,
saffron and honey, rosewater, mint, dates and sweet spices, Mrs
Leyel gave also in her book a little chapter of 'Dishes from the
Arabian Nights' which, no doubt because of its vagueness and
brevity contained the true essence of magic and mystery.

An Arabian way of cooking red mullet' – grilled in a sauce
composed of tomatoes, onions, spices, shallots, salt, pepper,
garlic, curry powder and saffron – sounded irresistible, so much
so that even if you barely knew whether a red mullet was a bird,
a flower or a fish you very quickly set about finding out. An
hors-d'oeuvre called *munkaczina*, alleged by Mrs Leyel to have
been brought from the East by Anatole France (maddeningly,
Mrs Leyel gives neither chapter nor verse), is a salad of sliced
oranges strewn with finely chopped onion which in turn is
covered with a layer of stoned black olives, the whole to be
sprinkled with red pepper, salt and olive oil. Mrs Leyel
certainly took one very far away indeed from the world of
grapefruit and Scotch eggs to which a bed-sitter cook so easily
succumbs. Her book turned out to be almost the equivalent in
cookery of Walter de la Mare's unsurpassed poetry anthology
Come Hither which had enlightened my childhood.

Mrs Leyel died in 1957 and *The Gentle Art*, many times
reprinted after its original publication, re-issued in Chatto's
pre-war three-and-sixpenny Phoenix Library and once again
reprinted in the fifties, has now been dropped by its publishers.*
Unaccountably the book has never been bought for a paperback and for its loss we are the poorer. As a book for the young
with minds and tastes of their own I cannot believe that *The
Gentle Art* was entirely out of date – to me it seems a good deal
less dated than for example the 1960 so-called Mrs Beeton, and

*Since this was written, Chatto have reprinted the book in its original format.

certainly a great deal more stimulating, but the book has another quality which I have only now properly perceived. Its excursions into far Arabia make it quintessentially a book about one particular facet of English food and English tastes.

*

Seven years have passed since that moment of comprehension which sparked off a train of thought, an idea. The train of thought has crystallized in this book, still incomplete, still no more than a glance into the English preoccupation with the spices and the scents, the fruit, the flavourings, the sauces and condiments of the orient, near and far.

February 1970   E.D.

* *

Spices and Condiments

'*The grocers were descended from the pepperers of Sopers Lane and the spicers of Cheap, who amalgamated in 1345, and in 1370 adopted the more comprehensive title of engrosser or grocer from the Latin grossarius. In a grocer's shop at that time was to be found every sort of medicine, root and herb, gums, spices, oils and ointments. Syrups and waters, turpentine and plaisters, ranged side by side with dried fruit and confectionery, pepper and ginger.*'

The Magic of Herbs, Mrs C. F. Leyel, 1926

ALLSPICE: This is the dried berry of *pimenta officinalis*, also called *eugenia pimenta*, an evergreen of the myrtle family. Also known from its place of origin as Jamaica pepper and from its botanical name as pimento, it is neither a true pepper nor has it any relationship to the capsicum or sweet red pepper which we call, wrongly, pimento. Nor is it, as is often thought by those who have seen it only in its powdered form, a mixture of spices. It is called allspice because it is thought to have something in its aroma of the clove, cinnamon and nutmeg combined. I cannot myself see where the nutmeg or cinnamon come in. A hint of clove is certainly there, and more than a hint of pepper. It can indeed do duty for the clove – and often does, in my kitchen – and at a pinch, a pretty tight one, for pepper.

The main use of allspice in English cooking is to give an aromatic scent to marinades and pickling mixtures for soused herrings, salt beef, pickled pork and the like. It is an important ingredient of the spice mixture for dryspiced beef (the recipe is on page 172), and is a muchused spice in the cooking of the Levant and Asia Minor. Since this cooking has particular appeal for me I find it useful to keep a special pepper mill – of a different colour or shape from the one filled with pepper proper – for allspice, which is at its best freshly ground or pounded.

Mention of Jamaica pepper is very frequent in English cookery books of the Edwardian period, when peppers with a number of alluring names, such as Coralline, Nepal and Malagueta made their appearance under proprietary labels. Coralline and Nepal pepper were variations on cayenne. Guinea and Malagueta pepper were made from the seeds of *afromomum melegueta*, a plant related to the cardamom.

Allspice was much used in English *pot pourris*, and there are those who use lavish quantities of this spice in Christmas puddings.

ANISEED: Fruit of the *pimpinella anisum,* one of the umbelli‑ferae, is little used nowadays in the English kitchen, although at one time aniseed sweets and comfits were the delight of English children.

French anisette liqueur is flavoured mainly with star anise or *badiane*, a totally different variety,* beautiful when dried and with a very bitter liquorice‑like taste not at all evident in the finished product. Unexpectedly a few drops of this liqueur do wonderful things for the flavour of certain fish sauces and soups. Some cooks use Pernod, also anise flavoured, for the same purpose. Anisette is more subtle. Spanish anise drinks, usually diluted with water, like Pernod, come in two versions, dry and sweet. Both are very potent and too coarse for delicate sauces. The traditional Spanish anise bottles, made to resemble moulded glass with hobnail patterns of endless variety, are a never‑failing source of interest and the labels often collectors' pieces.

Aniseeds are used in some of the more interesting of the old Indian recipes, particularly to flavour fish.

CARAWAY SEEDS: *Carum carvi*, another of the umbelliferae. Apart from seed cake, (why were those cakes always so dry?) once the great English favourite, and caraway sweets or comfits,

* *Illicum verum*, a tree of the magnolia family.

caraway appears little in English cooking. In Germany, Austria and in Jewish cookery it is greatly used for flavouring bread, cabbage, and cream cheeses. In Alsace, Munster cheese, the province's great dairy product, is always accom-panied by a little saucer of caraway seeds to sprinkle on to the cheese. In another Alsace cheese, Geromé, the seeds are already incorporated. Swiss cheese fondues are also sometimes flavoured with caraway, or indirectly so by means of kummel liqueur instead of the more usual kirsch.

Confusion sometimes arises over the French nomenclature of caraway. The correct word is *carvi*, but it is also known as *cumin des prés* or wild cumin. It is not however to be confused with what we know as cumin seed. Caraway and carraway are by the way alternative spellings.

CARDAMOM SEEDS: Essentially a spice of oriental cookery, these diminutive but potent and pungent black seeds are to be bought in Indian spice shops. They are marketed mainly in their pale cream-coloured or greenish pods which are some-times put whole into Indian dishes of lentils and other pulses, but more often and more effectively are extracted from the pods (there are some half dozen seeds varying in colour from brown to almost black in every pod) and pounded with other spices to make a flavouring for rice, chicken and meat dishes. Cardamoms are one of the important ingredients of curry powders, so although we may not know them by sight, their flavour and aroma should be familiar in an indirect way. I find cardamoms delicious and essential, although not often and not in quantity, a fortunate circumstance since they are among the most costly of spices. Perhaps for this reason they are some-times confused, both in old French and English recipes, with grains of paradise, the seeds of a related plant, *afromomum melegueta*.

The botanical names of the cardamom are *elettaria cardamo-mum,* and *amomum cardamomum*, plants of the ginger family, their habitats are Malabar and Ceylon, and, although not a plant native to their countries, the Arabs of the Near East have a great taste for cardamom, and flavour their coffee with this most interesting of spices.

CASSIA: The inner bark of a variety of cinnamon, *cinnamomum cassia*, is inferior to cinnamon in delicacy and subtlety, although strong in flavour. Cassia is frequently mentioned in old recipes and Sir Kenelm Digby,* who was by way of being something of an alchemist, was fond of putting it into his mead and metheglin. In the pharmacy of many countries oil of cassia, distilled from the leaves and twigs of this plant, substitutes for oil of cinnamon, although according to English law, oils of true cinnamon and of cassia must be differentiated. Cassia's native habitat is China, but in pharmacy there is another cassia plant called *cassia fistula*, grown in the East and West Indies and in Egypt, the pods of which are used, like senna pods, as a laxative. According to Potter,† the English vernacular name of this plant is Pudding Stick.

CAYENNE PEPPER: An umbrella term for various manifestations of a fiery seed of the capsicum tribe. Two only of these capsicums, *capsicum minimum* and *capsicum frutescens* are recognized by the British Pharmacopeia as being sources of the true cayenne.

Like all products of capsicum plants, cayenne pepper is notoriously difficult, not to say impossible, to track down in its ideal manifestation. This is said to be the cayenne pepper of Nepal, a tiny violet-red pepper or chilli, of which the seeds, when ground, yield a brown rather than a red powder. Since no cayenne pepper I have ever bought in England has failed to gum up within a week or two the shaker in which it is purveyed, and since it is a potential killer of taste unless used in the most infinitesimal quantity, it looks as though it were high time that somebody had a bright idea about the marketing of this spice, which the English regard with a great affection. Were it to be bought, like saffron, in thimble-size packs or little sachets,

---

* See p. 243.   † See p. 251.

I fancy that the sale would be enormous. Firms who pack salt and mustard for the airlines might perhaps take note?*

If and when you can find cayenne in viable form – most of it now comes from Africa rather than from Nepal – it does add an important zest to cheese sauces, the beloved English cheese straws (Parmesan biscuits, page 230, are an alternative), to plain unadorned sardines, potted fish pastes, crab and lobster dishes, and some people think – I do not – to oysters.

Cayenne Salt: 'Take two ounces of finely powdered dried birds'-eye chillies or capsicums, and mix them well in a mortar with two table-spoonfuls of clean salt; add a glass of white wine and two of water; put it into a corked bottle, and place in the sun for a week or more daily; then strain the whole through a fine piece of muslin; pour the liquor in a plate, and evaporate it either by a stove or in the sun; you will then have crystals of cayenne and salt; a much finer article than the cayenne powder.'

Indian Domestic Economy and Receipt Book, Madras, 1850

One way of solving the problem of cayenne pepper.

CHILLIES: There are numerous variations of these hot little peppers which are also known as bird peppers, Guinea peppers, African peppers, birds'-eye Cayenne peppers, and Zanzibar chillies. The seeds and fruit of the *capsicum minimum* or of the *capsicum frutescens* are ground to make cayenne pepper, while the chilli powder of commerce may be a mixture of varieties. Chilli powders and cayenne peppers are much used in herbal remedies as well as in chutneys, bottled sauces and ketchups. Whole birds'-eye peppers or Zanzibar chillies are one of the components of pickling spice.

CINNAMON: The inner bark of *cinnamomum zeylanicum*, a tree of the laurel family. Ceylon is the source of the cinnamon we

*The Canadian firm of Schwartz are currently marketing cayenne in a practical shaker.

buy today. The whole bark, in pale-brown slim quills rolled one in another rather like those crackly wafers called *cigarettes russes*, was used at one time in English cookery to flavour creams and custards, much as we now use the vanilla pod. Since cinnamon bark is very difficult to pound to a powder it is preferable, unless you intend using it in the old-fashioned way, to buy it in ground form, but in very small quantities, for it is not a spice which keeps its aroma over a long period.

With the recipe for chocolate chinchilla on page 223, will be found a note on cinnamon as the original aromatic used to flavour chocolate – it is one of the happy affinities which should not be forgotten – and a reminder of how greatly cinnamon varies in quantity and strength, a circumstance which explains the marked discrepancy in quantities pre-scribed in recipes for an almost identical cake or pudding but written by different hands and perhaps in different countries.

Cinnamon butter is a wonderfully useful little preparation. The recipe is on page 86.

At one of my favourite London Cypriot restaurants a bowl of powdered cinnamon is offered with the hot egg and lemon soup, the delicious *avgolémono* of Greece. A beautiful idea. And cinnamon sprinkled on courgettes (zucchini) and on honey and cream-cheese pie are other Greek delights. It is relevant that many of the elegant silver casters which once adorned our sideboards were intended not for sugar, but for the sprinkling of cinnamon on toast and muffins.

CLOVES: The flower buds of an evergreen of the myrtle family, called *eugenia caryophyllus*.

One of the great spices of the Moluccas, subsequently introduced into Penang, Amboyna, Madagascar and, in spite of the Dutch colonists who took every step including the systematic destruction of the shrub wherever possible to main-tain their monopoly, into Zanzibar. The whole world now relies upon Zanzibar for its supply of cloves. When the crop fails, as happened recently, the price of cloves soars. At the time of writing (1970) cloves are by a long way the most costly of spices with the sole exception of saffron. Fortunately, a small amount of cloves goes a long way, at least to my taste. I do not buy whole cloves, beautiful though they are, since for me they spoil the taste of apple pie, which is their main destination in the English kitchen. Perhaps the best use I have ever experienced of the whole clove is in the extraordinary candied walnuts of Turin in Northern Italy. Picked green, like our own pickled walnuts, they turn black and soft when cooked and half-crystallized. At first sight in the confectioner's shop these black fruits look like sugar-dusted prunes, or nuggets of some marvellous quartz, with a little aromatic nail – a whole clove – pushed into the stalk end of each fruit.

Ground cloves keep their aroma fairly well. They are, as few English cooks would need to be told, indispensable for Christmas puddings, mincemeat and hot cross buns. The venerable English cream cheese mixture described on pages 213 and 214 is less familiar. It is a dish of great character and allure.

CORIANDER SEEDS: The fruit of *coriandrum sativum*, a plant of the umbelliferae family. The coriander grows in Southern Europe, Sicily, Africa, India, Mexico, Malta, Cyprus, Spain, and was once cultivated in Southern England. The seeds, aromatically sweet and orangey when crushed but rather unattractive when unripe (they smell of bugs some say; others liken the smell to rubber) were sugar-coated to make the little sweets called comfits.

Coriander seeds make a delicious mild and spicey flavouring for stuffings, for sweet-sour pickles and chutneys and are one of the components of English pickling spice. A great Cypriot speciality is green olives crushed and heavily spiced with coriander seeds. Cyprus sausages are also aromatized with this spice.

A recipe for ham cooked in milk spiced with coriander seeds was given by William Verral in his delightful little book, *The Cook's Paradise*, 1749.* Verral was master of the White Hart Inn in Lewes, and probably obtained his coriander locally, for

* Reprinted by Sylvan Press, 1948

27

Sussex was one of the counties where the plant was cultivated. Vincent la Chapelle, chief cook to the Earl of Chesterfield and subsequently to the Prince of Orange, whose book* was written and published in English before being translated into French, gives a basting liquor for spit-roasted turkey made from two glasses of champagne or Rhenish wine aromatized with cloves, bayleaves, garlic, sliced lemon and coriander seeds.

Coriander leaves in their fresh state are much used in Cyprus, in Spain, in Mexico and in the Middle East.

Very large quantities of coriander seeds are used in curry powders. And, with juniper berries, coriander is one of the flavouring agents of gin.

Whenever possible buy coriander seeds in whole form. They are very easy to pound.

CUMIN or CUMMIN: One of the endless tribe of umbelliferae, *Cuminum cyminum* is indigenous to the Upper Nile, and cultivated along the North African coast and in India.

The seeds of cumin, or more properly speaking, the fruit, provide one of the most characteristic flavourings of Middle Eastern and of Moroccan cooking. The warm spicy scent of cumin pervades the souks of North Africa and of Egypt, gives the grilled lamb kebabs of Morocco their typical flavour (there is a recipe on page 139), goes into a hundred and one Levantine vegetable, meat and rice dishes, and is often, although not invariably, an ingredient of Indian curry compounds.

To me cumin is one of the more important spices. Both the whole seeds and ground cumin are in frequent use in my kitchen, for spicing chicken, rice dishes, lamb, and aubergines. It is one of the many spices which should be warmed to bring out its aroma before it is put into the cooking pot or sprinkled on meat for grilling. Although cumin looks so similar to fennel, aniseed and caraway seeds, its aroma is quite unmistakable.

* *The Modern Cook*, 3rd edition, 1736.

CURRY POWDER: Although there are so many made-up curry powders on the market, I find that I seldom use any of them. To me they are unlikeable, harshly flavoured, and possessed of an aroma clinging and as all-pervading in its way as that of English boiled cabbage or cauliflower. Too much hot red pepper, too much low-grade ginger, too much cheap white pepper, too much mustard seed and fenugreek, in fact too much of too many spices, probably inferior and certainly far from fresh, make commercial curry powders an unattractive proposition, however traditional they may be to the English kitchen.

I learn from the excellent book on food plants* published by the Oxford University Press that pepper, i.e., ordinary pepper, black or white, was the most pungent ingredient in Indian curries 'until chillies were introduced from America in the sixteenth century'. This explains a good deal about the evolution of Indian curries. It must have taken genera-tions for the cultivation of and the taste for chilli to spread throughout the vast sub-continent of India, and for the inhabitants of all the widely differing provinces and states to accustom themselves to the new fiery condiment. For as long as three centuries there would have been many isolated pockets of resistance where the old mixtures remained, accounting for stories of the elegant and subtle food of the Moghuls, for the ingenious and mild vegetarian dishes of the non-meat-eating sects of India. The cookery book of which I have written on page 191 describes Indian dishes which sound utterly delicious, far far removed from the curries of London Indian restaurants and of English recipes; and Mrs Balbir Singh's *Indian Cookery*, published in 1961 and still, happily, in print, gives many fascinating, beautiful recipes for Indian dishes made with just a few mild spices and never a sniff of bought curry powders.

As a nation we are not slow to adapt the food and the ingredients of other countries. We do seem to be possessed of an unhappy capacity to absorb the worst aspects of any given

*See p. 253.

cooking tradition while remaining deliberately blind to the true nature of the dishes we make our own.

In the case of curries, the complexity and the preparation of the correct spices must have been a bit daunting for even the kitchen staffs of eighteenth- and nineteenth-century England, accustomed though they were to pounding and bashing, mashing and sieving. Some curry ingredients such as poppy seeds and fenugreek are indeed so hard that it is impossible to pound them in an ordinary mortar. Indians grind their spices on a stone, although for commercial sale the job is no doubt performed by machine. An ordinary household electric mixer is of little avail for the more intractable of Indian spices; the hand-turned poppy-seed grinder mentioned on page 45 is quite effective, while a small electric coffee grinder is successful for peppercorns, allspice and juniper berries, coriander and cumin seeds.

Given the difficulties, it is not surprising that ready-prepared curry powders found and find such immediate acceptance in England, but for those who appreciate something a little less crude than dishes made with curry powders, a mixture of freshly pounded cardamom seeds, coriander, cumin, turmeric, and black or white pepper makes the basis of a very excellent spice compound, to my taste all the better for the absence of chillies, mustard seed, fenugreek and garlic. But *forget not the salt*. Forget not, also, that the development of the aromas of spices and spice mixtures is dependent upon the cooking process. If you want to flavour a cooked dish, a sauce, a soup, or a kedgeree, say, with even just a sprinkling of a ready-made curry powder, the flavour will be enormously improved if the powder is put on a heat-proof plate in a low oven or in a dry frying pan over gentle heat for a few minutes before it is used.

For those interested, the following table, reproduced from *Indian Domestic Economy*, shows four different compounds of spices to be made into curry powders.

It has to be borne in mind that British residents in India were fond of sending home to their families and friends in England their own particular brews of curry powders, pastes and chutneys. This would perhaps account for the rather large proportions in which the formulas are given.

INGREDIENTS FOR CURRY POWDER

	No. 1 lb.	No. 2 lb.	No. 3 lb.	No. 4 lb. oz.
Coriander seeds (to be well roasted, pounded)	20	12	3	1
Turmeric	4	2	1	1 2
Cummin seeds (dried and ground)	1	2	½	—
Fenugreek	1	1	½	0 4
Mustard seed (dried and cleaned of husks)	1	1	½	—
Ginger, dried	2	2	½	1
Black pepper	2	1	1	1
Dried Chillies	1	2	1	12
Poppy seed	2	2	—	—
Garlic	2	1	—	—
Cardamoms	—	—	—	0 8
Cinnamon	—	—	—	0 8

'Salt in proportion to be added when using the curry stuff. The whole to be cleaned, dried, pounded, and sifted; then properly mixed together and put into bottles, well corked. A table-spoonful is sufficient for a chicken or fowl curry.'

Indian Domestic Economy, Madras, 1850

In the light of this most remarkable work-out of curry-powder formulas – probably forerunners of commercially exported powders – it is with gratitude and relief that I turn to Mrs Balbir Singh.* Curry powder, or *garam masala*, says Mrs Balbir Singh firmly, 'is a mixture of cinnamon, cloves, carda-moms, black cumin seeds, nutmeg and mace'. The recipe for making 2 oz. (60 gr.) of garam masala is as follows:

* See p. 29 and Bibliography, p. 252.

'¾ oz. (20 gm.) brown cardamom seeds (illaichi), ¾ oz. (20 gm.) cinnamon (darchini), ¼ oz. (7 gm.) cloves (laung), ¼ oz. (7 gm.) black cumin seeds (kala zeera), good⁄sized pinch mace (javatri), good⁄sized pinch nutmeg (jaiphal).

'Grind the ingredients together with the help of a mortar and pestle or in a coffee grinder. Pass through a fine sieve and store in an air⁄tight bottle. It has better flavour than the commercial curry powders and keeps well for a fortnight provided the bottle is capped immediately after use.'

Indian Cookery, Mrs Balbir Singh, 1961

For a recipe for curry paste see page 164.

CURRY LEAVES: Come from a tree called *bergera koenigii*, cultivated in Indian gardens. The grey⁄green leaves have an aromatic curry⁄like scent, and under the name of *curry pak* or *neem* are indeed used in curries and curry pastes.

DILL SEEDS: Another of the umbelliferae, *anethum graveolens* similar in appearance to common fennel but distinctly different in aroma and taste. Dill seeds and dill leaves are rare in English cooking, but much beloved in Scandinavian countries and in Russia where pickled cucumbers and fish are traditionally flavoured with them. In the United States, pickled cucumbers have become so identified with the dill flavouring that they are known as dill pickles.
French for dill is *aneth*.

FENNEL SEEDS: Again the umbelliferae, *foeniculum vulgare*. Although fennel grows wild in England, and the leaves are well known in English cooking, the seeds are ignored. They have a slightly anise⁄like aroma, but less sweet. They are less brutal than caraway and could be more used than they are.
In Italian cooking, fennel seeds flavour a highly excellent salame called *finocchiona*, a speciality of Tuscany.
A few fennel seeds, a very few, which means not more than

three or four, scattered on a red mullet before it is grilled add a most subtle flavour to this fish. This trick I learned from M. Charles Bérot, patron-chef of l'Escale at Carry-le-Rouet near Marseilles. It is from small touches such as this that one learns about flavourings and begins to apprehend the infinite richness and variety of the scents and aromas of cooking.

In French, fennel seeds, or *graines de fenouil*, are often called *cumin* or *cumin des prés*, thus adding to the caraway–carvi–cumin confusion.

FENUGREEK: The seeds of this plant, *trigonella foencum-graecum*, a member of the pea family, are an ingredient of nearly all curry powders. They are yellowish-brown, look rather like a breakfast cereal of my childhood called grape-nuts, have very little aroma until subjected to heat, and are exceedingly hard. It is fenugreek, little known in England in the direct sense, which is responsible for the ugly smell – no doubt to many a whiff of Paradise – and to some extent for the coarse taste of made-up curry powder. Fenugreek is to curry much as malt vinegar is to English salads.

GINGER: In its many manifestations as a spice and as a sweet-meat, all ginger comes from the root or more properly the rhizome, in old English called a race or hand, of *zingiber officinale*.

Although Chinese ginger preserved in syrup is highly prized (mainly I suspect because of the charm of the jars in which it is exported to the West) the finest quality dried root ginger comes from Jamaica. It is from the dried root that we get the ground or powdered ginger which goes into our cakes and gingerbreads and puddings. Jamaican powdered ginger is easily distinguishable from the coarser varieties by its very pale colour and an aroma which is quite delicate and distinguished compared to the hot ginger of Cochin and the harsh peppery taste of the African varieties. The latter are the ones used to make the essences and extracts which flavour ginger beer and other such soft drinks, and no doubt also the ginger cakes and biscuits and confectionery of commerce. It is probably the preponderance of these cheaper varieties used as flavourings which has made ginger unpopular with those who value their palates, and certainly a little of even the finest ginger goes a long way. It can be a revelation, though, to taste a mild ginger and saffron spiced chicken or rice dish, or a delicate Grasmere gingerbread mixture as described in the recipe on page 221.

For once it was not the crusaders who introduced this spice to England for it was known here before the Conquest. Probably it was brought via their African colonies by the Romans, who used it in massive quantity. By the fifteenth century the popularity of ginger must have been tremendous, at any rate if one is to believe the cookery books. In every other recipe of the time one finds instructions to mix together 'canelle (cinnamon), pepir, gyngere and safroun', 'clowes (cloves), maces, and marow, and pouder of gyngere', 'take wyne and caste thereto pouder of gyngere, pepir and safroun, and salt'. This last is part of a formula for a dish called 'cha-wettys', made of minced veal or pork, mixed with the wine and spices already listed, plus egg yolks, verjuice (juice of unripe grapes or crab apples – in effect a kind of fruit vinegar), dates, currants, cloves and mace, all baked in pastry. In fact a kind of mincemeat pie – but then nearly every dish, meat, fish or fowl, from a 'crane rosted' to 'a custarde' of veal and herbs and 'sole, boiled, rost or fryed', has the same or a similar litany of spices, although ginger and 'safroun' seem to win out over the mace and cloves. Nutmeg, spelled notemygge, hardly gets a look in at all. Small wonder that in English ginger became a synonym for hot and lively, while racy in this context probably came from the same source – a race of ginger.

By the eighteenth century the ginger mania appears to have simmered down considerably, since it now figures mainly in cakes and puddings and creams (a ginger ice cream can be excellent) which would be recognizable today, although one eighteenth-century housekeeper, Charlotte Mason, from whose receipt book a volume entitled *The Ladies Assistant* was compiled and published in about 1780, puts ginger in her

Yorkshire pudding. Gingerbreads and cakes have long been great favourites in Yorkshire, and no doubt there would always have been ginger handy in the spice boxes of local housekeepers.

In my childhood it was customary to hand round a bowl of powdered ginger when melon was served as a first course for lunch. The ginger was necessary we were told to counteract the chilling effects of the melon, a tradition which still survives.

Crystallized ginger and candied ginger are attractive sweet/meats, especially at Christmas/time when they can be arranged in beautiful little pyramids with dark delicacies such as Bordeaux prunes and greenish Elvas plums, sticky brown dates, pale frosted *marrons glacés* and a few silvered almonds to glimmer in the candlelight. And ginger with chocolate – if it is good ginger and very bitter chocolate – is one of the happiest of inventions.

Green root ginger, so important in Chinese, Malay and Indian cooking, is hard to come by and harder still to keep. A method of storing it, and the ways in which it is used, are described on page 107.

JUNIPER BERRIES: The fruit of *juniperus communis*, shrub of the cypress family, native to the British Isles. The berries ripen every second year only.

It was the highly aromatic and pungent berry of the juniper, in Latin *ginepro*, which gave its name to gin and is the most important of the aromatics which go to make up its character/istic flavour.

Juniper berries make a wonderful seasoning for pâtés, stuffings for small game birds, and pork dishes. The dried berries should be used in small quantities and should always be crushed in a mortar or chopping bowl before they are added to a pâté mixture or a stuffing, or mixed with salt, olive oil and garlic as a seasoning for pork chops. Juniper berries are also used to flavour wine marinades for venison and mutton, in brines for hams and salt pork, and in the mixture for curing dry-spiced beef.

An interesting recipe for a dish of veal kidneys called *rognons à la liégeoise* was given by Ambrose Heath in *Good Food*.* The kidneys are rapidly cooked in butter, and just before they are ready to serve you throw in a few crushed juniper berries, then a wineglass of gin warmed in a ladle, ignited, and poured blazing over the kidneys. This, adds the author, is 'quite wonderful'. The gin, I should add, gives a terrific blaze and a most excellent flavour. It is a spirit which could be used more often in the kitchen.

'I conceive,' wrote Sir Kenelm Digby,† 'that Hydromel made with juniper berries (first broken and bruised) boiled in it, is very good. Adde to it Rosemary and Bay Leaves,' and Marcel Boulestin observed that 'these are neglected in English cooking, but much appreciated in Flanders and the North of France, where they are used as flavourings in dishes like partridge or pheasant braised with cabbage or *choucroute*.‡' Boulestin also mentions the 'aromatic flavour' imparted to veal kidneys by juniper berries.

MACE: In English cooking a most important spice, mace comes from the outer covering of the nutmeg (*myrista officinalis* or *myristica fragrans*). Potter§ describes it in technical terms as follows: '. . . the arillus known as Mace is a growth outside the shell of the nutmeg seeds . . . net-like . . . when dry of an orange-brown colour . . . is brittle and exudes oil when pressed by the nails. Taste, strongly aromatic, pungent . . .'

How mace came to be the hundred per cent traditional, invariable and indispensable spice of all English potted meats and fish compounds is not at all clear. One explanation could be that owing to the brittle, horny quality of that net-like arillus, mace is next to impossible to grind or pound in a household mortar, and is therefore habitually bought in

---

*Faber & Faber, 1932, reprinted by Neville Spearman, 1965. † See p. 243.
‡*Herbs, Salads, and Seasonings*, Marcel Boulestin and Jason Hill, 1930.
§See p. 251.

powdered form more often than in whole pieces. It would have been handy in the spice box or cupboard whereas the nutmegs had to be grated and were perhaps scarcer than mace, although the price of the latter seems to have been only very little less than that of nutmegs. A curiosity occurs in a recipe given by E. Smith in *The Compleat Housewife: or Accomplished Gentle-woman's Companion*, 1727. For a veal forcemeat or stuffing for a turkey, this author demands a whole nutmeg and a *dram* of mace. Now a dram or drachm was an apothecary's measure, and oil of mace – expressed more often from fragments of inferior nutmeg than from mace – was considered valuable for the relief of insomnia. (Nutmeg extract is now regarded as a potentially dangerous addiction). Where spices and flavourings, oils and essences, were concerned there must often have been little distinction between which belonged properly to the medicine cupboard and what to the housekeeper's provision store, from which expensive commodities such as sugar, dried fruits and spices kept under lock and key would be dispensed only as required.

Ground mace is a spice which should be bought in small quantity and used while fresh. And if it happens to be missing at the moment it is needed to spice potted tongue or some other delicacy of the kind, then I would use nutmeg without further ado.

MUSTARD: 'The list of herbs and vegetables included sage, parsley, fennel, dittany, hyssop, borage, leek, garlic, mustard, onions and porray.* The countess's account mentions fennel, parsley and enormous quantities of mustard. The countess's cook was not alone in his liking for mustard. The Goodman of Paris says that a wedding supper of only forty people would require two quarts of mustard, and Roger Leyburn bought a gallon of mustard at a time.'

A Baronial Household of the Thirteenth Century,
Margaret Wade Labarge, 1965

*Porray was a general term for green vegetables, or potherbs, and was also applied to the soup made from them.

A display of mustards, English, French and false French, at a Delicatessen Exhibition held in London in 1962 was responsible for the following paragraphs on the subject, originally published in the *Spectator*.

A restaurateur who worked at Boulestin's in the nineteen-thirties, once told me that Boulestin and his friend Robin Adair, having their own lunch one day in the restaurant, were looked after by a new waiter brought over from France. As the man left their table Boulestin was heard to gasp, '*Tu vois cela, Robin*? He offers us English mustard with the entrecôte. He must go.'

From the day I heard the story, now some years ago, I started experimenting with various kinds of mustard, a condiment which until then I had used only rarely. I still do not want it neat with my food. To some, mustard is a stimulant; to others an irritant. That it has both properties is, I see, confirmed by Potter,* a reliable source of reference in such matters. In dishes made with English or Gruyère cheeses, in cream sauces for chicken and fish, in a parsley butter to eat with steaks or grilled salmon, and to spread on food such as pig's trotters, breast of lamb, chicken, rabbit, destined subsequently to be breadcrumbed and grilled or baked, certain kinds of mustard can be immensely enhancing.

Like Boulestin I prefer French mustard to English because I find it less brutal and more aromatic, while English-made copies of French mustards – and I have tried a good many – all seem to me lacking in resemblance to their French counter-parts in strength, flavour and aroma. In any case there should not now be any need to buy imitations, there is a plentiful supply and variety of the genuine article on the market. Most respectable delicatessen and grocery shops stock one brand at least. The ones I prefer come from Bocquet or from the old Dijon firm of Grey-Poupon. Both companies make a *moutarde forte au vin blanc*, a yellow mustard packed in glass jars or in those familiar blue and white china mustard pots.

*See page 251.

The colour, when mustard is to be used as a flavouring for a white or other pale-coloured sauce, is important; brown mustards may taste as good as yellow ones, but tend to turn the sauce a rather unattractive colour.

The reason that French cooks give instructions to add mustard to sauces only in the final stages of cooking is the rapidity with which mustards lose their aromas when subjected to heat. Then there is the strange case of a mayonnaise or remoulade for a shredded celeriac salad; this needs a flavouring of mustard so strong that by itself it would be uneatable. For this purpose pure yellow mustard flour, English or the Canadian product now sold in some supermarkets, does excellently.

Robert May, author of *The Accomplisht Cook*, first published in 1660, the year of the Stuart restoration, gives interesting instructions as to the different ways in which mustard was then mixed in England and France (where he had received part of his training).

'Have good seed, pick it, and wash it in cold water, drain it and rub it dry in a cloth very clean; then beat it in a mortar with strong wine-vinegar; and being fine beaten, strain it and keep it close covered. Or grind it in a mustard quern, or a bowl with a cannon bullet.'

'*Mustard of Dijon, or French mustard*. The seed being cleaned, stamp it in a mortar with vinegar and honey, then take eight ounces of seed, two ounces of cinnamon, two of honey and vinegar as much as will serve good mustard not too thick, and keep it close covered in little oyster barrels.'

Incidentally, two of the dishes to which Robert May is insistent that mustard should be an accompaniment are herrings and brawn; things haven't changed all that much.

May's Dijon method is confirmed by Alexandre Dumas* over 200 years later. He quotes a recipe which explains what is not made quite clear by May, that the mustard seed was first steeped overnight in vinegar, *then* pounded with more vinegar, plus whatever spices, wine, honey, you might choose to add.

Grand Dictionnaire de Cuisine, 1873.

Today, the Dijon firms (Dumas asserts that the founder of the Maille condiment firm invented ninety-two kinds of mustard) have simplified matters. White wine, mustard seed, salt, spices and citric acid are the sole ingredients listed on the Grey-Poupon label. In bizarre contrast, an English product of the nineteen-sixties, a tomato mustard manufactured by a London firm using the brand name La Favorite, contains 'tomato ketchup, spirit vinegar, mustard seed, flour, salt, sugar, edible oil, spices, tragacanth, flavouring'.

Criticisms of the ingredients used in made mustard are nothing new. Here is Sir Hugh Plat on the subject, three and a half centuries ago.

Mustard Meale 'It is usuall in Venice to sell the meale of Mustarde in their markets, as we doe flower and meale in England: this meale by the addition of vinegar in two or three daies becometh exceeding good mustard, but it would bee much stronger and finer, if the huskes or huls were first divided by searce* or boulter,† which may easily be done, if you drie your seeds against the fire before you grinde them. The Dutch iron handmils, or an ordinarie pepper mil may serve for this purpose. I thought it verie necessarie to publish this manner of making your sauce, because our mustard which we buy from the Chandlers at this day is many times made up with vile and filthy vinegar, such as our stomack woulde abhorre if we should see it before the mixing thereof with the seeds.'

Delightes for Ladies, Sir Hugh Plat, 1600

MUSTARD SEEDS: There are two distinct variations of mustard, *brassica nigra* and *brassica alba*, black mustard and white mustard. Both have been used as condiments since about A.D. 300, at any rate according to Potter.‡

English white mustard, considered to be very fine, is grown in Cambridgeshire and Essex, the black in Lincolnshire and Yorkshire. Mustard seeds appear to be used in our kitchens

*Sieve. †Straining cloth. ‡See p. 251.

40

only as a component of mixed pickling spice, although in the days before the invention of powdered mustard for making into a paste – this is said to have been originated by a Mrs Clements in Durham, about 1720 – there must have been quantities of mustard seeds in every store cupboard in the land, the white being less prized than the black which contain a much higher proportion of the important volatile oil, while the white seeds contain an acrid substance known as 'sinalbin'. At one time good English mustards were made from a judicious mixture of the two varieties (approximately 37 per cent of brown to 50 per cent of white mustard flour), plus spices, such as pepper, chilli pepper, and even ginger, and about 10 per cent of rice flour.

English mustards are popular in France, while in England we import large quantities of the less ferocious French mustards. Brand names of some of the best of these are mentioned in the list of branded products at the end of this book.

NUTMEG: The inner kernel of the fruit borne by a tree called *myristica officinalis* or *myristica fragrans*.

The Moluccas and the islands of the Dutch East Indies were for centuries the great source of nutmeg production, the spice marts of Holland, Amsterdam and Rotterdam maintaining a virtual monopoly of the nutmeg and mace trade. This in no way prevented the English from becoming quite serious nutmeg addicts. Along with a number of other spices nutmeg was used – piteously – as a fumigant against the plague. At the same time it was immensely popular in the kitchen. During the seventeenth, eighteenth and nineteenth centuries English sweet dishes and cakes appear to have been crammed with nutmeg, mace, cinnamon and cloves. For nutmegs, English silversmiths devised marvels of pocket graters, little boxes hinged and folded, with sharp grating surfaces and a compartment for the nut. No fastidious traveller need ever have been without a nutmeg to grate upon his food, his punch, his mulled wine, his hot ale or comforting posset.

In 1966 a collection of these silver nutmeg graters, oval,

round, thimble-shaped, rectangular, octagonal, egg-shaped, heart-shaped, tubular, all of them rubbed and worn and loved, was auctioned at Sotheby's.* Prices fetched were anything from £40 to £160.

Somewhere I have read that English silver nutmeg graters were carried on the chatelaines worn by the housekeepers in great country houses, and that nutmegs were used for making a nutmeg tea. Curiously, I have never seen an old nutmeg grater with a ring by which it could be hung from a chain, nor have I ever come across any other mention of nutmeg tea. A secret addiction possibly?

Another odd point about nutmegs in English cookery is that recipes repeatedly call for 'slic'd nutmegs, a nutmeg sliced', sometimes two or three to one spice cake – admittedly very large ones. Now, it is not really possible to slice a nutmeg although it can be cut into little crumbs which today we certainly would not want to find in our creamed spinach or cheese sauce. Possibly, given the high price of good-quality nutmegs, and the quantity demanded for the kitchen, the inferior or wormy specimens† which were broken up for sale to the apothecaries for making extracts and tinctures (nutmeg oil was used to relieve a number of ailments, including insomnia) were also bought by economically minded house-keepers. There could hardly have been any question of lack of graters for although obviously not every household possessed a silver nutmeg grater – such a trinket would not in any case have been kept in the kitchen – a grater of some sort, usually called a rasp, was part of the equipment of most kitchens. The rasp was used mainly for breadcrumbs and was perhaps too rough for nutmegs, but there was also the housekeeper's spice box, probably kept under lock and key, with compartments for some half dozen spices and in the centre a little tubular box containing a grater and a place for the nutmegs.

---

*There is also a small collection in the Victoria and Albert Museum.

† The worm to which the fruit of *myristica* is subject has always pushed up the price of nutmegs, for it necessitates treatment with lime wash or by fumigation of the nuts before they are acceptable for sale.

Nutmeg is one of the spices which quickly loses its aroma when ground, so should be bought in whole form. In cheese sauces and soufflés, with all cream cheese mixtures, with spinach, a great number of egg dishes and in Christmas puddings and cakes, nutmeg is indispensable. In Italian cookery the nutmeg – *noce moscata* – is essential, and it flavours also a good deal of the food of Northern France, a circumstance due perhaps to the proximity of the Flemish and Dutch ports, as well as to Nantes, the Breton port which was at one time the headquarters of the French colonial spice trade.

The value set upon the nutmeg in the Near East might be summed up in a sentence written by Joseph Addison in the *Spectator* of 3 September 1711. 'The present Emperor of Persia,' writes Addison, 'denominates himself "the sun of glory and the nutmeg of delight".'

PAPRIKA PEPPER: The ground seeds of *capsicum annuum,* the sweet pepper which we call pimiento or pimento. The best paprika pepper is Hungarian; there are several grades between mildly hot, mild, and sweet; several shades from a rosy-brown to scarlet – the brown is said to be the best. Unending arguments as to which is best for what kind of goulash or other central European speciality are a Hungarian pastime; don't ever ask a Hungarian food expert to tell you about paprika unless you are prepared to hear more about the subject than you want to know. In other words, this is not the place for me to write about paprika, nor indeed do I use it very much in my cooking. It is a spice which could be useful, since it is mild and sweet, but it keeps badly. Those charming little red tins in which the best *edel-süss* or noble-sweet paprika is packed and exported from Hungary invariably end in my dustbin long before a quarter of the contents has been used. It should be borne in mind that paprika is *not* a substitute for cayenne, nor cayenne for paprika.

Pimentón is the Spanish version of paprika, and in English cookery books of the Edwardian period paprika is sometimes referred to as Krona pepper.

PEPPERCORNS:* The world's most valuable although not most expensive spice. While whole peppercorns which are the berries of the pepper tree, *piper nigrum*, retain their aroma and savour almost indefinitely, once ground, pepper rapidly deteriorates. For this reason all pepper, both for cooking and for the table, should be freshly ground in a pepper mill at the moment of use. There are very many different qualities of pepper, the most valuable and the hottest of the ordinary peppers being the white ones. White peppercorns are the inner part only of the berry gathered when fully ripe, while black ones are picked immature and retain their outer covering. While milder than white peppercorns, black ones have a more aromatic scent and flavour and are preferable for general kitchen use. One of the best qualities of black peppercorns is Malabar Black.

The peppery taste which is so overwhelming in many of the foods of commerce – English sausages in particular – is due to the inferior and mixed peppers used. These produce a hot and prickly sensation in the mouth without the true aromatic smell and taste of good pepper. When buying peppercorns, look to see that the grains are of an even size and colour. If some are large and black and others very small and brownish looking, this means that poor quality peppercorns have been mixed with the good ones.†

It should be added that when it comes to seasoning white cream sauces and other pale dishes, many cooks prefer freshly ground white to black peppercorns. The black specks of the latter do perhaps look a little rough in a delicate sauce, although I do not think the point of great import.

In France a mixture of black and white peppercorns – black

*Green peppercorns in their unripe and undried state have recently appeared on the European market. In consistency, these green peppercorns are soft, in taste and aroma they are delicious – pungent and at the same time very fresh and clean.

A further note on this very interesting new form of an ancient spice will be found on page 257.

†The above paragraphs were written in 1960 for *French Provincial Cooking* (Michael Joseph, Penguin).

for aroma, white for strength – is often used in cooking and for the table. No bad idea. (See the recipe for steak au poivre, p. 151.) This mixture of peppers – both can be put into one pepper mill – is sometimes known as mignonette pepper.

PICKLING SPICE: A uniquely English mixture, varying according to each spice-purveyor's own formula, but basically made up of mustard seeds, coriander seeds, allspice berries, a very small proportion of tiny hot red chillies, sometimes broken bayleaves, and little pieces of dry ginger root.

For the spicing of chutneys and pickled fruits and vegetables it is advisable to tie the spices in a little piece of muslin which can be extracted when cooking is complete. I still remember, from my earliest cooking days, picking red chillies out of about fifteen pounds of plum chutney rendered uneatable because the recipe had not included instructions to tie the chillies in a bag – and had clearly trebled the quantity of chillies needed. That author was one I did not trust again for a long long time.

POPPY SEEDS: These do not contain opium. They are the seeds of *papaver rhoeas*, very widely used in Jewish cookery and throughout central Europe to sprinkle on bread, salt sticks, rolls and biscuits. Ground, they flavour cakes and puddings, and are one of the ingredients of curry pastes and powders. The grinding of poppy seeds is easier said than done. They are one of the hardest of spices, requiring a special grinder, common in Austria and Germany, but hard to come by in England.

PUDDING SPICE OR MIXED SPICE: Fairly obviously, a compound of the sweet spices of English cookery – cinnamon, cloves, nutmeg, sometimes coriander, occasionally Jamaica pepper or allspice, depending upon each spice-purveyor's recipe, and which spices are plentiful and cheap when the time comes to make up the spice mixture in bulk.

For those who make rich fruit cakes and puddings or who are much addicted to dishes such as the cream-cheese mixtures described in this book, a little jar of mixed sweet spices is useful –

but do make it a little one. These powdered and mixed spices quickly lose their strength.

SAFFRON: Saffron is a 'useful aromatic, of a strong penetrating smell, and a warm pungent bitterish taste'. Culpeper's very exact description contains its own warning. There are few spices or aromatics which possess *and* impart scent, taste and colour in such a high degree as saffron. Properly administered, it can make a rice dish, a soup, a sauce, most wonderfully attractive; incautiously used, that penetrating smell, that pungent, bitterish taste can turn the same dish into something quite repellent. On the other hand, anybody unfamiliar with the appearance and the smell of true saffron may find himself landed with an adulterated or falsified version of saffron powder which produces an effective yellow stain but makes little difference to the scent or flavour of a dish, a circumstance which has led to odd misconceptions as to the properties of saffron, the quantities in which recipe writers prescribe it, and the methods advised for adding it.

True saffron, as we know it for cooking or pharmaceutical purposes, consists of the dried styles of *crocus sativus,* the lilaccoloured autumnflowering crocus. Some 85,000 flowers are needed to make up one pound of dried styles. One grain, or one 437th of an avoirdupois ounce of these tiny, fierylooking orange and red threadlike objects scarcely fills the smallest salt spoon, but provides flavour and colouring for a typical Milanese risotto, Spanish paëlla, or bouillabaisse, for four to six people.

A reader once asked me if a recipe calling for 2 oz. of saffron could be quite correct. No wonder. She had discovered that at the then current retail price of 3d. a grain, 2 oz. would add about £11 to the cost of the dish. A misprint? Or a howler on the part of the recipe compiler?

The way Italians use the little saffron filaments is to pour over them about a coffeecupful of hot water or of whatever stock is being used for the dish in question – usually a Milanese risotto. Leave this infusion until it has turned a deep bright orange and is giving out its characteristic unmistakable smell. When your rice is about two-thirds cooked, strain the liquid into it. This tiny quantity will turn three-quarters to one pound of rice a fine bright lemon colour, and will give it a flavour sufficiently pungent for most people's palates. Too strong an infusion will produce a bitter taste, and so would the little threads themselves if put whole into any dish, cake, soup or sauce.

For dishes where the additional liquid of an infusion may not be practical, powdered saffron can be stirred directly and with a little trouble, evenly, into a mixture, although ready-powdered saffron in little packets, if genuine, comes, weight for weight, at least twice as expensive as whole Valencia saffron. This is the quality considered by the trade to be the best. It is to be bought at good chemists and from spice and herb specialists.

When you are using saffron only for an occasional dish the difference in cost between the whole and the powdered product may seem small. For caterers and restaurateurs who claim to provide Spanish, Italian, Provençal and other saffron-flavoured dishes in their genuine form and on a large scale, it could be considerable. As the bulk price of the best quality Spanish whole saffron before it enters this country is upwards of £7.50 a pound and rises to £5.50 an ounce by the time the customs, wholesalers, distributors, and retailers have taken their toll, it seems unnecessary to double it again by paying for ready-ground saffron. It is not surprising however if caterers and restaurateurs economize by using diluted saffron or the so-called paëlla powder which is quite commonly used in Spain. Nobody familiar with saffron could mistake this tangerine-coloured substance for the real thing, nor indeed does it make any pretence to containing any saffron at all. It is simply for producing the right yellow colour, and its taste is faintly salt. Customers who've never tasted the original dishes may well prefer them without saffron.

If I myself had to choose just one type of dish in which saffron makes an important difference it would be Mediterranean fish soups and stews rather than rice dishes.

As an alternative to saffron, genuine or imitation, some cooks use the ground root of turmeric, a plant of the ginger family, which gives commercial curry powders their yellow colour. Without the bitter pungency of saffron, turmeric has a quite attractive spicy flavour and smell, is comparatively cheap (at spice counters and Indian grocers) and can be added direct without preliminary infusion. A teaspoonful, approximately, will do the job of colouring a rice dish for four people, but the resulting flavour is very different from that produc-ed by saffron. An oriental rather than a Mediterranean accent.

Even in the days when saffron growing was a quite flourish-ing English agricultural activity with a centre at Saffron Walden in Essex and extensive cultivations in Suffolk and Cambridgeshire, saffron was an expensive aromatic drug and colouring agent.

From an engrossing account* of the household expenses and the daily life of Eleanor, Countess of Leicester, wife of Simon de Montfort, we learn that the Countess paid between 10s. and 14s. a pound for saffron, as against 10d. to 2s. 4d. for pepper (56 lb. were bought during six months), about the same price for ginger, and only 4d. for coriander. Cloves, on the other hand, evidently in that year of 1265 going through one of their periodical fluctuations in price, cost nearly as much as saffron of which Miss Labarge notes that the de Montforts 'never bought more than a pound' at a time, and only a pound and a half of cloves as compared with six of cinnamon.

Taking into account the size of a great feudal household with family, domestic servants, retainers, cooks, bakers, body-guards, horsemen, falconers, messengers, and all the rest of the train forever on the move between one establishment and another (Dover Castle was the de Montfort stronghold), carry-ing with them the necessary supplies of food, the spice-buying does indeed seem rather modest. One hundred and ten pounds of rice bought between Christmas and April and two hundred

---

* *A Baronial Household of the Thirteenth Century*, Margaret Wade Labarge, 1965.

and eighty of almonds during the same period put the quantity of spices into reasonable proportion.

'A few threads of saffron', says *Law's Grocer's Manual,** 'put in the water for canaries occasionally makes a good stimulant'.

SALT: *Forget not the salt.* Elizabeth de Grey, Countess of Kent, writes this final instruction at the end of a recipe for spice cake included in a little cookery book called *A True Gentlewoman's Delight,* posthumously published in 1653.

There seems little to add to the Countess of Kent's reminder, although I cannot help remarking that it is odd that, in books and treatises on spices, salt is so seldom accorded space in its own right.

Though we may have at our command all the spices grown between Trebizond and Malabar and every aromatic harvested from the Lebanon to Mexico, we cannot ignore our need for salt. Salt is a mineral and regarded as a condiment rather than as a spice, since all spices are of vegetable origin. So for that matter are all other traditional condiments, so the prime importance of salt in our food and in our lives is an interesting point.

In England we use salt mined from the rocks, salt evaporated from the sea, and salt from the earth which is called saltpetre or nitre (potassium nitrate, or KNO_3), which is the all-important ingredient that gives our bacon and hams, our salt beef and our pickled ox-tongues† their familiar dark-pink colour and without which these cured meats would be an unappetizing grey. A Victorian writer on the chemistry of cookery calls saltpetre‡ the cosmetic of the preserved-meat industry. Sal-prunella is a chemical variant of saltpetre, often specified in old recipes, probably because (due to the fusion of the saltpetre into small hard balls) it contained a minute quantity of potassium nitrite and so started the curing process more rapidly. So far as

---

*See p. 251.

†Formulas for brines are quoted on pp. 167 and 168, and others, special to ox-tongues, on pp. 175 and 176.   ‡ See also note on p. 167.

I know, sal-prunella is no longer used in England, but salt-petre proper is to be bought from chemists and can be used where sal-prunella is specified. Beware of overdoing the dose, for saltpetre has a hardening effect on meat.

Freezing salt, often referred to in the old instructions for ice-cream making, is a coarser version of salt in crystals or *gros sel*. Proportions for the old hand-cranked *sorbetière* are approxi-mately 1 lb. of salt to 3 lb. of ice. A sprinkling of saltpetre is said to hasten the freezing process. Freezing salt is hard to come by; demand is now so small and the salt so bulky that few grocers can find room for it; and it cannot, by Board of Trade food regulations, be sold for human consumption. A coarse crystal salt – not the costly Maldon salt – does just as well but does make the cost of ice-cream rather high.*

Our table salt is mainly produced from the salt springs of Cheshire and Worcestershire. Nowadays it is refined and made free-running by the addition of magnesium carbonate, a chemical no doubt harmless but all the same suspect to many people who feel that our daily food is already quite sufficiently unnatural without even our salt being tampered with.

Old-fashioned block or kitchen salt, also known as cut lump salt, is rock salt refined but without additives, and is the salt which is meant when recipes, usually those for pickling hams and curing beef, call for 'common salt' or 'kitchen salt'. Stocked by health food stores, kitchen shops and the more enterprising grocers, this pure Cheshire rock salt is also packed in 3 lb. and 6 lb. containers. I use it for all my cooking.

Rock salt in crystals is less refined than kitchen salt. In France this is known as *sel-gemme*, and in the heyday of our own salt production the term sal-gem was also common English usage. (The great Cheshire mines were first discovered in 1670, and so mightily did the English salt industry flourish that two hundred years later we were producing two million

*F. E. Charman Ltd, British Rail Depot, Lots Road, London S.W.10 (01-352 3591) sell salt suitable for freezing in minimum quantities of 1 cwt. Customers can collect, or Charman's will deliver locally, but a charge is made for carriage.

tons of salt a year, supplying a third of all the table salt con-
sumed in Europe, and exporting to America to the tune of
something like a million tons yearly.) In recent years the
English production of rock salt in crystal form has dwindled
almost to vanishing point, a Northwich firm being the only
one still active in this branch of the salt business. As far as sea
salt is concerned, since 1970 the only English-produced one
comes from Maldon in Essex. This latter salt, evaporated by a
process which has remained unique, was already renowned for
its quality and purity at least two hundred years ago, for
Hannah Glasse mentions it twice in her celebrated *Art of
Cookery Made Plain and Easy*, first published in 1747. Mrs
Glasse avers that York hams owed their excellence to the salt
used in the cure, 'a large clear salt ... gives the meat a fine
flavour. I used to have it from Maldon in Essex, and that salt
will make any ham as fine as you can desire.' Mrs Glasse was
also of the opinion that Suffolk butter was finer than any other
in England, and that the quality was due to the Maldon salt
used to preserve it. She does, however, allow that rock salt from
Nantwich in Cheshire is good for salting meat, and the 'right
sort is called Lounds's salt'.

   The editor of *Cassell's Dictionary of Cookery*, published some
hundred and thirty years later, was of a different opinion,
although the importance of the quality of salt is still stressed. 'It
is not a matter of indifference what kind of salt is employed for
curing meat and fish. Bay-salt is preferred. This is in large
crystals – it is obtained by spontaneous evaporation of salt
water. The superiority of Dutch cured herring has been
ascribed to the use of bay-salt.' Can 'spontaneous evaporation'
be quite correct? In a sense it is.

   The differentiation between bay-salt and sea-salt is or was
that the former was obtained by evaporation of sea water in pits,
and by the natural heat of the sun, whereas sea-salt is evaporated
by artificial heat. The best bay-salt available in England came
at one time from Portugal, and again we have the theory that a
certain type of preserved fish owed its reputation to the excellence of the salt – in this case it was a question of Portuguese

sardines. The French on the other hand attribute the delicacy of their sardines partly to the fine olive oil in which they are canned, but mainly and predictably, to the greater finesse of the fish caught in French waters. What few people seem to realize about the canned sardines which we take for granted is that they are the direct descendants of the old salted sardines of Brittany. Before the discovery of the canning process, in the eighteen-twenties, these salted sardines, stored in jars and sealed with butter, were one of the many marine delicacies enjoyed by the merchant families of the port of Nantes on the Loire estuary. Hence, it was in Nantes that the sardine canning industry was evolved.

Claims regarding the superior nature of Gorgona anchovies over any other have been based on the fine salt of Tuscany, which is rock salt, exceptionally potent, or so it seemed to me when I brought some home from Volterra, where the salt springs are worked. In Italy, incidentally, salt is a State monopoly and is bought not from a grocer but from tobacconists' shops.

No doubt the Sardinians, who have immense sea-salt pans in the south-eastern end of their island, could make out a case for the connection between this circumstance and the ancient fame of their *botargo,* the compressed and salted mullet roe of the Mediterranean. (This delicacy, well known in Jacobean England, was offered at the coronation feast of James II in 1685.)

Scottish haddock curers have – or had – their own sea salt and with their Arbroath smokies could certainly stake a claim to producing one of the most subtle of all salt and smoked fish delicacies. Salty black olives of Provence, salted pistachio nuts of Persia, firm white ewes'-milk cheese of Greece, stored in brine, salt lemons of Morocco, sharp and penetratingly aromatic, all these . . . a score of foods – which are obviously not necessities, but are among the small luxuries of life – owe their existence to the preservative properties of salt, every grain of it doubtless regarded in its own locality as the finest, the cleanest, the purest, the most salty salt.

In other words, forget not the salt, whether it be a question of your bread dough, your salad dressing, your béchamel sauce, your omelette, your rice, your spice compounds – and do forget the salt when it comes to making a stock or broth which is to be concentrated by reduction, or you take the risk of making it uneatable by anybody's standards.

This brings us to a point which I find odd. The gastronomically knowing tend to be abusive about the Englishman's habit of adding salt to his food at table. Why, when as is universally accepted, everybody's palate for salt differs so widely? No doubt it is more mannerly, not to say more prudent, to taste a dish before reaching for the salt, the pepper mill, the mustard, but to claim that any cook however masterly and subtle his touch can season all dishes to suit every palate seems to me to attribute to him the powers of a magician. Ah well, not even this super-being can get the salt into a boiled egg before it gets to your egg cup. .... And do remember by the way that those who habitually eat more vegetables, eggs, and cheese than meat need more salt in their food than those whose chief sustenance is steak, roast meat and chicken.

As for salt for the kitchen, and the table, keep the former, if it is rough or *gros-sel*, in a non-porous and open stoneware jar or wooden box near to your stove, so that you can reach out to seize a handful to throw into your saucepan of vegetables, or rice. (Talking of rice, a grain or two in the salt jar helps to keep the salt dry.) Perhaps the proximity of the salt will remind you also to rub it over your steak *immediately* before you cook it, to season your fish *in advance*, to crush your garlic and a little salt with the flat of a knife on a wooden board instead of fiddling about with the lethal garlic squeezer. (I say lethal because to me the extraction of the potent and acrid juices so ably performed by this instrument spells death to any dish into which garlic is thus introduced.)

For the table, the present-day tendency – all the go, as Edwardian gossip writers used to say – is to have a salt mill to grind sea or rock salt. Personally, I think it not worth the bother. I crush my salt in a wooden mortar – which takes a few seconds – and put it upon the table in an old-fashioned salt cellar. If you use Maldon salt, the flakes do not need grinding, and in any case are so formed that they slip straight through the mechanism.

I have to admit that I do not even bother with a salt spoon. I am not able to see what is unmannerly or wrong with putting one's fingers into the salt.

SESAME SEEDS: In Greek, Middle Eastern and Arabian cooking these seeds of *sesamum indicum* are freely strewn on cakes and bread and sweetmeats, giving a characteristic sweet-scorched flavour which belongs unmistakably to the Levant. A thin clear and light oil used in Chinese and Indian cooking and for curry pastes is also made from sesame seeds, but it is in the thick oily paste known as *tahina* or *tahini* that sesame really comes into its own. It is tahina which, diluted with water, makes the sauce in which Egyptians, Syrians, Lebanese and Cypriots dip their flat unleavened bread, and it is tahina mixed with sieved, cooked chick peas which nowadays figures daily on the menus of the scores of London-Cypriot taverns and restaurants. (I suspect that much of it comes out of tins imported from Israel.) An ancient dish, this *hummus bi tahina* of Egypt and Asia Minor, and a most delicious one – and it must not be forgotten that a sprinkling of dried mint is the essential finishing touch.

Indian, Chinese, and African cooking are also rich in recipes using sesame seeds and sesame oil, but the tahina paste appears to be unique to the Levantine countries and the Eastern Mediterranean. Halva, the great sweetmeat of these countries is also based on sesame-seed paste. A description of the ancient method of mashing the seeds is given in *Law's Grocer's Manual* (*circa* 1892), already quoted in these pages:

'Sesame is also widely cultivated in Syria, where, in preparing the oil, the grain is soaked in water for 24 hours, and then placed in an oblong pot, coated with cement, on which two men work a wooden hammer of 20 lb. weight. Efforts are not made to mash the kernels. The skins are separated in a tub of water, salted to a degree sufficient to float an egg. The bran sinks, while the kernels remain on the surface. The sesame seeds are now broiled in an oven, and sent to the mill to be ground. From the millstone the oil drops into a jar, and is thick, of a dark yellow colour, and sweet. It is used extensively by the poorer classes in place of cheese, syrup, honey, etc., and is popular on account of its saccharin properties.

'Confectionery is made by mixing sesame oil with syrup and other elements.'

TURMERIC: A root or rhizome of the ginger family, *curcuma longa*, turmeric yields the yellow spice powder which gives curry compounds their characteristic colour and a small part of their aroma. A mild, warm and attractive spice, turmeric is much loved in Moroccan as well as in Indian cookery. For those who like mild spices but do not care for curry proper, likewise for those who cannot take saffron, turmeric provides a most useful alternative for flavouring and colouring rice, chicken and lamb dishes.

Ground turmeric retains its colouring properties for a long time but quickly loses its aromatic strength. A young friend once brought me a little phial of a spice bought the day before in a Moroccan spice bazaar. It was called *kharkoum*, she told me. It smelled delicious and unfamiliar, and it was only when I sprinkled a little into a lamb stew the same evening that I realized it was turmeric, so fresh and aromatic that it was hard to believe that this was the same spice as the one which had obviously spent far too long in my cupboard. A good lesson. One ounce of turmeric is more than enough to buy at one time – unless you live on spiced rice and curries.

VANILLA BEANS: The pods of a climbing orchid called *vanilla planifolia*, vanilla deriving from the Spanish *vaina*, a pod, sheath or scabbard, and *planifolia* indicating flat leaves. The plant and its product are said to have been known to the Aztecs and used by them as a flavouring for chocolate. It is odd there⁄ fore that when the Spaniards took chocolate, or rather cocoa beans to Spain in the sixteenth century, they appear not to have known about vanilla, for until the eighteenth century and even later cinnamon was the common flavouring for both drinking chocolate and chocolate as a sweetmeat. Indeed cinnamon complements chocolate more suitably than does vanilla which is overpowered by the heavy cocoa taste, although the synthetic vanilla of commerce has such a coarse aroma that it surmounts any such considerations. Plain chocolate, so the manufacturers declare, is today scarcely acceptable without a vanilla flavouring.

It is in the characteristic rime or 'frost' which forms on the outer surface of vanilla pods when they are dried that the fragrance of this aromatic bean is concentrated and by which they should be judged when bought.

In the nineteenth century the French sugar growers of the island of Réunion or Bourbon made the cultivation of vanilla an important secondary industry; scarcely a sugar estate on the island, we learn from a handbook of about 1890, had not 'more or less land under vanilla' and 'the occupants of almost every hut cover their yards, courts, and plots with vanilla creepers.' To this colonial enterprise is due the popularity of vanilla in France, its association with *les îles Bourbon* – nearly all vanilla sold in France bears a label declaring it to be *vanille Bourbon* – and its presence in so many cakes, creams, biscuits, pastries and preserves. Vanilla ice cream was more probably popularized by the Americans, for during the latter decades of the nineteenth century immense quantities of vanilla – something like 100,000 lb. a year – were exported from Mexico to New York. At one time the vanilla ice cream of the city of Philadelphia was said to be the best in the States.

The following recipe for a vanilla ice-cream mixture from *Gunter's Modern Confectioner* (1861) gives some idea of the lavish way in which this powerfully scented and highly prized bean was used before the discovery of synthetic essence:

'Chop up half an ounce of vanilla, pound it very fine in a metal mortar. Take five or six ounces of sugar, and add it by degrees to the vanilla, and pound together. When done, put this into a pint of fresh cream, with the yolks of seven or eight eggs, make hot over a fire, but do not boil. Strain through a sieve. When sufficiently cool put it in the freezing pot and work it well.' Half an ounce of vanilla is about six pods. I find that two or three are ample to flavour a mixture made from one and a half pints of cream, four ounces of sugar and four egg yolks.

To make vanilla sugar for flavouring sweet pastry and fruit dishes, it is not necessary to pound the vanilla beans. Simply cut one or two into halves or quarters, store these in a jar of caster sugar. After a few days the sugar will be strongly scented.

To make a vanilla-flavoured custard or cream put a whole bean into the milk, egg and sugar mixture. Extract it when the custard is thickened and cooled. Vanilla beans can be used many times. Dry them in the plate drawer of the oven and return them to the caster sugar jar.

Do not try to strain out the tiny black specks left by the vanilla bean after cooking. They are the visible signs of the authenticity of flavouring in a vanilla ice cream, custard or soufflé.

A piece of vanilla bean baked with sliced apples, whole plums or apricots gives the fruit an extraordinary and haunting scent.

An unusually early mention of vanilla in an English cookery book occurs in Hannah Glasse's *Art of Cookery*, 1756 edition. She specifies 'three good vanelos', 2 oz. of the best cinnamon, half a dram of cardamom pods, and 3 oz. of sugar to flavour and sweeten the extract of 6 lb. of cocoa nibs.* Odd proportions, and an odd mixture of aromatics. This must have been the transition period from cinnamon to vanilla. Mrs Glasse was using both, as cooks so often do, just to make sure.

French vanilla notwithstanding, the best beans still come from Mexico. Harvesting takes place in the late autumn and winter. Drying and treating take four or five months, so the new season's vanilla pods reach the European markets in the spring.

* The rough form in which cocoa for drinking chocolate was marketed. The equivalent, in a sense, of coffee beans. The extract took several hours to brew and must have been bitter and very thick.

* *

Aromatic Herbs, Dried or Fresh

When a recipe says 'herbs', when can I use dried and when must I use fresh ones (must because the latter are more difficult to get)? Can I use the herbs such as fennel and marjoram which I see growing wild? If so, which parts, fresh and/or dried? Into what dishes to put which different herbs, and, roughly, in what quantities?

Questions, all these, put to me by a reader, good questions, but not ones to which there are any short answers. As briefly as possible, however, and to deal with the commonest herbs only, I'd outline the matter as follows: among those herbs which it is essential to have fresh, or rather, which are not worth bothering with in dried form are parsley, chives, chervil, fennel *leaves*. Fresh tarragon, provided it comes from the true French plant and not from the Russian variety, more prolific but scentless, has considerable strength, flavour and aroma all of which are weakened, although not radically altered, when the herb is dried, so a good dried tarragon (such as the one put out by the Chiltern Herb Farm) used within a few months – very few dried herbs last as long as a year – is very adequate in Béarnaise sauce, in stuffings and sauces for chicken, in fish dishes, and in herb butter for steak or fish. It is a passable substitute for fresh tarragon in a vinaigrette sauce, so long as you have fresh parsley to supplement it. As to quantities, if a recipe prescribes a teaspoon of fresh tarragon leaves, I use double the amount of dried.

Basil is a herb which is incomparably superior in its fresh form. One little bunch or plant will fill a whole room with its rich and spicy scent; but the plant is notoriously difficult to rear in our climate and, when it does succeed, is in season during a few weeks of the late summer only. There are some dishes, such as the famous *soupe au pistou* of the Niçois district, and the *pesto* sauce of the Genoese which depend entirely on fresh basil, and plenty of it, for their existence, and these it would be pointless to attempt with the dried version, which not only loses a deal of its pungency but also undergoes a change in flavour. Good ones, such as the one dried on the stalk in Provence and the Chiltern home-grown – when available – still give out an attractive and quite pronounced scent when used in meat stews, sauces for pasta, soups, and Mediterranean vegetable dishes. I find basil indispensable and use it lavishly, but it isn't everybody's taste, so quantities must be decided by trial and error.

With fresh mint we are on more familiar ground. Any self-respecting English cook knows that if she wants mint sauce then the fresh herb is essential. Dried, the crumbled leaves of common garden spearmint make a typical and equally essential Middle Eastern flavouring for curd-cheese fillings for pastry, yogurt dressings and sauces, salads, stuffed or stewed aubergines, tomatoes and peppers, pilaffs, carrots, fish stewed in oil, soups. Quite often, in this type of cookery, mint can be substituted for dried basil, which is a member of the mint family and when dried takes on something of the same flavour.

*

An important but often overlooked category is that of herbs which are used dried, or semi-dried, on the stalk. These include all kinds of thyme, bayleaves, rosemary and sage, and (stalks only) fennel.

Fresh wild thyme from the South Downs and most of the cultivated varieties, and also bay leaves, rosemary and sage, can be left, without water, in a big bowl, or spread out on newspaper. In due course they become sufficiently dry to be stored, on the stalk, in tall glass jars; or they can be kept anywhere handy in the kitchen – although the bunches of herbs which look so picturesque hanging up in the kitchens of Mediterranean houses tend, in smoky cities, to get a bit musty and begrimed. Since these herbs, picked and packed in Provence are now so widely sold in English kitchen shops, it is useful to know that stored in glass jars or in Porosan bags they will retain their aromatic properties for a long time.

Twigs of thyme and bayleaves tied together with fresh parsley make up the routine bouquet of French stewed and braised dishes; to this bouquet some cooks add rosemary. I don't. With sage, this herb figures in my kitchen as a decoration only – with their grey-green and reddish leaves both herbs are beautiful in a jug of country flowers but in cooking I don't want either. Many Italians stuff joints of lamb and pork almost to bursting with rosemary, and the result is perfectly awful. The meat is drowned in the acrid taste of the herb and the spiky little leaves get stuck between your teeth. Once, in an out-of-doors Capri café I saw an old woman basting her fish – it was grilling over an open charcoal fire – with a branch of rosemary dipped in olive oil. That's about as much of rosemary as, personally, I want.

The use of herbs is very much a matter of association, taste, and prejudice, and cooks whose work I respect recommend a branch or two of rosemary in the dish with veal, chicken and lamb roasts (I prefer branches of wild Provence thyme); others suggest that the meat be spiked with the minutest pieces of dried rosemary and garlic. As for sage, Italian cooks, like ourselves, are fond of it, and use it for a number of veal dishes. To me, it deadens the food with its musty, dried-blood scent. Instead of sage, it is worth trying dried mint or basil, especially in a sauce or stuffing for duck. Summer savory (*sarriette* in French, *poivre d'âne* in Provence) is another rather potent herb, good with haricot beans and bean soups. It is also worth knowing that this herb can be used rather as is a condiment, and provides a little help for those on a salt-free diet.

For pork roasts and grills, for fish stocks and soups, for pot-roasted chicken and grilled fish, the sun-dried stalks of wild or garden fennel make a wonderfully aromatic flavouring. But it is essential they be tinder dry, or they will give no scent as they cook. The feathery leaves of fennel, so delicate when fresh and cooked for a second or two with veal escalopes, fish fillets and egg dishes, don't survive the drying process. They are worth neither trouble nor money.

*

When it is a question of bought herbs, dried and rubbed, the rougher looking ones are usually the best. The more finely powdered the herbs, the more the aromas tend to get lost. Lemon thyme (at its most delicious when fresh), common thyme, and marjoram are all good and much used dried herbs for poultry and veal stuffing and for meat stews. Dried wild marjoram, usually sold as oregano (*origanum* being the botanical name of all marjorams) or *marjolaine,* is a splendid herb to sprinkle on lamb and pork for roasting and grilling. In Greece, grilled lamb kebabs owe much of their character to the combined flavours of *rigani* and lemon juice freshly sprinkled over the meat before cooking. An important point though about the Greek wild marjoram is that the Greeks dry the *flower heads* for cooking purposes whereas here, in France, and in Italy, it is the *leaves* which are used. The difference in scent and keeping quality is immense, the Greek version being in both cases on the winning side.

In other words, dried herbs should not necessarily be regarded as a substitute for fresh ones. Very often the dried version is more useful than the fresh, and when an essential fresh herb is out of season or unobtainable try an *alternative* rather than waste time on a substitute.

In the eager rush to meet the growing demand for kitchen herbs more enlivening than the musty mixtures in a cardboard packet of the old greengrocer's shop, the new generation of packers and suppliers – and customers – has forgotten that dried herbs should be purveyed in small quantities.

Do you need to invest in dried herbs to bequeath to your grandchildren? Jars or packets of dried herbs should not contain more than one ounce, or approximately 30 grammes – and even that is a generous allowance for many of the lesser-used herbs. It is preferable to pay proportionately more for a small quantity than to be landed with a whopping jar, adorned with a fancy label, which you will throw into the dustbin long after the contents have become useless for any purpose whatsoever.

On the other hand it is relevant to bear in mind that many of the herbs normally bought in dried form – thyme, tarragon, mint, basil, marjoram, fennel, savory – flower once a year only and that the season's crop reaches the shops in the early autumn. With the exception of bayleaves and possibly rosemary the dried herbs you buy at Christmas or Easter or in June will be of the same vintage as the ones you bought in October. It is unreasonable to expect freshly dried herbs in May. It is unreasonable given our climate to expect even fresh herbs other than chives and parsley in May. Tarragon is rarely ready before June, and basil is at its most prolific in the later summer, mid-July to September.

One herb which we can get nearly all the year round is watercress. Perhaps because we regard this plant as a salad and soup or garnishing herb rather than as a flavouring or aromatic, we forget about delicious things like watercress butter, and about the useful properties of a little chopped watercress as an alternative to mustard and pepper in a cream sauce (especially good with fish), and as a filling for omelettes instead of the fresh *fines herbes* so hard to come by.

'*In plain Bag-puddings it makes them much more savoury, to put into them a little Penny-Royal shreded very small, as also other sweet-Herbs. You must put in so little, as not to taste strong of them, but onely to quicken the other flat Ingredients.*'

The Closet of the Eminently Learned
Sir Kenelm Digby Knight Opened, 1669

As so often, Sir Kenelm sums up the whole matter of how to use herbs in a couple of memorable lines. Pennyroyal by the way is *mentha pulegium*, a variety of mint.

* *

More flavourings

LENGTHY though they may appear, the foregoing notes on spices, aromatics and condiments used in the English kitchen are very far from complete. The list could go on to include many more important aromatics such as the zest of lemons and oranges, orange-flower water, almonds both sweet and bitter, candied fruit peels and angelica (one of my favourites) and all the essences which go into cakes and confectionery. Apart from the essential condiments – salt, mustard, – there is sugar, and there is honey, all the vinegars and the concentrated sauces such as walnut, mushroom and tomato ketchups, anchovy essence, soy, tabasco, Worcester sauce, and its few surviving imitations, there is horseradish, there are capers, in fact an armoury of flavouring aids through which we consume, indirectly, a formidable quantity of spices, condiments and herbs, not to mention quite a few synthetic substances. There are faddy flavourings, once beloved of the slightly manic English military gentleman who cherished secret compounds such as sherry in which chillies had been steeped, there is the juice of fresh limes – a condiment rather than a flavouring or aromatic – there are dried mushrooms and anchovies preserved in salt brine or in olive oil, and above all there is Parmesan cheese, for it should not be forgotten that the uses of grated Parmesan as a condiment have been appreciated in English cooking for some centuries, certainly since the Stuart period. Not even the most drum-bashing British patriot would attempt to pretend when it comes to a concentrated and subtle flavouring, that any English cheese can substitute for Parmesan. Not even the French can claim, although they have been known to try, that used as the Italians use it, any known cheese is possessed of the remarkable seasoning powers, seasoning without overpowering, of this entirely marvellous product of the province of Parma.*

There are flavouring vegetables and fresh herbs – tarragon, basil, parsley, chives, lemon, thyme, mint, watercress, carrots, onions, leeks, shallots, garlic, mushrooms, which could all be included in this list. Going back only a little way into the past, we should find sorrel, nasturtium and violet leaves, marigold petals, and clove carnations, pomegranate seeds, pennyroyal, galingale,† rocket‡ and rue. Kipling knew what he was talking about when he said *Anything green that grew out of the mould / Was an excellent herb to our fathers of old.*

This little volume started out as a twenty-page booklet and has already turned into a fully grown book. Were I to attempt the inclusion of all the aromatics and spices, herbs, condiments and flavourings of English cooking, past and present, not to mention those of the national styles of cookery with which we are becoming newly familiar – the Chinese, the Greek and Cypriot, the Spanish, Italian and North African and West Indian – what would emerge would be an encyclopedia, a weighty reference book. I would not be capable of compiling such a volume, and this present one is intended primarily as a cookery book. The history and the theory must not swamp the practice. It is the recipes which are the core of the book.

BOUQUET GARNI

To make a bouquet garni, the little bunch of herbs required in so many meat, game and poultry recipes, simply tie together a couple of whole bayleaves, a sprig or two of dried thyme on the stalk, a few fresh parsley stalks, and, for certain dishes such as *daubes* of beef, a strip of orange peel and a piece of celery. For fish dishes make the bouquet of fennel stalks, lemon peel and

---

*Not all Parmesan cheese comes from the province of Parma, or even from Italy. Much of the so-called Parmesan provided by caterers and restaurateurs hails from the Argentine.

† The root of a plant of the ginger family.

‡ A peppery salad herb, *eruca sativa*.

bayleaves. Leave a long string on the little bunch so that it can be easily extracted from the pot when cooking is completed.

To make a bouquet of herbs in leaf form (for those who do not care to find the little leaves in their soup or stew) put a teaspoon of mixed basil, marjoram, thyme and savory, with a crumbled bay leaf, in a 4 inch square of muslin. Add three or four whole peppercorns and, if you like, a peeled clove of garlic crushed with a knife. Tie the little bundle with thread, discard it when the dish is cooked.

For chicken and fish dishes, vary the flavouring by using tarragon or fennel instead of the mixed herbs; for pork and game dishes add crushed juniper berries to the mixture.

Either of the above methods gives results so superior to the anonymous, slightly musty-smelling sachets or so-called bouquets garnis of commerce that it is really worthwhile taking the scarcely noticeable extra trouble. Personally I find the little ritual of preparing herb bouquets one of the minor pleasures of cooking. Nothing would persuade me to relinquish it in favour of a bought bouquet made up in a factory and sold by the dozen, all as like as two – or rather twelve – teabags.

*

It is interesting to recall, in connection with aromatic herbs, that they were not necessarily always used for cooking and medicine, or even for love potions, magic spells, oils, essences, and perfumes. Many of them were valued as strewing herbs to make a clean smell in the house, and as rough and ready dis-infectants. Making up the ritual bouquet for the pot, or igniting the fennel and bayleaves underneath a sea-bass, a piece of pork, a chicken, it is pleasing to think of Andrew Boorde, sixteenth-century doctor, sometime monk, and author of *The Dyetary of Helth* (1542), who recommended that juniper, rosemary, rushes, bayleaves, or frankincense be burned 'to expel all corrupt and contagious air in the buttery, the cellar, the kitchen, the larder-house . . .'

Measurements and Temperatures

How much cheese is a handful? How much more or less is a cupful? What is the capacity of a glass, a tumbler, or soup ladle? What is the difference between a suspicion and a pinch? How much more is a good pinch? How much wine is a little, how many olives a few? When the book says a tin of chopped almonds or pomegranate juice what are you supposed to understand by that?

The answer to that one, at least, I know. A tin is an English round fifty-cigarette tin, at one time a fairly common unit of measurement in Egypt and other parts of North Africa and the Middle East. It holds 8 fl. oz., the same as an American measuring cup. When I see this unit occurring in a traveller's cookery book I feel reassured that the recipe is genuine, probably written down from dictation by some Berber, Persian or Sudanese cook. Infuriating instructions, though, to anyone not in the know. In the same way, some of the best of old French recipes are the kind which specify '*un bol de crème fraiche*' or '*un verre de farine*'. Maddening until one twigs that the French have a different word for every kind of bowl they use, and a '*bol*' is not a salad bowl or a mixing bowl of unspecified capacity, but the bowl from which you drink your morning café au lait, in fact a cup: so to use it as a measuring unit is perfectly reasonable since every French household possesses – or did possess – such bowls, and their capacities, ½ pint near enough, vary little.

Those glasses of flour, it can usually be taken, are tumblers of 6 oz. capacity, because if French cooks mean a wine glass they say '*un verre à Bordeaux*' and if they mean a small wine glass they say '*un verre à porto*' – a sherry glass to us.

English teacups, breakfast cups and coffee cups used as measuring units make sense to us; there could hardly not be a teacup in the house; give or take a spoonful its capacity is always about 5 oz.; a breakfast cup is 7 to 8 oz.; a coffee cup is an after-dinner coffee cup, or 2½ oz.; but not to Americans, who are baffled by these terms in English cookery books. To them a cup is a measuring cup of 8 fl. oz. capacity and there the matter ends. They don't know what a teacup holds, nor what a breakfast cup looks like, and a coffee cup is a morning coffee cup, which might be a teacup or a breakfast cup, whereas an after-dinner coffee cup is a demi-tasse.

As for scales and weights, in American household cooking they scarcely exist. The American system of measuring liquids and dry solids in standard cups and tablespoons is not very accurate but eliminates clutter in the way of measuring apparatus and means that everyone knows where they are when they read American recipes. Except, that is to say, ourselves. Because when we are told that the American measuring cup contains exactly a half pint of liquid we are often not told also that the American pint is 16 oz. whereas our Imperial pint is 20 oz. Although it wasn't, until 1878; a point which one has to remember when attempting to adapt recipes from eighteenth- and the earlier nineteenth-century books. Subtract 8 oz. from each of those quarts of stock and wine, milk and cream specified in the older books and it makes quite a difference. Anyone, therefore, who uses American cookery books and American translations of foreign cookery books published in England, without clear indications as to the system of measurement used, needs to remember that the American pint is the pre-1878 English one of 16 oz., and that a quart in American terms means 32 oz.

Where I find the American measurement system messy, unreliable and time-wasting is when it comes to cramming sticky things like butter or fat into a cup – incidentally, a stick of butter, sometimes specified in American recipes, means 4 oz., a unit in which you can buy butter in the States – and I have never been very successful in measuring cooked ingredients such as chopped meat or diced potatoes in cups. Do you cram the stuff down? Do you give it a good rattle so that it settles –

or alternatively flies all over the place? Just press lightly, my American colleagues tell me. How light is lightly? And how much does it matter?

Recipes in which every last drop of lemon juice and grain of pepper are specified are often no more logical than the ones which throw out instructions to 'chop a handful of shallots' or 'braise a nice piece of beef'. If you are going to be told exactly how much of everything to use, at precisely what stage each ingredient is to be added, plus cooking temperatures and timing down to the final minute, then you require to be told also the weight and dimensions of the cooking pot you are to use and the material of which it is to be made; variations for every type of fuel would have to be allowed for, not to mention qualifications such as the temperature of your kitchen and the altitude at which you are cooking; after all you might want to know how long it takes to boil an egg when you reach the top of Mont Blanc.

There is surely a happy medium. It is quite possible to combine the exercise of one's five senses in the kitchen with the use of measuring devices as guides. By temperament a non-measurer, I have myself, first through the wish to communicate recipes and now by force of habit, become the reverse. I find that the discipline of weighing and measuring does one's cooking nothing but good, provided that one does not waste time messing about with quarter-saltspoons and five-eighths of pints, nor, above all, expect that precision will eliminate the necessity to keep one's head or train one's eye and palate.

SOLID MEASUREMENTS

Metric	English
1,000 gr. (1 Kg.)	= approx. 2 lb. 3 oz.
500 gr.	= approx. 1lb. 1½ oz.
250 gr.	= approx. 9 oz.
125 gr.	= approx. 4¼ oz.
100 gr.	= approx. 3½ oz.

Measurements and Temperatures

LIQUID MEASUREMENTS

1 litre   = 1,000 gr. = approx. 35 fl. oz. = approx. 1¾ pints

½ litre   =   500 gr. = approx. 17½ fl. oz. = approx. ¾ pint plus 5 tablespoons

¼ litre   =   250 gr. = approx. 8¾ fl. oz. = approx. ½ pint less 2½ tablespoons

                170 gr. = ¼ pint

1 decilitre =   100 gr. = approx. 3 fl. oz. = 6 tablespoons

1 centilitre =   10 gr. = approx. ⅓ fl. oz. = 1 dessertspoon

TABLE OF EQUIVALENT AMERICAN MEASUREMENTS

English	American
¼ lb. butter or fat	= approx. ½ cup solidly packed
2 oz. butter or fat	= approx. ¼ cup = 4 tablespoons
1 oz. butter or fat	= approx. 2 tablespoons
½ lb. caster sugar	= approx. 1 cup plus 3 tablespoons
¼ lb. caster sugar	= approx. 8 tablespoons
2 oz. caster sugar	= approx. 4 tablespoons
1 lb. plain flour sieved	= approx. 4½ cups sieved cake flour
¼ lb. plain flour sieved	= approx. 1 cup plus 4 tablespoons
2 oz. plain flour sieved	= approx. 8 tablespoons
¼lb. dry grated cheese	= approx. 1 cup
6 oz. rice, raw	= approx. 1 cup

LIQUID MEASUREMENTS

English	American
1 gallon = 4 quarts = 8 pints	= 10 pints = 1¼ gallons
1 quart = 2 pints = 40 oz.	= 2½ pints = 5 cups
1 pint = 20 oz.	= 1¼ pints = 2½ cups
½ pint = 10 oz.	= 1¼ cups
¼ pint = 5 oz. = 1 gill	= ½ cup plus 2 tablespoons
2 oz. = 4 tablespoons	= ¼ cup
1 tablespoon = ½ oz.	= ½ oz.
1 teaspoon = ¼ tablespoon	= 1 teaspoon = ⅓ tablespoon

TABLE OF EQUIVALENT GAS AND ELECTRIC OVEN TEMPERATURES

Solid Fuel	Electricity		Gas
Slow	240°–310°F.	115°–155°C.	¼–2
Moderate	320°–370°F.	160°–190°C.	3–4
Fairly Hot	380°–400°F.	195°–205°C.	5
Hot	410°–440°F.	210°–230°C.	6–7
Very Hot	450°–480°F.	235°–250°C.	8–9

Sauces

COLD SAUCES

CUMBERLAND sauce is certainly one of our most delicious sauces. What basis there is for the story that it was named after Ernest, Duke of Cumberland, that brother of George IV's who became the last independent ruler of Hanover, nobody has ever explained. Still, as legends concerning the origins of dishes go, it's as good as another, and better than some: the sauce itself being as obviously German in origin as was its supposed royal namesake of the House of Hanover. All the same it is odd that no recipe for Cumberland sauce as such appears in any of the nineteenth-century standard cookery books in which one might expect to find it.

Eliza Acton's *Modern Cookery*, 1845, doesn't mention it; neither does Mrs Beeton's *Household Management*, 1861, nor Francatelli's *Cook's Guide* of the eighties. When the recipe does get into print it is in a book about English cooking written in French by a Frenchman, a chef called Alfred Suzanne who had worked in two great English households of the period, those of the Duke of Bedford and of the Earl of Wilton. Possibly in one of these aristocratic kitchens the sauce, already familiar, had been re-named in honour of a royal visit or some such festivity. In any case, it is the recipe in Suzanne's book *La Cuisine Anglaise*, 1904, which seems to have been popularized in the Edwardian period by Escoffier, who was also responsible for the commercial success of Cumberland sauce. Another highly respected French writer, Ali-Bab, describes a similar mixture of redcurrant jelly, port and orange peel which he says is called Sauce Victoria, asserting that it is eaten with grouse.

Was it that it took French cooks to perceive the possibilities of a sauce so very alien to French cooking? Evidently. At any rate another great chef and writer of French birth, Alexis Soyer, had in fact preceded his compatriots by fifty years. What is without doubt Cumberland sauce, although a rather simpler version than the one most of us know nowadays, is to be found incorporated in a three-page recipe for boar's head given in this author's *Gastronomic Regenerator*, 1853. (A summary of this recipe will be found on page 184.)

Acknowledged by Soyer to be the German method of making a sauce to be eaten with boar's head his instructions are to '*cut the rind, free from pith, of two Seville oranges into very thin strips half an inch in length, which blanch in boiling water, drain them upon a sieve and put them into a basin, with a spoonful of mixed English mustard, four of currant jelly, a little pepper, salt (mix well together) and half a pint of good port wine.*'

Among Soyer's extraordinarily versatile gifts was his great capacity for devising simple recipes of this kind, recipes which are quite timeless, and which anyone with no more than a single gas ring to cook on could still use today. (His *Shilling Cookery for the People*, 1855, is a little mine of instructive information for a lone, unskilled, and impecunious cook.) And as far as Cumberland sauce is concerned, Soyer's recipe is the one I habitually use these days; it produces results which if anything are better than Suzanne's more complicated formula (the shallots both he and Escoffier add are perfectly unnecessary). The only alterations I make are to use French mustard instead of English and to quarter the quantity of port; a half pint to four tablespoons of jelly produces a sauce which would be excessively liquid for modern tastes, although it probably suited Soyer's contemporaries. In his day that tendency to thicken all sauces which has since contributed to the ruin of our cookery had scarcely started; for example, plain port wine, simply warmed, could be served as an accompaniment to game birds such as wild duck and teal; any cook who offered such an unthickened sauce today would consider himself disgraced.

A recipe for modern, unthickened, version of the sauce follows.

CUMBERLAND SAUCE

This best of all sauces for cold meat – ham, pressed beef, tongue, venison, boar's head or pork brawn – can be made in small quantities and in a quick and economical way as follows:

With a potato parer cut the rind, very thinly, from two large oranges. Slice this into matchstick strips. Plunge them into boiling water and let them boil 5 minutes. Strain them.

Put them in a bowl with 4 tablespoons of redcurrant jelly, a heaped teaspoon of yellow Dijon mustard, a little freshly milled pepper, a pinch of salt and optionally a sprinkling of ground ginger.

Place this bowl over a saucepan of water, and heat, stirring all the time, until the jelly is melted and the mustard smooth. It may be necessary at this stage to sieve the jelly in order to smooth out the globules which will not dissolve. Return the sieved jelly to the bowl standing over its pan of hot water.

Now add 7 to 8 tablespoons ($2\frac{1}{2}$ oz.) of medium tawny port. Stir and cook for another 5 minutes. Serve cold. There will be enough for four people.

Made in double or triple quantities this sauce can be stored in covered jars and will keep for several weeks.

N.B. On no account should cornflour, gelatine or any other stiffening be added to Cumberland sauce. The mixture thickens as it cools, and the sauce is invariably served cold, even with a hot ham or tongue.

SWEET-SOUR CHERRY SAUCE FOR COLD TONGUE

Ingredients are a breakfast cup (about $\frac{1}{2}$ lb.) of bottled, tinned or fresh cherries, $\frac{1}{4}$ lb. of redcurrant or rowanberry jelly, 3 tablespoons of wine vinegar, 2 teaspoons of yellow French mustard, 1 teaspoon of ground cinnamon, freshly milled pepper.

Stone the cherries, and if they are large halve them. In a bowl over boiling water melt the jelly. Stir in the mustard, then the vinegar, and a little pepper. When the jelly is liquid and smooth add the cherries and the cinnamon. Serve cold.

When using commercial redcurrant jelly for sauces it is often necessary, or at any rate desirable, to sieve it after it has melted and before adding the solid ingredients. Otherwise a few undissolved globules of jelly may remain in the finished sauce. In any case it is always preferable to melt the jelly by the bain-marie system rather than over direct heat, for if allowed to come to the boil the jelly will produce a scum of which it is difficult to rid the finished sauce.

In the summer when fresh cherries are in season use, if you can find them, the dark juicy variety which English fruiterers call 'bigaroons' – a corruption of the French *bigarreaux*. They make a sauce vastly better than tinned cherries, but if you have to use these the best are of Polish origin.

FRUIT SAUCE FOR GAME

'1 lb. red plums or damsons, ½ lb. sugar, 1 inch cinnamon stick, 2 cloves, 2 tablespoons redcurrant jelly, 1 glass port wine, 1½ oz. butter.

'Choose ripe plums and wash or wipe them carefully. Put them into a lined or earthenware saucepan with the sugar, cloves, and cinnamon, but without any water, and stew them slowly until reduced to a pulp. Then rub the fruit through a fine sieve and return the purée to a clean saucepan. Add the red-currant jelly and port wine, bring to the boil and simmer for a few minutes. Then draw the saucepan to the side of the fire and add the butter in small pieces. Do not boil again after the butter is added. The sauce may be used either hot or cold.'

Cookery for Every Household, Florence B. Jack, 1931

Sauce of Horse-radish

'Take Roots of Horse-radish scraped clean, and lay them to soak in fair-water for an hour. Then rasp them upon a Grater, and you shall have them all in a tender spungy Pap. Put

Vinegar to it, and a very little sugar, not so much as to be tasted, but to quicken (by contrariety) the taste of the other.'

The Closet of Sir Kenelm Digby Knight Opened, 1669

MINT SAUCE

Although I find mint such a sweet-smelling herb, I cannot say that I care for mint sauce. For those who do like it, the best formula is given by Florence Jack whose *Cookery for Every Household* first published in 1914 was for about fifty years one of the faithful friends and advisers of just that – every household. Miss Jack was Principal of the Edinburgh School of Domestic Arts, her book was crammed with instruction, and with informative drawings which have never been bettered.

What makes Florence Jack's mint sauce different from the routine English one is the brown sugar – and her injunction to leave the sauce to mature before it is served. A less good idea is the brown vinegar. White wine vinegar is less savage and to me makes the sauce more acceptable, even if less authentically English. And a quarter pint of *any* vinegar does seem to me rather too much.

'2 tablespoons chopped mint, 1 tablespoon brown sugar, 2 tablespoons boiling water, 1 gill (¼ pint) brown vinegar.

'Put the sugar into a basin or sauce-boat, pour over it the boiling water and stand until dissolved. Wash the mint, which should be young and fresh, pick it from the stalks, dry and chop it finely. Mix all the ingredients together and stand two or three hours before serving. Serve with roast lamb.'

OXFORD BRAWN SAUCE

Put two tablespoons of soft, dark-brown sugar into a bowl. Stir in 2 teaspoons of strong yellow Dijon mustard. Add ½ a teaspoon each of freshly milled black pepper and salt.

Now add, gradually, stirring all the time, 5 to 6 tablespoons of olive oil. Finally, add two tablespoons of wine vinegar. The sauce should be thick and translucent, looking rather like dark honey.

Except that I have reduced the amount of vinegar, this recipe is in all essentials the one given by Eliza Acton in her famous *Modern Cookery* of 1845. It is a splendid sauce to eat with cold spiced beef as well as with brawn.

ENGLISH SALAD SAUCE

Authentic mayonnaise is, as we all know, made with raw egg yolks and olive oil. In England it has never achieved true popularity, perhaps because as a nation we have always tended to regard olive oil as medicinal rather than as a marvel-lous and necessary table delicacy. It was English salad sauce, made with cooked egg yolks and cream, that was the basis of the commercial salad cream, wrongly called mayonnaise, which became, and remains, one of the major culinary disasters of this country. It is the acetic acid, the flour, the dried egg, the stabilizers, the emulsifiers and all the bag of trick ingredients which make English salad sauces, creams, and so-called mayonnaise the laughing stock of Europe. With the original recipe there was nothing wrong. Its name was per-fectly explanatory, its ingredients honourable. As a sauce in its own right it is exceedingly good. With some salads – not with lettuce or straight green salads, but with compound cooked vegetable salads – and particularly with fish salads and with rich fish such as salmon it is perhaps preferable to mayonnaise because the combination of cooked egg yolk with cream produces a lighter sauce than that made of raw yolks with olive oil. As against that point the sauce is very easy to make. Here is the authentic pre-1914 recipe:

Ingredients: 1 large or 2 small hard-boiled egg yolks and 1 raw egg yolk; seasonings of salt, sugar, cayenne; $\frac{1}{4}$ pint of double cream; 1 to 2 teaspoons of lemon juice or tarragon vinegar.

Pound the hard-boiled yolk to a paste, with a few drops of cold water. Stir in the raw yolk. Add seasonings with caution. Under-seasoning can be corrected later. Over-seasoning cannot.

Then stir in, little by little, the cream. Finally add the lemon juice or vinegar.

This sauce is best made an hour or two ahead of time, the acid of the lemon or vinegar causing the cream to thicken to the correct consistency. To the basic mixture can be added, according to what may be available and the food which the sauce is to accompany, chopped herbs, anchovy fillets, finely grated horseradish, mustard.

SAUCES FOR FISH

Is the fish or the sauce to play the star part? In traditional English cookery the answer to the question is taken for granted. As we see it, the fish is going to be so delicious that there is little need to bother about the sauce. Therefore the sauces appertaining to English fish cookery are very simple indeed. So far so good. Further on, a great deal less good. Somewhere along the line we began to confuse good plain cooking with plain bad cooking. At this stage our English melted-butter sauce became muddled, not so much with the French *sauce blanche* which is what it is, but with béchamel, which is very much what our white sauce never became. What it did become was billstickers' paste, and on this basis egg sauce, parsley sauce, caper, anchovy, shrimp, mushroom, lobster and some half dozen other perfectly respectable sauces fell toppling to their ruin. To restore them, we need to go back, far back, to the recipes of more than a century ago, to the early and mid-nineteenth century, when an authentic and still strong English cooking tradition flourished amid the ravages of the Industrial Revolution. So here they are, a few of the simple basic sauces of English fish cookery.

GOOSEBERRY SAUCE FOR BAKED MACKEREL

To the French, green gooseberries are known as mackerel gooseberries or *grosielles à maquereau* as opposed to *groseilles* proper, which are redcurrants. At one time, in France as well as in England, a green gooseberry purée seems to have been the accepted sauce for mackerel. I cannot claim ever to have encountered this particular sauce in France, where gooseberries are now far less common than they are in England. Recipes for a gooseberry sauce are, however, common enough in French cookery books of the seventeenth and eighteenth centuries, and linger on until the end of the nineteenth. The formula differs little from the one given in our own books of the equivalent periods; and we too, while cultivating our gooseberries for pies, fools and puddings, have allowed the sauce to fall into disuse. We should revive it. It is interesting, appropriately sharp with a rich fish such as mackerel, dead easy to make, and invested with the charm of the unexpected.

Here is what Jules Breteuil, nineteenth-century French chef and author of an interesting cookery book called *Le Cuisinier Européen* (*circa* 1860) and one of the few French writers to give accurate information concerning the cookery of countries other than his own, wrote about this particular English dish, which he calls *maquereau aux groseilles à l'anglaise*:

'This recipe, nowadays little used in France, is very current in England; it is one of the oldest dishes of ancient French cookery; from it derives the common name *groseilles à maquereau*.'

And here is the recipe for gooseberry sauce as given by Eliza Acton in the 1855 edition of *Modern Cookery*, first published in 1845.

'Cut the stalks and tops from half to a whole pint (i.e., 1 lb.) of quite young gooseberries, wash them well, just cover them with cold water, and boil them very gently indeed, until they are tender; drain and mix them with a small quantity of melted butter, made with rather less flour than usual. Some eaters prefer the mashed gooseberries without any addition; others like that of a little ginger.'

Miss Acton goes on to say that, in her opinion (I agree with her), the gooseberries should be sieved, slightly sweetened – the amount of sugar must depend on the acidity of the fruit – and softened by the addition of a bit of fresh butter about the size of a walnut. As an extra flavouring Miss Acton obviously prefers ginger to the fennel leaves which often go into the gooseberry sauce; they make a nice addition when the sauce has been made with preserved or bottled gooseberries, but on the fresh fruit, fennel makes little impact; and a pinch of powdered ginger is indeed an excellent spice for gooseberries.

The sauce is served hot, with hot baked or boiled mackerel; and the 'melted butter made with rather less flour than usual' is melted butter sauce, made as follows:

MELTED BUTTER SAUCE

2 teaspoons of flour, ¼ pint of water, 2 to 3 oz. of butter, salt.

In a small saucepan mix the flour and the water to a thin paste, adding a good pinch of salt. Stir the mixture over gentle heat without allowing it to boil. When it is smooth and hot add the butter, cut into small pieces. Stir vigorously with a wooden spoon until all the ingredients are thoroughly amalgamated and the sauce looks creamy and slightly thickened. It should be thoroughly hot, but at no time should it boil. If it does it will (a) taste of uncooked flour, and (b) the butter will oil. Badly made, melted butter sauce deserves all the scorn earned in the past by English sauce-cookery. When well cooked, it is an excellent and highly useful basic sauce. With a flavouring of a few drops of lemon juice it is good with grilled or poached salmon, trout, sole, and also with asparagus and broccoli. Melted butter sauce and all sauces based on it should be cooked as, and in the quantity, needed. They do not re-heat successfully.

CUCUMBER SAUCE

Melted butter sauce as above, plus cucumber, chives or parsley, lemon juice.

Discard the seeds from a two-inch length of peeled cucumber, and chop it finely. In a small frying pan heat a nut of butter. Put in the cucumber, sprinkle it with salt. Let it heat through. It must not shrivel or fry. Stir it into the prepared sauce. Add a good squeeze of lemon juice, and a sprinkling of fresh chives (cut with scissors) or finely chopped parsley.

This is a most delicate and fresh-flavoured sauce. It goes well with hot salmon, sea-bass, turbot, halibut, hake.

SHRIMP SAUCE

Melted butter sauce plus boiled fresh shrimps, ground mace, cayenne pepper.

Shell a half-pint of freshly boiled shrimps. Stir them into the prepared melted butter sauce, heat them through, add the seasonings.

English shrimp sauce is traditional with poached turbot. An alternative way of making it is to boil the shrimp shells and debris in water to cover, and to use a quarter pint of this stock, strained and cooked, to make the initial melted butter sauce. When freshly boiled shrimps (not to be confused with what the Americans call shrimp, which are prawns) are unobtainable, use the contents of a two-ounce carton of potted shrimps, from which the protective covering of butter should be removed. When potted shrimps are used, no additional spices will be necessary, but a good squeeze of lemon juice improves the sauce; a spoonful of chopped fresh fennel or parsley will also be an improvement.

EGG SAUCE

Melted butter sauce plus hard-boiled eggs
Have ready two hard-boiled eggs. Shell them. (To break the shells cleanly, roll the eggs on a table.) Separate the yolks from the whites, and chop them separately, using one white only. Add first the white then the yolks to the prepared melted butter. Season rather highly with salt and freshly milled white

pepper (unless very well seasoned, egg sauce is cloying), and serve as hot as possible.

In my childhood, egg sauce with boiled cod was routine schoolroom food. Fish and sauce were equally ghastly. It is only recently, since discovering that authentic English egg sauce is made with melted butter rather than on a basis of milk and flour paste that I have been able to bring myself to cook and eat egg sauce. With plain poached smoked haddock it is delicious. Boiled cod, fresh or salt, belongs, as far as I am concerned, to the past.

MUSTARD SAUCE FOR GRILLED HERRINGS

Melted butter sauce plus made mustard, English or French.

Have ready a warmed sauceboat. Into it put a heaped teaspoonful of strong yellow mustard (I use a strong yellow Dijon mustard made with white wine or genuine English mustard freshly mixed. The kind to avoid is the English imitation of French mustard.) Mix the prepared melted butter sauce, gradually, with the mustard. Serve it at once, without further cooking.

DRAWN BUTTER

We often find French cookery terms confusing. English terms can be every bit as baffling. If melted butter is not melted butter but a flour-thickened sauce, what is drawn butter? Melted butter – what else? And melted butter is about the simplest sauce you can have. With a delicate salmon trout or spotted brown trout, free-range variety, no sauce is so good as simple drawn or melted butter.

Here is a three hundred-year-old formula:

'Take your Butter, and cut it into thin slices, put it into a dish then put it upon the coals where it may melt leisurely, stir it often, and when it is melted, put in two or three spoonfuls, of water, or vinegar, which you will, stir them and beat it until it be thick.'

This recipe is from *A True Gentlewoman's Delight*, the receipt book, posthumously published, of Elizabeth de Grey, Countess of Kent, who died in 1651. The first edition of this book appeared in 1653; the recipe quoted is from the nineteenth edition dated 1687.

GRANVILLE SAUCE FOR SALMON

Instead of the mayonnaise or hollandaise which are the usual accompaniments of cold and hot salmon respectively, Granville sauce is worth a try. The recipe comes from Lady Llanover's *Good Cookery*, published in 1867. She advises it as a fine sauce for Welsh salmon.

First of all prepare the following ingredients: 1 chopped shallot, 4 chopped anchovy fillets, 2 tablespoons of sherry (I don't much like sherry in sauces so I use dry vermouth or white port instead), ½ tablespoon of wine vinegar, 6 whole black peppercorns, ground mace and nutmeg.

Cook all these ingredients (be cautious with the nutmeg and mace) in a small saucepan over hot water or in a heatproof bowl standing in a large pan, until the shallot is soft.

In the meantime prepare a butter and flour thickening – 1 oz. of butter worked with 1 dessertspoon of flour.

Stir this into the first mixture.

When the sauce has thickened and is very hot stir in about 6 tablespoons of thick fresh cream. Press through a fine sauce sieve.

This is enough only for 2 or 3 people. And personally I use either rather less anchovy or a little more cream – to make the sauce somewhat milder. Either way it is excellent, and as Lady Llanover says, even better if made the previous day and reheated – always of course over hot water.

Granville sauce is also good with grey mullet and grilled hake or cod steaks.

BÉCHAMEL SAUCE*

Although the preparation of this sauce is extremely simple many amateur cooks are frightened by it. Anyone who has sufficient perseverance to practise making the sauce a couple of times according to the recipe which follows should never again have cause to worry as far as the making of a béchamel is concerned. And mastering the preparation of this sauce opens up a large repertory of very excellent and often cheap recipes.

To make a half-pint of béchamel the ingredients are: ¾ pint of milk, 1½ oz. of butter, 2 heaped tablespoons of plain flour, seasonings of salt, freshly milled pepper (preferably white peppercorns for white sauces; but the point is a minor one) and grated nutmeg.

Choose a heavy saucepan of 2 pint capacity, and have ready a wooden spoon and a measuring jug. Measure out the milk, bring it to simmering point in your saucepan. Pour it back into the jug, rinse out the pan, and put in the butter. When it is hot, but before it turns colour take the saucepan from the heat and with a wooden spoon stir the flour into the butter. Within a few seconds the two ingredients will have amal-gamated into a smooth thick paste. Now, still keeping the pan away from the heat, start adding the hot milk, a little at a time, and stirring constantly; as each small quantity of milk is added, stir until the paste is again smooth. When you have added about half the milk, return the pan to the heat, turned very low and preferably with a mat over the burner, at least until all the milk has been added. Continue adding the milk. At this stage you begin to think you have already made the sauce too thin. Do not worry. Go on adding the milk and stirring, taking care, as always when making a sauce, that your spoon does not just move the sauce but reaches right to the base and sides of the pan.

When all the milk is added and the sauce is a smooth and thin cream, add seasonings of about a teaspoonful of salt, two

*Reproduced from the author's *Summer Cooking*, 1969.

or three turns from the pepper mill and a generous scraping of nutmeg. A well cooked béchamel requires 15 minutes' gentle cooking and stirring and almost imperceptible reduction and thickening, the time to be calculated from the moment when all the milk has been added.

Let us not pretend that a béchamel sauce never goes wrong even if you follow the directions exactly. Minor accidents happen to the best of cooks but remedies are usually very easy. If there appear any tiny lumps of flour in your sauce, sieve it while it is still very liquid and therefore takes only a few seconds to run through the sieve placed over a jug or bowl. Rinse out your saucepan, return your sauce to it, put it back over the mat on low heat, and when it is again warm it is sufficiently cooked. It is safe to leave it. But before doing so, put a piece of buttered paper right down inside the saucepan over the hot sauce. As the butter melts, it makes a little protective film which prevents a skin forming on the top of the sauce.

To re-heat béchamel, it is best to use the bain-marie system (i.e., with the saucepan standing in, not over, another one containing water) rather than direct heat.

TOMATO SAUCES

A world devoid of tomato soup, tomato sauce, tomato ketchup and tomato paste is hard to visualize. Could the tin and processed food industries have got where they have without the benefit of the tomato compounds which colour, flavour, thicken – and conceal so many deficiencies? How did the Italians eat spaghetti before the advent of the beloved golden apple of the South? Was there such a thing as a tomato-less Neapolitan pizza? What were English salads like before there were tomatoes to mix with lettuce? Could Provençal cooking be separated from the *pomme d'amour* which goes into so many of its most famous dishes?

Incredible though it now seems, the tomato, brought by the Spaniards from Peru to Spain at the close of the sixteenth century and shortly afterwards planted in France, Portugal, Italy and England, was well known to us as an ornamental plant for two hundred years before its culinary possibilities were perceived. The first English cookery-book recipes for tomatoes appear only at the beginning of the nineteenth century. They were for ketchup-type sauces. Since the tomato, being a member of the *solanacae* tribe which includes also the poisonous nightshades, was long regarded as a dangerous if not actually deadly fruit (the potato and the aubergine, also of the *solanacae* family, have in their time suffered from the same associations) presumably the mixture of vinegar and spices was regarded as a safety-device against the possibly toxic effects of the fruit itself. By the end of the nineteenth century, when tomato soup was already well on its way to immortality, a new legend had become attached to the tomato. It was reputed to induce cancer. It was also, wrote Miss Anne Buckland, the anthropological scholar and author of an entertaining book called *Our Viands* (1893), too expensive to be generally popular, and regarded with suspicion by the poor who 'despise and dislike it'.

In the seventy odd years which have elapsed since the publication of Miss Buckland's book the tomato has taken its revenge – and in no uncertain way – for three centuries of neglect and calumny. What we need now is the restraining hand implicit in the observation made in a French book of *Dissertations Gastronomiques* (1928) by Ernest Verdier, owner of the Maison Dorée, a restaurant celebrated in pre-1914 Paris. 'The tomato,' says M. Verdier, 'imparts its delicious taste, at the same time acid and slightly sweet, to so many sauces and dishes that it can fairly be classed among the best of condiments. Happy are those who understand how to use it judiciously.' Canners, freeze-dryers, packagers and restaurant cooks please copy.

FRESH TOMATO SAUCE

This is an excellent sauce to make when tomatoes, either home-grown or imported, are plentiful and relatively cheap. The method of cooking makes it particularly useful for people who cook with solid fuel stoves.

Put from 2 to 3 lb. or more, of very ripe tomatoes, whole and unskinned, into an earthenware or other oven pot. Add nothing whatsoever. Cover the pot. Put it into a moderate oven, gas No. 3, 330°F., and leave it for almost an hour, or until the tomatoes are soft and squashy. Press them through a sieve or a mouli.

Heat the resulting purée in a thick saucepan, adding, for every pound of tomatoes, a teaspoon each of salt and sugar, and optionally, a little ground ginger or cinnamon, dried or fresh basil or marjoram, and crushed garlic if you like. A tablespoon of port per pound of tomatoes has a wonderfully mellowing effect on the sauce. For immediate use, cook the sauce as little as possible so that it retains its freshness of flavour and bright colour.

This is, basically, the tomato sauce given by Mrs Rundell in *A New System of Domestic Cookery* published in 1806. (Such is the current interest in old English cookery books that in 1965 the rare first edition of Mrs Rundell fetched one hundred and thirty pounds at Sotheby's.) Mrs Rundell, whose formula appears to be one of the earliest published English recipes for tomato sauce, added chilli vinegar, pounded garlic and ground ginger to the tomato pulp, directed that the sauce should be stored in small, wide-mouthed bottles, well corked, and in a dry cool place. The sauce was intended for 'hot or cold meats'.

Mrs Rundell's method of baking the tomatoes is a most useful one to know. To my taste it is best minus the original vinegar and garlic. More or less reduced according to taste and stored in the refrigerator for current use (don't try to store it by Mrs Rundell's rather too rough and ready method) it is exceedingly good with pasta and with egg dishes. It can make also the basis of a luxurious and richly flavoured tomato soup.

THREE MINUTE TOMATO SAUCE

Pour boiling water over a half-pound of fine, ripe tomatoes. Skin and chop them. Put them with a teaspoonful each of butter and olive oil into a heavy frying pan or small saucepan. Cook them for three minutes, no more. Season them with salt, sugar and a scrap of dried basil or a teaspoon of freshly chopped parsley.

This is the sauce, or fondue of tomatoes, which makes the best filling for a tomato omelette.

BUTTERS

'*How to make sundry sorts of most daintie butter, having a lively taste of Sage, Cinnamon, Nutmegs, Mace, etc.*

'This is done by mixing a fewe drops of the extracted oile of Sage, Cinnamon, Nutmegs, Mace, etc., in the making up of your butter: for oyle and butter will incorporat and agree very kindely and naturallie together.'

Delightes for Ladies, Sir Hugh Plat, 1600

ANCHOVY BUTTER

Anchovy fillets in oil, milk, lemon juice, cayenne pepper, freshly milled black pepper, unsalted butter.

Soak the anchovy fillets in a little milk for about an hour, drain them, pound them to a paste, mix this with the slightly softened butter, allowing 2 oz. to a half dozen anchovy fillets; season with the lemon juice, cayenne and freshly milled black pepper; pack into a small jar, cover and store in the refrigerator for not longer than 10 days, or in the deep freeze for as long as you like.

This is a most delicious little mixture and a wonderful standby for serving with steaks or for adding to eggs en cocotte.

86

CINNAMON BUTTER

1½ oz. butter, 1 teaspoon of ground cinnamon, a squeeze of lemon juice, a sprinkling of cayenne.

Work the cinnamon into the softened butter, add the lemon juice and cayenne.

Put the spiced butter into the refrigerator to chill.

Excellent with white fish such as plaice, with plain braised or baked onions, with pancakes, or instead of plain butter for cream cheese sandwiches – or for cinnamon toast as described on page 223.

ORANGE BUTTER FOR FISH

The grated rind of one orange, 1 dessertspoonful of orange juice, 2 oz. of butter, ¼ teaspoon of paprika, salt.

Work the butter to a cream, mix in all the other ingredients. Leave the butter to harden. Serve in the same way as parsley butter, with grilled or foil baked fish. Especially good with red mullet, gurnard, John Dory.

TARRAGON BUTTER

Work together 2 oz. of butter, 2 teaspoons of fresh tarragon leaves or of Chiltern Herb Farm dried tarragon, a squeeze of lemon juice and a scrap of freshly milled black pepper.

Stored in a small covered jar in the refrigerator, tarragon butter will keep several days, so it is often worth making double quantities. Made with fresh tarragon and stored in the deep freeze, tarragon butter will retain its aroma all winter.

BRANDY BUTTER
For the Christmas plum pudding

For about a dozen helpings the ingredients are: 1 lb. *unsalted* butter, 8 oz. icing sugar, 2 or 3 tablespoons of brandy, a tea-spoon of lemon juice, a sprinkling of nutmeg.

If you have an electric blender, simply cut up the butter and put it with all the other ingredients into the goblet and let them whizz away for 2 or 3 minutes.

For those who haven't a mixer the most successful procedure seems to me to be as follows: soften your butter by putting it into a warmed bowl. In another bowl, also warmed, mix the icing sugar, brandy, nutmeg and lemon juice to a smooth cream.

Beat the butter, if possible in a big wooden mixing bowl, and with a wooden fork, to a soft cream; very gradually add the sugar and brandy mixture and beat or knead by hand until the butter is smooth. Store in a covered dish.

Readers familiar with brandy butter recipes will see that the proportions usually recommended – twice the weight of sugar to butter – are reversed in this recipe. This is because many people, myself included, find the normal brandy butter much too sweet. But whatever proportions are used, the method of making the sauce is the same.

Alternative names for brandy butter are 'hard sauce' and 'Senior Wrangler sauce'.

CLARIFIED BUTTER

In a large frying or sauté pan put a slab of butter. (I use a good quality butter and find that it pays to prepare 2 lb. at a time since it keeps almost indefinitely and is immeasurably superior to fresh butter for frying bread, croquettes, rissoles, fish cakes, veal escalopes, fish *à la meunière* and a score of other tricky cooking jobs.) Let the butter melt over very gentle heat. It must not brown, but should be left to bubble for a few seconds before being removed from the heat and left to settle.

Have ready a piece of butter muslin wrung out in warm water, doubled, and laid in a sieve standing over the bowl or deep wide jar in which the butter is to be stored. Filter the butter while it is still warm. For storage keep the jar covered, in the refrigerator.

The object of clarifying butter is to rid it of water, buttermilk sediment, salt and any foreign matter which for purposes of frying cause the butter to blacken and burn, and also render it susceptible to eventual rancidity. The clarification process also expels air and causes the butter to solidify as it cools, making it a highly effective sealing material, essential for preserving English potted meats and fish.

Butter and Oil to Fry Fish

'The best Liquor to fry Fish in, is to take Butter and Salet Oyl, first well clarified together. This hath not the unsavoury taste of Oyl alone, nor the blackness of Butter alone. It fryeth Fish crisp, yellow, and well tasted.'

The Closet of the Eminently Learned Sir Kenelm Digby Knight Opened, 1669

THE COLONEL'S SAUCE CUPBOARD

'– No store-room should be without tarragon vinegar, anchovy vinegar, French vinegar, and white wine vinegar.

'Amongst sauces I consider Harvey's the best for general use; Sutton's 'Empress of India' is a strong sauce with a real flavour of mushrooms; Moir's sauces and 'Reading sauce' are very trustworthy, and there are others which, no doubt, commend themselves to different palates, but I denounce 'Worcester Sauce' and 'Tapp's Sauce' as agents far too powerful to be trusted to the hands of the native cook. Sutton's essence of anchovies is said to possess the charm of not clotting, or forming a stoppage in the neck of the bottle. I have a deep respect for both walnut and mushroom ketchup, soy, and tomato conserve. Then as special trifles, we must not forget caviare, *olives farcies*, and anchovies in oil.'

Culinary Jottings for Madras,
'Wyvern' (Colonel Kenney-Herbert), 5th edition 1885

TAPP'S SAUCE

This is one of the sauces mentioned in the preceding passage by Colonel Kenney-Herbert as being 'too powerful to be trusted to the hands of the native cook'. The recipe certainly does have a ferocious ring. Those quarter pounds of chillies and garlic . . .

'Take of green sliced mangoes, salt, sugar and raisins each eight ounces; red chillies and garlic each four ounces; green ginger six ounces; vinegar three bottles; lime-juice one pint. Pound of several ingredients well; then add the vinegar and lime juice; stop the vessel close, and expose it to the sun a whole month, stirring or shaking it well daily; then strain it through a cloth, bottle and cork it tight.

'Obs. – The residue makes an excellent chutney.'

Indian Domestic Economy, Madras, 1850

MUSHROOM CATSUP

'These are procured in all parts of India during the rains, and to make your own catsup not only will be found economical but far stronger and better than can ever be purchased. Take as many as you please of large flap mushroom that are of a reddish brown inside (peel off the top skin) and lay in the bottom of a deep dish; sprinkle them over with clean salt; and so continue until the dish or pan is full; let them remain for about eight hours; then mash up the whole; strain off the juice, to each pint adding half an ounce of black pepper and about forty or fifty cloves; put the whole into a stone jar and place the jar covered over in a saucepan of water, and let it boil until about one-third or one-half has evaporated; then set the whole by to cool and settle; then strain it off clear into pint or half-pint bottles, adding to each pint a table-spoonful of brandy; if you have any claret that has been opened or otherwise, you may add a wine glass to each pint or more as you please – it makes the catsup keep better in this country.'

Indian Domestic Economy, Madras, 1850

PIQUANT SAUCE

'½ oz. of Mace, 1 oz. of Ginger, ½ oz. of Piminto*, ¼ oz. of Chillies, ½ oz. of Mustard seed, 1 oz. of Long Pepper,† ¼ pint of Soy, 1 quart of Vinegar.

'Bruise the spice and simmer them in the vinegar a few minutes. Strain it, afterwards add the Soy. *Excellent.*'

This recipe comes from a modest little manuscript cookery book in my possession. From the same source I obtained a recipe for snow cheese, a beautiful old English sweet cream cheese flavoured with lemon peel, and since the author has noted that her piquant sauce is excellent I feel inclined to believe her – at least in so far as it would be excellent of its kind. Compare the proportions of hot spices with those given for some of the foregoing brews quoted from cookery books written for British residents in India.

The date of the manuscript is probably early Victorian, so the quart of vinegar would be 32 oz. or 2 of the old English 16 oz. pints (4 cups U.S.) as opposed to our Imperial or 20 oz. pint.

*Allspice berries or Jamaica pepper.

†*Piper longum,* a variety of pepper used in Indian cookery. Black peppercorns are similar, although more pungent.

* *

Salads and First-course Dishes

'All the herbs of which we use the leaves are most delicate and fragrant when they are fresh-gathered, but only a few, such as Rosemary, Bay and Rue, keep their full flavour during the winter, even if they stay above ground; so that for winter use the others must be preserved by drying. This business of harvesting and drying the herbs was once important enough to have left its mark on the language in the phrase "cut and dried", and it still remains one of the pleasantest labours in the economy of the garden. It is best carried out just before the plants flower, for at that time the essential oils are present in greatest quantity and tend to be mobilised into the leaves and bracts of the flowering stems, where, in many spices, they undergo an elaboration which refines their fragrance.

'To preserve the herbs with a minimum loss of flavour it is necessary to dry them as quickly as possible at a low temperature. This is best accomplished by hanging them up in loose bunches or spreading them on sheets of paper (when they must be turned over twice a day), in some place where a current of air will play over them and where they will not be exposed to the direct rays of the sun. If the drying is carried out in the open air the herbs must be brought in at night to protect them from the dew. When the leaves are crisp they should be rubbed off the stalks, and stored in well-corked, wide-mouthed bottles that have been sterilised by baking in the oven.'

Herbs, Salads and Seasonings, X. M. Boulestin and Jason Hill, 1930

MUNKACZINA

This is one of the dishes given by Mrs C. F. Leyel in *The Gentle Art of Cookery** which so beguiled me when I read her book for the first time.

'Take one or more oranges and cut them in slices crossways. Peel the slices and remove the pips and white in the middle of the round. Arrange a bed of slices of orange at the bottom of the dish, and cover with finely chopped onion. On the onion place a bed of stoned black olives, and sprinkle them with red pepper, salt and olive oil.'

Mrs Leyel added a note to the effect that this dish was brought from the East by Anatole France.

CORIANDER MUSHROOMS

This is a quickly cooked little dish which makes a delicious cold hors-d'oeuvre. The aromatics used are similar to those which go into the well known *champignons à la grecque*, but the method is simpler, and the result even better.

Ingredients for three people are: 6 oz. of firm, white, round and very fresh mushrooms, a teaspoon of coriander seeds, 2 tablespoons of olive oil, lemon juice, salt, freshly milled pepper, and one or two bayleaves.

Rinse the mushrooms, wipe them dry with a clean cloth, slice them (but do not peel them) into quarters, or if they are large into eighths. The stalks should be neatly trimmed. Squeeze over them a little lemon juice.

In a heavy frying pan or sauté pan, warm the olive oil. Into it put the coriander seeds, which should be ready crushed in a mortar. Let them heat for a few seconds. Keep the heat low. Put in the mushrooms and the bayleaves. Add the seasoning. Let the mushrooms cook gently for a minute, cover the pan and leave them, still over very low heat, for another three to five minutes.

*See pp. 15 to 20.

Uncover the pan. Decant the mushrooms – with all their juices – into a shallow serving dish and sprinkle them with fresh olive oil and lemon juice.

Whether the mushrooms are to be served hot or cold do not forget to put the bay leaf which has cooked with them into the serving dish. The combined scents of coriander and bay go to make up part of the true essence of the dish. And it is important to note that cultivated mushrooms should not be cooked for longer than the time specified.

In larger quantities the same dish can be made as a hot vegetable to be eaten with veal or chicken.

Cooked mushrooms do not keep well, but a day or two in the refrigerator does not harm this coriander-spiced dish. It is also worth remembering that *uncooked* cultivated mushrooms can be stored in a plastic box in the refrigerator and will keep fresh for a couple of days.

PARMESAN EGGS

For this original dish of cold stuffed eggs ingredients are 6 hard-boiled eggs, ¼ lb. of fresh spinach, 2 tablespoons of grated Parmesan cheese, 3 or 4 tablespoons of cream, salt, freshly milled pepper, and grated nutmeg.

Clean and cook the spinach, drain it, squeeze it dry and chop it thoroughly.

Shell the eggs, cut them in half lengthways, scoop out the yolks, mash them with the spinach. Add the cheese, the cream, and the seasonings. Stuff the half eggs with this mixture, piling it up in a mound in the centre of each, so that the whites are left clear.

With their decorative and fresh green and white appearance, these eggs make an attractive little first course, or part of a mixed hors-d'oeuvre, for 4 people.

SWEET PEPPER AND WATERCRESS SALAD

1 large fleshy red pepper, 1 shallot, a half bunch of watercress.

Cut the stalk end from the pepper, remove the seeds, then rinse the pepper in cold water to ensure that not one seed is lurking. Sometimes these seeds are very fiery. Even one can spoil a dish or a salad. Slice the pepper into strips. Mix these with the shallot peeled and sliced paper thin.

Rinse the watercress, discard the muddy and ragged part of the stalks, cut the rest with scissors into rather large pieces.

The dressing should be made with salt, a scrap of sugar, olive oil, lemon juice or mild wine vinegar.

A good salad to offer with veal escalopes or pork chops.

CUCUMBER AND GREEN PEPPER SALAD

A cool salad with a mint-flavoured yogurt dressing, excellent with or after spiced dishes such as Moroccan kebabs.

Peel a small cucumber, cut it in half, then quarter these halves lengthways. Discard the seeds, slice the cucumber into thin strips, no longer than matchsticks. Sprinkle them with salt and white sugar.

Cut half a green pepper, seeds and core discarded, into very fine strips. Mix these with a few small and paper-thin raw onion rings. Season with salt and lemon juice.

Mix the pepper and cucumber together.

Into a carton of plain yogurt (if possible, the goats'-milk yogurt sometimes to be bought at health-food stores; failing this the French Danone is quite good) stir a tablespoon of olive oil, a pinch of salt and of sugar, a drop or two of wine vinegar, a teaspoonful of dried mint.

Mix the dressing with the prepared cucumber and green pepper at the last moment. Serve it in a small shallow bowl or soup plate.

When no green peppers are to be found, it is best to make the salad with cucumber only, rather than attempt a substitute.

AVOCADO SALAD

We tend to think of the avocado pear as a fruit which has come into our lives only very recently. It is true that before the early nineteen-sixties it would not have been found listed on almost every restaurant menu in the British Isles. (Listed it may be. How often can it be actually produced, and in proper condition?) So it is interesting to find Sir Francis Colchester-Wemyss, whose *The Pleasures of the Table* was published in 1931, deciding that the avocado makes the ideal salad to go with pressed beef.

This is his recipe: 'Make an ordinary well-seasoned oil and vinegar dressing, pour a dessertspoonful or so into the middle of each half, and then with a teaspoon detach the flesh in small pieces till nothing but the thick skin is left, and the flesh is all in the centre. Mix this well with the dressing, and serve, as it is, in the skin.'

I agree with Sir Francis about the rightness of the avocado with salt beef.

SPICED BEETROOT SALAD

A freshly boiled or baked beetroot, skinned, cut into cubes, seasoned with salt and ground allspice, dressed with olive oil, a very little wine vinegar, and chopped parsley makes an excellent little salad. The allspice or Jamaica pepper is a particularly good seasoning for beetroot.

To compound an excellent sallat
and which indeede is usual at great feasts, and upon Prince tables:

'Take a good quantity of blauncht Almonds, and with your shredding knife cut them grosly; then take as many Raisyns, and the stones pickt out, as many figges shred like the Almonds, as many Capers, twice so many Olives, and as many currants as of all the rest, cleane washt; a good handful of the small tender leaves of red Sage and Spinage; mixe all these well together with good store of Sugar, and lay them in the bottome of a great dish, then put unto them Vinegar and Oyle, and scrape more Suger over all; then take Orenges and Lemons, and paring away the outward pills, cut them into their slices, then with those slices cover the sallat all over; which done, take the thinne leafe of the red Coleflowre, and with them cover the oranges and lemons all over, then over those red leaves lay another course of olives, and the slices of well pickled coucumbers, together with the very inward heart of your Cabbage Lettice, cut into slices, then adorne the sides of the dish and the top of the Sallat with mo slices of Lemons and Oranges, and so serve it up.'

The English Hus-Wife, Gervase Markham, 1615

PRAWN PASTE*

An excellent little first course dish for three to four people.

½ lb. peeled cooked prawns; 4 to 6 teaspoonsful of olive oil; seasonings of dried basil, cayenne pepper, and the juice of a fresh lime or lemon. For a more spiced flavour add a saltspoon of crushed coriander or cumin seed.

Mash or pound the prawns to a paste. Very gradually, add the olive oil. Season with cayenne pepper and about a half teaspoonful of dried basil warmed in the oven and finely crumbled. Add the strained juice of half a lemon or of a whole fresh lime (when available, the lime is much the better choice). When the mixture is smooth, and is seasoned to your satis-faction – salt may or may not be necessary, that depends upon how much has already been cooked with the prawns – pack it into a little jar or terrine. Cover and store in the refrigerator. Serve chilled, with hot thin toast. Do not attempt to store for more than a couple of days.

If using freshly boiled prawns in the shell, allow approxim-

*From the author's *Dried Herbs, Aromatics and Condiments*, 1967.

ately 1½ pints gross measure. The shells and heads will make the basis of a good shellfish soup.

N.B. In an electric blender or automatic chopper the prawns and olive oil can be mashed to a paste in a couple of minutes.

POTTED TONGUE*

To my mind this is the best and most subtle of all English potted-meat inventions. My recipe is adapted from John Farley's *The London Art of Cookery* published in 1783. Farley was master of the London Tavern, and an unusually lucid writer. One deduces that the cold table at the London Tavern must have been exceptionally good, for all Farley's sideboard dishes, cold pies, hams, spiced beef joints and potted meats are thought out with much care, are set down in detail and show a delicate and educated taste.

Ingredients and proportions for potted tongue are ½ lb. each of cooked, brined and/or smoked ox tongue and clarified butter, a salt-spoonful of ground mace, a turn or two of black or white pepper from the mill.

Chop the tongue and, with 5 oz. (weighed after clarifying) of the butter, reduce it to a paste in the blender or liquidizer,† season it, pack it tightly down into a pot or pots, smooth over the top, cover, and leave in the refrigerator until very firm. Melt the remaining 3 oz. of clarified butter and pour it, tepid, over the tongue paste, so that it sets in a sealing layer about one eighth of an inch thick. When completely cold, cover the pots with foil or greaseproof paper. Store them in the refrigerator.

The amount given will fill one ¾ to 1 pint shallow soufflé dish, although I prefer to pack my potted tongue in two or three smaller and shallower containers.

*Reprinted from the author's *English Potted Meats and Fish Pastes*, 1968.

†Of these machines by far the most effective for potted meats, as also for raw pâté ingredients, is the French Moulinette automatic chopper. This device does the job of chopping and pounding without emulsifying the ingredients or squeezing out their juices.

POTTED SPICED BEEF

With a half pound of cooked spiced beef including a good proportion of fat, and approximately 6 oz. of clarified butter, a most excellent potted meat can be made. No extra spices are needed.

Cut the beef with its fat, into chunks, reduce them to paste in a blender or with an automatic chopper,* adding 3 oz. of the clarified butter as chopping proceeds.

Pack the paste into a pot or pots (it will fill a ¾ pint dish) press it well down, smooth the top with a palette knife, chill thoroughly before warming the remaining 3 oz. of clarified butter, and pouring it over the top of the beef to form a complete seal.

Cover the pot or pots with foil and store in the refrigerator.

Potted meat should be eaten very cold with hot thin toast. Originally a breakfast dish, it makes a delicious first course for lunch.

PORK AND SPINACH TERRINE

Pâtés and terrines have become, during the past decade, so very much a part of the English restaurant menu as well as of home entertaining that a variation of formula would sometimes be welcome.

At Orange, that splendid town they call the gateway to Provence, I once tasted a pâté which was more fresh green herbs than meat. I was told that this was made according to a venerable country recipe of Upper Provence.

The pâté was interesting but rather heavy. I have tried to make it a little less filling. Here is the result of my experiments:

1 lb. of uncooked spinach, spinach beet or chard, 1 lb. of freshly minced fat pork, seasonings of salt, freshly milled pepper, mixed spices.

Wash, cook and drain the spinach. When cool, squeeze it

*See footnote, p. 98.

as dry as you can. There is only one way to do this – with your hands. Chop it roughly.

Season the meat with about three teaspoons of salt, a generous amount of freshly milled black pepper, and about a quarter teaspoon of mixed ground spices (mace, allspice, cloves).

Mix meat and spinach together. Turn into a pint-sized earthenware terrine or loaf tin. On top put a piece of buttered paper. Stand the terrine or tin in a baking dish half filled with water.

Cook in a very moderate oven (gas No. 3, 330°F.) for 45 minutes to an hour. Do not let it get overcooked or it will be dry.

This pâté *can* be eaten hot as a main course, but I prefer it cold, as a first dish, and with bread or toast just as a pâté is always served in France.

The interesting points about this dish are its appearance, its fresh, uncloying flavour and its comparative lightness, which should appeal to those who find the better-known type of pork pâté rather heavy.

You could, for example, serve a quite rich or creamy dish after this without overloading anybody's stomach.

A MACARONI DISH

It may seem surprising that a number of such typically French dishes as *bœuf miroton* and pork pâté are included in a book devoted mainly to English cooking. It should not seem so. Consider the case of the cookery writer who was reported, only five years ago, as having declared 'I am the man who brought French cuisine to the British.' In the year A.D. 1965 that seemed a pretty large claim. It was difficult not to wonder what-ever became of 1066 and the nine centuries during which French cooking has taken root, grown, and flourished in English kitchens.

The gentleman did, however, raise a point. Who are, who were, the writers responsible for the propagation of the gospel of French cooking in these islands? To me it would seem that

English and French traditions of cookery are too inextricably interwoven to allow of arbitrary division into two separate streams. To say that *this* cookery writer wrote only of French cookery, *that* one exclusively of English cookery, is to attempt to divide the indivisible. Every author who writes about cookery in the English language and for English readers is, by implication, writing about English cookery. If he is not, then he might as well write his book in Chinese or Armenian. At the same time, however staunchly British and John Bull-ish he might be, he will find it a practical impossibility to avoid altogether any reference to French cooking and French methods, even if it is only for the sake of comparison, and to discover in what fashion a nine-hundred-year-old tradition has developed.

Toward appreciation of these points, increased familiarity with our own cookery history and its literature, so astonishingly rich, varied, and illuminating, would help.

To take just one example out of scores, there is the case of William Verral, whose little book *The Cook's Paradise* was published in 1759. No man could have been more English by birth, breeding, occupation, outlook. To be precise, Verral was a Sussex innkeeper, Master of the White Hart at Lewes. At this inn, still flourishing, Verral's father before him had presided, the young Verral being apprenticed to St Clouet, a French chef in the service of Thomas Pelham Hollis, Duke of Newcastle, member of the great Sussex landowning family of Pelham, and for thirty years George II's notoriously incompetent Minister of State.

Most of William Verral's recipes, were, so he tells us, learned from St Clouet, and indeed from Verral's phonetic French spelling (nantiles for *lentilles*, glass for *glacé*, pauvrade for *poivrade*) it is easy to deduce that they were noted down from direct dictation, and subsequently rendered into Verral's own breezy, colloquial English. From *The Cook's Paradise*, however allegedly French the recipes, emerges a vivid little picture of what we should now consider honest old-fashioned English country cooking as practised in the chief coaching inn of an

important county town. Here, for example, is Verral's version
of macaroni cheese, a dish which perhaps came to us from
French rather than from Italian kitchens, for Verral calls
macaroni *macarons* or macaroons, and includes two recipes for
them among his sweet dishes and *entremets*, or what we should
now call savouries. These days, macaroni cheese would be
served as a hot first course dish and with a béchamel or cheese
sauce, or hot cream rather than with the meat sauce advocated
by Verral.

WILLIAM VERRAL'S MACARONI WITH PARMESAN CHEESE

'These are to be had at any confectioner's in London and the
newer they are the better – this is not what we call macaroons
of the sweet biscuit sort, but a foreign paste, the same as
vermicelly, but made very large in comparison to that – for this
you must boil them in water first, with a little salt, pour on
them a ladle of cullis,* a morsel of green onion and parsley
minced fine, pepper, salt and nutmeg; stew all a few minutes,
and pour into a dish with a rim, squeeze a lemon or orange,
and cover it over pretty thick with Parmesan cheese grated very
fine, bake it of a fine colour, about a quarter of an hour, and
serve it up hot.

'The French serve to their tables a great many dishes with
this sort of cheese, and in the same manner, only sometimes with
a savoury white sauce, such as scallops, oysters, and many of the
things you have among these entremets.'

On pages 150 and 228 there are two more of William Verral's
recipes.

Macaroni again figures as a 'second dish' at one of the
famous Parson Woodforde's dinners:

* Coulis or cullis was the basic brown sauce of highly concentrated meat
stock thickened with flour and butter, which was all-important in eighteenth-
century cookery.

April 8, (1796) FRIDAY: Mr Custance, Mr and Mrs Corbould, Mrs Mellish of Tuddenham, and Mr Stoughton of
Sparham, dined and spent the Afternoon with us, and did not
leave us, till after 9. in the Evening. Each Gentleman had a
servant with him. It was very near 4 o'clock before we sat
down to dinner, Mr Corbould coming very late to us. Mr
Custance was with us by half past two. He brought us a brace
of Cucumbers, very fine ones, and the first we have seen this
year. It was extremely kind of Mr Custance. We had for
dinner, a fine Cod's Head and Shoulders, boiled, and Oyster
Sauce, Peas Soup, Ham and 2 boiled chicken, and a fine Saddle
of Mutton rosted, Potatoes, Colli-Flower-Brocoli, and Cucumber. 2nd Course, a rost Duck, Maccaroni, a sweet batter
Pudding, & Currant Jelly, Blamange, and Rasberry Puffs.
Desert, Oranges, Almonds & Raisins, Nutts, & dried Apples,
Beefans.* Port & Sherry Wines, Porter, strong Beer & small.
After Coffee & Tea, we got to Cards . . .'

The Diary of a Country Parson 1758–1802, James Woodforde, edited by John
Beresford, World's Classics, 1963.

*Biffins, or beaufins, at one time the variety of apple used for drying, parti-
cularly in East Anglia.

* *

Fish

THE late Sir Harry Luke's *The Tenth Muse* was first published by Putnams in 1954, and was re-issued in a revised edition in 1962. The following notes on this original book appeared in the *Spectator* in December 1962.

During a lifetime spent – and uncommonly well spent, one deduces from this book – in the Colonial Service, Sir Harry collected recipes from British Residences and Government Houses, from their chatelaines, their cooks – cooks Maltese and Cypriot, Hindu and Persian and Assyrian, cooks Goanese and Polynesian, cooks naval, military and consular, cooks in Union Clubs at La Paz and Santiago di Chile, cooks of French pioneers and Brazilian countesses, Turkish Grand Viziers and Coptic Archimandrites. The marvel is that in setting down his recipes Sir Harry acknowledged the source of each and every one – Government House, Springfield, St Kitts; Government House, Fiji; Sant Anton Palace, Malta; the Goanese cook at the Residency, Bahrein; Government House, Wellington, New Zealand; Count Haupt Pappen-heim, Sao Paolo, Brazil; Lloyd, the butler at Kent House, Port of Spain.

Sir Harry must have been an ideal guest. The wife of the British Resident in Brunei prefers to mix her own curry powders, so off Sir Harry goes with her to market, noting that she buys, separately and in varying quantities, black pepper, aniseed, cardamom, chillies, cinnamon, cloves, coriander, cumin, mace, nutmeg, poppyseed, saffron, tamarind, turmeric ... As British Chief Commissioner in the Trans-Caucasian Republics of Georgia, Armenia and Azerbaijan he attends a banquet (it is 1919) at Novo Bayazid; there he eats a species of salmon trout unique to Lake Sevan and called *ishkhan*, the prince; it is served 'surrounded by its own amber-coloured caviare, accompanied by a sauce made of the cream of water-buffalo's milk, mixed with fresh peeled walnuts ... with somewhere a touch of horseradish (a condiment to which Sir Harry appears much addicted) ... the dish was subtly and incredibly delicious.' And it *sounds* delicious, so much so that one would like to be off to the shores of Lake Sevan in search of that princely fish, that water-buffalo cream and those fresh-peeled walnuts – but even supposing that the water buffaloes have not all been turned into tractors, I'll bet there's only one week of the entire year when all these delicacies coincide – and Sir Harry doesn't reveal which week it is.

I am relieved to find, since I intend to try it, that he is more forthcoming about how to steep a goose in a salt-and-sugar brine as it is done in the south Swedish province of Scania, how to cook it and what sauce to serve with it (recipe from the British Vice-Consul at Malmo); how to *try* to make the most delicious coffee cream cake which, the author says, is one of the best sweets he has ever tasted (in fact it is a meringue confection, and a tricky one); that a combination of fresh grapefruit segments and chestnuts is surprisingly good; that medlar and guava jellies to be served with meat and game are vastly improved by the inclusion of a little Worcester Sauce and fresh lemon juice in their composition; that a lady who lives at Dramea below the medieval castle of Buffaventa in the Kyrenia Mountains of Cyprus uses the leaf of the *persica* or wild cyclamen instead of vine leaves for her dishes of rice-stuffed dolmas.

Don't look here for infallible instructions; the quality which urges one to cook something new is rarely combined with that of technical precision, and Sir Harry himself disclaims knowledge of kitchen practice; few authors are as modest, and fewer still provide the ideas, the stimulus, the unexpected information, the sense of other people's horizons, which to me make this book so entrancing and transporting.

One of Sir Harry Luke's well-observed recipes is reproduced below. Others will be found on pp. 130, 155, and 245.

FRESH FISH

CRAB GRATINÉ

'1 medium-sized crab, ½ oz. butter, ½ oz. flour, ½ pint boiling milk, nutmeg, a little cream, a pinch of grated Parmesan.

'Remove the flesh from the crab and flake it. Make a cream sauce with the flour, butter and milk, adding seasoning, Parmesan, nutmeg and cream. Heat the crab meat gently in the sauce, using enough sauce to make the substance thick. Pour the whole back into the crab shell, sprinkle with white bread-crumbs and melted butter, and brown in the oven or under the grill. Serve with brown bread and butter.

'As the flavour of the crab is a very delicate one, the Parme-san must be used sparingly. For the same reason crab should never be submerged by such high-powered flavourings as curry powder, onion, Worcestershire sauce or red peppers, which often find their way into it.'

The Tenth Muse, Sir Harry Luke, 1954

MUSSELS IN SAFFRON SAUCE

From an Avignon restaurant, via a generous reader, comes a recipe for a saffron-flavoured mussel dish which contains more than one excellent idea.

For two people cook 3 to 4 pints of carefully cleaned mussels with a small onion, chopped, a bayleaf, parsley stalks, a scrap of thyme, three or four fennel seeds and a teacup of water. As soon as the mussels open, remove them, strain the liquid and add a scant ½ pint of it to a ¼ pint of very thick béchamel.* Then add enough saffron, either in powder or infusion form (in the latter case subtract the coffee-cupful of liquid from the total amount of mussel stock) to make the

*See p. 82.

sauce 'a good butter colour'. Next, just *one* tablespoon of cooked and very finely chopped spinach. Then stir in the shelled mussels and turn all into a fireproof dish. Spread with breadcrumbs and tiny pieces of butter. Reheat in a pretty hot oven for about 10 minutes, until the top surface is golden.

TO SPICE A FISH OR CHICKEN

I have made several attempts over the years to use, or rather to adapt, some of the extraordinary and fascinating and obviously authentic recipes given by the anonymous author of *Indian Domestic Economy*, published in Madras in 1850, and described on pages 190–91. Translating the spice quantities into workable measurements is not at all easy, and another difficulty is the question of green ginger root, a highly important ingredient in this kind of spice-cookery. It is obtainable in Indian and Chinese grocery shops but it is highly perishable, so it is useless to lay in a supply, unless you care to scrape it, slice it, and store it in a little jar of dry sherry which should be kept well-stoppered in the refrigerator. I learned of this method from Mrs Grace Zia Chu, author of *The Pleasures of Chinese Cooking* (Faber, 1964), and mighty grateful I am for the information.

If you have a freezer, it's easy to keep green ginger. Provided that the roots are really fresh, there is no need even to peel them. Simply wrap them separately in foil and put them all in one bag so that one or two can be extracted as and when you need them. If you use only a small piece, the remainder of the root can be put back in the freezer.

When one needs green ginger nothing else will do. On occasion, I *have* used as a substitute a small piece of stem ginger in syrup plus a little bit of crushed dried ginger root. This works quite well, but it does lack the characteristic tang of the green root (which *is* faintly green when it is peeled; outside it looks like a withered old Jerusalem artichoke).

*

Supposing then, that you have the green ginger, a spiced fish or chicken (not so subtle, I'm afraid, as the originals, but the recipe provides a good working basis) can be made with the following mixture: 2 teaspoons of coriander seeds, 6 cardamom pods, ½ oz. of green ginger (which sounds a lot, but there's a great deal of waste when you peel it; if tinned green ginger, which is already peeled and sliced, is being used, about ¼ oz. or 4 slices is enough), half a teaspoon of ground cloves, half a dozen or so black peppercorns, 2 teaspoons of salt.

The coriander seeds should be put in a warm oven for two or three minutes, a process which brings out their sweet aromatic orangey scent in a remarkable way. The cardamom pods you break, retaining only the tiny seeds (a very pungent and also very expensive spice, cardamom). All the ingredients, including the peeled ginger, you then pound together; moisten the mixture with a little oil and then work in half an ounce of butter. The resulting paste you spread under the skin of your chicken for pot-roasting, baking or grilling, or into incisions made across each side of a whole fish for grilling or baking. This makes an admirable way of dealing with a large grey mullet and with fresh-water fish such as carp.

The spice mixture ought to be made, and rubbed into your fish or chicken, about 2 hours before you intend cooking it. not much longer though, unless you intend to give yourself or somebody else a demonstration of the vagaries of spices in cooking. Once they are ground and mixed they alter and weaken in flavour in a very perceptible way even after a few hours – which is one reason for buying, whenever feasible, whole rather than ready-ground spices. Another is that whole spices are cheaper. You aren't paying the pepper and spice grinders' profit. One sees why good Indian cooks make their curry and spice mixtures fresh for every meal. The difference in aroma between whole fresh spices and stale powdered ones is enormous.

SPICED FISH CROQUETTES

First mix 12 to 16 oz. of cooked white fish, weighed when already freed of skin and bone, then flaked, with 2 tablespoons of chopped parsley, salt, coarsely milled pepper and 1 whole large beaten egg. Form the mixture into little cork shapes, roll them in flour and leave them on a floured dish or board. There should be about 2 dozen croquettes.

Now chop finely 1 small onion with a tablespoon of parsley; add ½ teaspoon each of powdered saffron, ground ginger, cumin seeds or ground cumin, and freshly ground pepper; and ¼ teaspoon each of cayenne pepper and salt.

Melt 3 oz. of butter in a big frying pan. In this gently cook the spice and onion mixture without letting the butter brown. Add ½ pint of water or fish stock. Bring gently to simmering point. Put in the fish croquettes, and let them cook gently for about 15 minutes, turning them from time to time and shaking the pan so that they do not stick. If the sauce gets too thick add a little more water or stock.

Turn the fish croquettes and the sauce on to a heated serving dish. As a first course serve simply with lemon, or as a main course with a salad of sliced tomatoes and lettuce dressed with oil and lemon, or if you prefer have a dish of pilau rice.

BAKED SPICED MACKEREL

In an oven dish or baking tin arrange four to six medium-sized mackerel, cleaned but not split. (I prefer to cook them whole, heads and all. The point is not important. It rather depends upon the shape and dimension of your dish.) The fish should be well sprinkled, inside and out, with salt. Add a few slices of lemon or orange, a half-dozen bayleaves, a teaspoon-ful of allspice berries or black peppercorns, a few parsley stalks and, if available, three or four dried fennel stalks.

To every three mackerel add a couple of tablespoons of wine vinegar. Now pour in a little water, from a quarter to a half-pint, depending on the size of the dish. There should be enough to prevent the fish drying out during cooking.

Cover the dish with a piece of oiled paper or foil. Cook the mackerel in the centre of a moderate oven, gas No. 4, 350°F., for 25 to 30 minutes.

Gooseberry sauce as described on page 76 goes particularly well with mackerel cooked in this fashion.

As an accompaniment have plain boiled new potatoes or, when available, a salad of raw Florentine fennel sliced into thin strips, and dressed with salt, lemon juice and olive oil.

SALTED AND SMOKED FISH

SMOKED HADDOCK

What Englishman exiled in a foreign land has not at some time yearned for a kipper on his breakfast table or bloater paste for his tea? At the thought of a kedgeree made with smoked haddock and plenty of hard-boiled eggs English eyes grow dreamy and the smell of an English country house dining-room at breakfast time, the blue flame of methylated spirits burning under a plated dish warmer, comes back to tease and tantalize.

These smoked, dried and salted fish, to which as a nation we are so attached, are by no means always easy to come by in prime condition. Neither are they very well understood by the average customer at the fishmonger's counter, who rarely knows the difference between a true haddock and a dyed whiting fillet, although the true and the false are so easily distinguished, since the skin of the haddock bears the two black marks on each side of the backbone known as St Peter's thumb mark (the John Dory also bears these marks); and a real Finnan smoked haddock is pale with a dull surface, whereas the artificially coloured, bright yellow fillets called golden cutlets, which may be haddock fillets and may be whiting, are treated with a chemical which gives them a 'smoke' flavour.

TO COOK SMOKED HADDOCK

'Aberdeen haddocks are considered the best. Remove the fins and cut the fish in convenient-sized pieces. If very salt, steep it in hot water for a few minutes. Then place the fish on a well-greased baking dish, sprinkle it with pepper, cover with greased paper and bake in a moderate oven from 10 to 15 minutes, according to the thickness of the fish. Serve the fish very hot and in the dish in which it was cooked.'

Cookery for Every Household, Florence B. Jack, 1931

KIPPERS

Although kippers are one of these foods brought forward whenever somebody thinks it time to come to the defence of British culinary achievements, they are of much less ancient origin than one might suppose. It is only about a hundred and twenty years since the kipper was invented by a Northumberland man called Woodger, who copied the idea from the kippered salmon, already known in the North for at least three centuries. Kippers eventually replaced in popularity the old red herring, which was more like a bloater, but inclined to be excessively salt and dry.

A much-discussed question is that of the dyeing of kippers. Since we are becoming a nation which eats by visual appeal rather than by taste and smell, the plain, pale, undyed kipper is now regarded by the general public as in some way defective, and the large chain of fish merchants in the country find that they cannot sell it, except in one or two isolated areas where old eating habits die hard.

In the Isle of Man the dyeing of kippers is actually forbidden by law, but the kipper season is so short there – about two months in the summer – that the small delicious little kippers they produce are hard to come by.

On the whole, it looks as though in the case of the kipper the deterioration is less serious than is sometimes supposed. The dyeing process is harmless, and on the other hand, were we confronted with the dry salt fish of a hundred or even fifty years ago the chances are we should find it quite uneatable.

To cook kippers, put them flat in a baking dish, or heads downward in a tall jug, pour boiling water over them and leave them five minutes. Pour off the water, put them in a warm oven with a piece of butter on each, until the butter has just melted. Some people prefer to put them straight under the grill, with butter. This is alright providing the grill can be controlled. Too hot a fire makes the kippers curl up and they become hard.

ARBROATH OR ABERDEEN SMOKIES

These are haddock, gutted and decapitated, but not split like the Finnan haddock. With dark golden skins and firm sweet white flesh they are the most delicious of the smoked-haddock family. As they are hot-smoked they are already cooked, and can be eaten exactly as you buy them, or if you like them hot simply put them in the oven, with a good pat of butter on each, until they are warmed through. The market for smokies has hitherto been mainly in their native Scotland, but recently the excellence of these fish has become more widely appreciated, and quite often nowadays they are to be found at large London stores and in the shops of enterprising fishmongers in the bigger provincial towns.

SMOKED TROUT, MACKEREL, BUCKLING AND SPRATS

Smoked mackerel, although cheap, is the rarest of the smoked-fish tribe in England. Small quantities are smoked, over chips, on the Scottish coast, and sometimes they are to be found in London shops, notably at Hamburger Products, No. 1

Wardour Street, where a good variety of smoked fish is always to be had.

Smoked mackerel are best perhaps, like smoked trout, served just as they are, and the same applies to buckling which are herrings hot-smoked, and therefore in no need of further cooking.

Smoked sprats are also delicious and cheap little morsels for an hors-d'oeuvre.

YARMOUTH BLOATERS

Bloaters are – or were, since they are now very rare – herrings, salted and smoked without being split or gutted, a process which is responsible for their characteristic gamey flavour.

One way of preparing bloaters was to cut off the heads and tails, open the fish down the back, lay them flat, grill them on both sides, and serve them with fresh butter and a Captain's biscuit heated in the oven. This was the system recommended by Francatelli, author of *The Cook's Guide*, 1888, and once, for a brief period, head chef to Queen Victoria.

Another system is to open the bloaters down the back, bone them, sandwich two fish together, flat and with skins outward, wrap them in buttered paper or foil, and heat in a slow oven for about 20 minutes. A similar but more fancy method was suggested by Soyer, who used one bloater and one fresh herring clamped together.

* *

Rice and Vegetables

'To turn to spices, mace – that aesthetically beautiful by-product of the nutmeg-tree, a network husk of deep and brilliant lacquer-red while it is still fresh on the nut – enriches thick soups and the stock-pot generally with its singularly piquant aroma. Nutmeg itself, grated, is also a help in soups (as has been noted elsewhere) no less than in bread sauce and a rum punch. Saffron is as indispensable to a good Milanese risotto as it is to a bouillabaisse and a paella. A touch of cardamom or coriander seed transforms a humdrum stew with the aroma of a Middle Eastern suq. And what a rich evocative aroma they have, those ancient vaulted bazaars of Aleppo and Damascus and the Old City of Jerusalem, of Qazvin and Meshhed and Isfahan, as you approach the streets of the vendors of spices. Here you inhale an amalgam of all the aboriginal savours and smells of the Orient: the pepper and cloves; the cinnamon and turmeric and coriander.'

The Tenth Muse, Sir Harry Luke, 1954

PILAU RICE

There are Egyptian, Turkish, Persian, Indian, Chinese and goodness knows how many other systems of cooking and flavouring pilau rice. This is one of my own recipes, evolved by combining an Indian method with flavourings which are predominantly Levantine.

Measurements for pilau rice cookery are nearly always based on volume rather than weight. The use of a cup or glass for measuring the rice simplifies the recipes because the cooking liquid is measured in the same vessel, the success of the process depending largely upon the correct proportions of liquid to rice. The cooking pot is also important, especially to those unfamiliar with the routine. Choose a saucepan or a two-handled casserole not too deep in proportion to its width. Whether of aluminium, iron, cast iron, copper or earthenware is not important provided the base is thick and even.

Those unfamiliar with rice cookery are advised to start by making a small quantity of pilau, enough for say two or three people. The recipe once mastered, it is easy to increase the quantities, in proportion, and to experiment with different flavourings.

Using the best quality thin-grain rice sold in the Indian shops under the name of Basmati* the initial ingredients and preparations are as follows: 1 tumbler of rice, 2 tumblers of water.

Put the rice in a bowl and cover it with water. Leave it to soak for an hour or so.

Cooking and flavouring ingredients are 1 oz. of clarified butter (or ghee bought from an Indian provision store), 1 small onion, 4 cardamom pods, 2 teaspoons of cumin seeds, or ground cumin, a teaspoon of turmeric powder, 2 teaspoons of salt, a bayleaf or two, 2 tumblers of water.

Melt the butter in your rice-cooking pot or saucepan (for this quantity a 2½ to 3 pints one is large enough) and in it cook the sliced onion for a few seconds, until it is translucent. It must not brown. This done, stir in the cardamom seeds extracted from their pods and the cumin seeds, both pounded in a mortar, and the turmeric. The latter is for colouring the rice a beautiful yellow, as well as for its flavour, and the object of cooking the spices in the fat is to develop their aromas before the rice is added. This is an important point.

Drain the rice, and put it into the butter and spice mixture. Stir it around until it glistens with the fat. Add the salt. Pour in the two tumblers of water and let it come to the boil fairly fast. Put in the bayleaf.

Let the rice cook steadily, uncovered, over medium heat

---

* There are three grades of this rice. The secondary qualities are white, while the first is brownish, and the grain perceptibly longer than in the second-quality grades. A third, packed in cartons, is good, but not the best, which is usually sold loose.

until almost all the water is absorbed and holes begin to appear in the mass. This will take almost 10 minutes.

Now turn the heat as low as possible. Over the rice put a thickly folded absorbent tea cloth, and on top of the cloth (use an old one; the turmeric stains) the lid of the pan. Leave undisturbed, still over the lowest possible heat, for 20 to 25 minutes. At the end of this time the rice should be quite tender and each grain will be separated. Fork it round, turn into a warmed serving bowl.

The rice should be a fine yellow colour and mildly spiced.

The pilau can be eaten as an accompaniment to spiced lamb or beef kebabs, but to my mind is even nicer on its own, with the addition of a few sultanas or raisins, soaked for an hour in water, heated up in a little saucepan and mixed into the rice just before it is turned out of the saucepan for serving. Oven-toasted almonds or pine kernels make another attractive addition.

The tumbler I use for measuring holds 6 oz. of Basmati rice and 6 oz. or just over ¼ pint of water.

In the following recipe the rice is simply washed under running cold water rather than soaked. I find that it does not produce quite such well-swollen and delicious rice, but many people hold that the quicker method is the better one.

QUICK PILAU RICE

If you are in a hurry, or have forgotten to soak the rice, simply put it in a sieve or colander, wash it very thoroughly under cold running water, and cook it as described for pilau rice – with or without spices – allowing a little longer, say five extra minutes, for the first part of the cooking.

SAFFRON PILAU RICE

To make a dish of plain yellow rice which is to be a back⁄ground for kebabs or some other meat, chicken or fish dish, the rice is cooked as for the pilau on page 114. Instead of all the spices, use saffron to colour the rice, and leave out the onions.

To prepare the saffron for colouring the rice proceed as follows: put as many whole saffron filaments as will cover a pre⁄decimal sixpenny piece upon a fireproof plate. Heat it for 5 to 10 minutes in a *very* moderate oven. The saffron filaments can now be crumbled between the fingers and can then be stirred into the rice when it is in the saucepan and already glistening with the warmed clarified butter or fat.

The saffron does not immediately colour the rice, even when the water is added. The yellow stain and the pungent aroma develop gradually. So do not panic and add a double dose until you have experience of the performance of this very pungent aromatic.

SAFFRON OR MILANESE RISOTTO

A saffron risotto is a kettle of rice very very different from a saffron pilau or saffron rice. In the first place whereas Basmati rice for pilau is long and thin⁄grained, risotto rice has a large round grain with a hard white central core. It can be cooked by a method not feasible for other rice grains and still remain slightly resistant; although basically the whole dish is liquid as compared to the essential dryness of a pilau rice. This is a point rarely appreciated. Nor is the relevance of the differing cooking qualities – not to mention the flavours – of the two types of rice. And it is not easy to cook a good risotto for a party. It is a dish for a small number of people and must be made on the spot, for a risotto cannot really be kept waiting any more than can a soufflé, or more relevantly perhaps, scrambled eggs. For as there is a moment in the cooking of scrambled eggs when it is necessary to remove the saucepan from the heat although the eggs may look under-cooked, so it is with the rice for a risotto, which at a given moment is cooked but appears far too soupy. All the same you do not leave it over the heat for another two minutes because during the two, or three, or four minutes which elapse before you get the risotto from the pan to the serving dish and from the serving dish to your plates, the rice will have absorbed, through its own heat, the excess liquid. If it has absorbed too much it will be stodgy.

Just as for the pilau on page 114, I suggest that the way to learn to make a risotto is to cook it for two or three people only, and to experiment until you get it right. It does need practice and a very watchful eye.

Ingredients, then, for two people are 1 teacupful (5 to 6 oz. or 1 cup) of Piedmontese Arborio white rice of the quality called *superfino,** 2 oz. of the very best butter you can buy, 1 very small onion or shallot, 1 to 1¼ pints of clear mild chicken stock (if you have none, use water, not a cube), enough saffron filaments to cover a sixpence, salt, 2 tablespoons of grated Parmesan cheese, and more to put on the table.

After trying scores of different pans, I have come to the conclusion that a heavy aluminium or tinned copper saucepan of conventional shape is the best pot for cooking a risotto. For the quantities given a 2½ to 3 pint saucepan is the right capacity.

First put the saffron in a little cup, cover it with a little boiling water or stock and leave it to infuse. Then peel and chop the onion. Melt 1½ oz. of the butter, put in the onion, let it cook a minute, until it is translucent. It must not brown. Put in the rice. Stir it around until it glistens with butter. *On no account let it fry*, or your finished risotto will have an un-attractive scorched taste. Pour in about ¾ pint of the boiling stock or water. Leave the rice to cook, uncovered, over medium heat until the liquid is all absorbed. This will take approxim-ately 15 minutes.

*In grocers' shops in Turin, Milan and Venice, the three great risotto-eating towns of Italy, there are usually three different grades of risotto rice to choose from. Superfino Vialone or Arborio are the most expensive. The yellow-coloured crystal rice sold in many English delicatessens is good but not the best.

When the rice begins to look dry, pour in approximately another ¼ pint of boiling stock or water. Add about 3 teaspoonfuls of salt and the strained saffrontinted stock or water.

At this stage the risotto needs a fair amount of watching and stirring. Use a wooden fork, which doesn't break the grains, and taste the rice to see if it is reaching or has reached the proper degree of tenderness. A grain *must retain* a slight resistance as you bite it. And the risotto must be liquid. Not soup, but only just not. Stir in the Parmesan cheese. Taste for seasoning. Add the reserved halfounce of butter when you have transferred the rice to its serving dish.

The risotto should be cooked in approximately 25 minutes.

In restaurants in Venice, Turin and Milan, and indeed anywhere else in Italy from Rome northwards, where the cooking is conscientious, the risotto is made freshly at frequent intervals during the busy hours of lunchtime and dinner. More than six portions are seldom made at once, and usually the waiter will tell you that your order will take 20 minutes. (It does, and it is rare that a risotto is not worth waiting for.)

It is essential to serve risotto on a hot dish, and to eat it from hot plates, and they should be soup plates.

It is the saffron which makes this risotto a dish of Milan rather than of Turin or Venice. Curiously, considering their ancient history as the spice traders of Europe prior to the Portuguese discovery of the sea route to India, the Venetians use very few spices in their cooking.

A point not fully understood in England is that Italians do not use risotto as a vehicle for leftovers, nor is it treated – with one exception – as a background for meat, poultry, fish or game. It is a dish in itself, served as a first course and on restaurant menus invariably listed among the soups. Equally invariable is the Milanese saffrontinted risotto offered as an accompaniment to *ossi buchi* (literally hollow bones), that very fine and filling dish of veal knuckles sawn into short lengths, slowly simmered with wine and aromatics, all the pieces carefully arranged so that the marrow in the centre does not fall out. A dish which it is very difficult indeed to make in England because the young veal needed to make *ossi buchi* successfully is not obtainable.

N.B. For a risotto, rice is *never* washed, and the liquid, whether water or stock, should be boiling when poured over the rice.

For a pilau the rice *is* washed or soaked, and the water or stock can be cold or hot when added.

PAËLLA VALENCIANA

There are countless versions of this celebrated Spanish rice dish. The only constant ingredients in every recipe are rice and saffron or the saffron substitute sold in Spain as paëlla powder. A mixture of pork, chicken and shellfish is characteristic, although not invariable.

Here is a simple paëlla recipe given me by a native of Valencia.

First, the size and shape of the utensil in which the paëlla is cooked are important. It should be a wide, round, shallow pan – and if you are cooking on gas or electricity a heavy one with a flat base – measuring approximately 10 to 12 inches in diameter, about 2 inches deep, and with a minimum capacity of 4 pints, to make a paëlla for 3 or 4 people. The typical Spanish paëlla, which originally gave the dish its name, has two handles, and may be made of earthenware, but more usually of rather lightweight raw iron, which rusts all too easily in the English climate. A large heavy frying pan or sauté pan, aluminium or copper, of approximately the same dimensions does perfectly well for the purpose, but bear in mind that the paëlla *should* be brought to table in the pan in which it has cooked.

Ingredients are one small roasting-chicken weighing about 1½ lb. or half a larger one, about a ½ pint of unshelled prawns or 4 oz. shelled or 6 giant Mediterranean or Pacific prawns, 12 French beans (about 2 oz.), 2 teacupsful (10 to 12 oz.) of Valencia rice (this is obtainable from Ortega's, 74 Old Compton

Street, London. Italian Arborio or very good-quality Patna-type rice make a better although less authentic paëlla.); 2 tomatoes; and seasonings of saffron, *pimentón* (this is the Spanish version of paprika pepper, which is sometimes used instead), salt and freshly milled pepper; and olive oil for cooking.

Cut the chicken into about 8 pieces. In the pan warm 4 tablespoons of olive oil. Put in the pieces of chicken, seasoned with salt and pepper. Let them cook very gently for about 12 minutes, mainly on the skin side, as this should be fried to a nice golden colour. Set aside on a plate.

In the same oil fry the peeled and chopped tomatoes; stir in a teaspoon of *pimentón* or paprika. Now add 2 pints of water. When it comes to the boil, put back the pieces of chicken and simmer gently for 10 minutes. Add the rice, the prawns (Spanish cooks don't shell them; this is a matter of taste, I prefer them shelled) and the beans topped and tailed and broken into inch lengths. Cook steadily for 15 minutes; sprinkle in half a teaspoon of powdered saffron* and a little salt. In another 5 to 7 minutes the rice should be cooked, but timing depends upon the quality of the rice, and the size and thickness of the pan and so on. If the water has evaporated before the rice is cooked, add a little more. If on the other hand there is still too much liquid by the time the rice has cooked, increase the heat and cook fast until the rice is dry. Finally, taste for seasoning, and serve the paëlla in the pan in which it has cooked.

The rice should be a beautiful yellow colour, and although moist, each grain should be separate. And if it is necessary to stir, use a fork, not a spoon, which might break the rice.

To this basic mixture, can be added other ingredients such as small dice of salt pork, mussels, or any other shellfish you please, artichoke hearts, green peas, sweet peppers, snails, rabbit; and, traditionally, the paëlla is eaten with a spoon. Knives and forks are not supposed to be required.

In south-eastern Spain, in the regions of Valencia and

*Or subtract a small coffee-cupful of water from the 2 pints used for cooking the rice, steep saffron filaments in it, add, strained, at the appropriate moment.

Alicante, paëlla is the favourite Sunday lunch dish. During the summer, in the country and seaside restaurants which cater for the locals as well as for summer visitors there is a brisk Sunday trade in paëllas. Late in the afternoon, when the so erroneously named midday meal is at last over, you will see rows of iron or aluminium paëlla pans, of assorted sizes, all scrubbed and shining, arranged in orderly ranks and left drying in the sun outside the kitchens or in the courtyards.

Truth demands the admission that for me every once in a while is quite enough for the paëlla ritual. The making of it is a drama which is instructive and entertaining but Valencia rice is of poor quality; dishes made with it are not to be compared with the much simpler risotto of Northern Italy – that wonderful melting risotto which relies for its appeal on the fine rice of Piedmont, on the finesse of authentic Parmesan cheese, good butter and a well moderated flavouring of saffron. Not so colourful as a paëlla. But infinitely more subtle.

BOILED RICE

Nothing is easier than to produce a dish of plain boiled rice and to serve it in perfect condition even as long as 30 minutes after it has been boiled.

4 to 6 oz. best-quality rice; salt; olive oil; butter.

The first essential is to buy the best-quality rice, either long-grained Indian Basmati or so-called Patna, or the Italian large and round-grained variety. Fill a 6 to 8 pint saucepan three-quarters full of water. Bring it to the boil. Throw in 2 tablespoons of salt. Put in the rice (don't wash it first). When the water comes back to the boil, float 2 tablespoons of olive oil on the top. This helps to prevent the water boiling over. Boil the rice for 14 to 18 minutes (Italian rice takes longer than Patna and Basmati). Time it carefully, and after 15 minutes test it by tasting a grain or two. When it is tender but still slightly firm, it is ready. Drain it in a colander. Have ready a casserole or a deepish fireproof serving dish, well buttered. Put in the rice. Add a good lump of butter, and stir it around. Cover the rice with a clean dry folded teacloth. Cover this with the lid. Thus protected (the cloth absorbs the steam) the rice can be left in a low or medium oven for 30 minutes or more.

Enough for 2 people.

*

It should be noted that neither this method, nor any other, will work unless you have good rice. Small round-grained pudding rice will not do. In my opinion the American Uncle Ben rice lacks flavour, and it is not worth bothering with any of the various brands of instant rice.

Boiled Rice Dry

'The manner of boiling Rice to eat with Butter, is this. In a Pipkin pour upon it as much water, as will swim a good fingers breadth over it. Boil it gently, till it be tender, and all the water drunk into the Rice; which may be in a quarter of an hour or less. Stir it often with a wooden spatule or spoon, that it burn not to the bottom: But break it not. When it is enough, pour it into a dish, and stew* it with some Butter, and season it with sugar and Cinnamon. This Rice is to appear dry, excepting for the Butter, that is melted in it.'

*The Closet of the Eminently Learned
Sir Kenelm Digby Knight Opened*, 1669

QUICK KEDGEREE

For a party I make a kedgeree with rice boiled in advance, then kept hot, with all its extra ingredients, in a big bowl standing in a saucepan of simmering water.

For an impromptu dish for two or three people I use a quick and easy method which, once you've understood the principle, has infinite possibilities. You can apply the same system to prawns, mussels, vegetables, chicken, meat – with one

*I fancy that this was a printer's error and should read 'strew'.

proviso. Good-quality rice, either long-grained Basmati or the hard round-grained Italian variety is essential. Soft pudding rice will turn to just that – pudding.

Ingredients are 3 smoked haddock fillets, 2 tablespoons of olive oil, 1 medium onion, 4 heaped tablespoons of rice, a scant teaspoon of curry powder, 2 tablespoons of sultanas or currants, seasonings, 2 hard-boiled eggs, parsley, water; a lemon and chutney.

First pour boiling water over the haddock fillets. Leave them two or three minutes, drain them, peel off the skin and divide the fish into manageable pieces.

Heat the oil in a heavy 10 inch frying or sauté pan. In this fry the sliced onion until pale yellow. Stir in the curry powder. Add the rice (don't wash it). Stir all round together. Add the washed sultanas or currants. Pour in 1 pint of water. Cook steadily, not at a gallop, and uncovered, for 10 minutes. Put in the haddock. Continue cooking until the liquid is all absorbed and the rice tender – approximately 10 minutes. But keep an eye on it to see it doesn't stick, and stir with a fork, not a spoon which breaks the rice. Taste for seasoning. Salt may or may not be required. Turn on to a hot serving dish. On the top strew the chopped eggs and parsley – and, if you like, a nice big lump of butter. Surround with lemon quarters and serve with mango chutney.

KHICHRI

The dish from which the English evolved kedgeree. The original contains no fish, and is simply a mixture of lentils and rice cooked with spices. It is very cheap and filling.

Spices are a quarter teaspoon each of ground ginger and cloves, 6 allspice berries, 6 white peppercorns, the seeds from 6 cardamom pods. Other ingredients are 1 oz. of clarified butter or ghee, ¾ of a glassful (approximately 4 oz.) each of ordinary red lentils and Patna or Basmati rice, salt, 3 glasses of water, a tablespoon or two of the liquid part of rather sharp mango chutney, or more correctly, of tamarind pulp, 1 small onion.

Pound the peppercorns, allspice and cardamoms. Mix them with the ground spices.

In the clarified butter or ghee melt the thinly sliced onion. Do not let it brown. Stir in the spices, let them fry for a minute or so. Add the lentils, then the rice. Stir both round in the fat. Season with salt – about 1 heaped dessertspoonful. Add the chutney or tamarind pulp. Pour in 3 glasses of cold water.

Cook, uncovered, over medium heat. Stir from time to time with a fork, for about 15 minutes, until all the water is ab/sorbed. By this time the lentils are nearly cooked but the rice is not. Turn the heat as low as possible, put the saucepan on a heat/diffuser mat, cover the rice and lentils with a folded tea cloth and the lid of the saucepan. Leave for 20 minutes. Turn into a heated dish, squeeze lemon juice over and serve at once, very hot. There should be enough for three or four, depending upon what other dishes are to be given.

Khichri can be eaten on its own or as an accompaniment to a meat or chicken curry. In either case a little dish of chutney and another of fresh cucumber with a yogurt and mint dressing or some other such refreshing little preparation should be offered at the same time.

The spices can be altered to suit individual taste. Those who do not like ginger (a little green ginger root is far better than the powdered variety) or cloves could substitute cumin and turmeric, and if you have no cardamom seeds – well, perhaps you will invent some new and perfect spice mixture. If English kedgeree can evolve from khichri, then in cookery anything at all can happen.

CARROTS STEWED WITH RICE

An excellent little dish, which makes a course on its own.

Scrape 1 lb. of young carrots, and cut each in half length/ways.

Heat a little olive oil in a 9 inch skillet or other heavy frying pan. Put in the carrots and turn them over and over so that they are well coated with the oil.

Add 2 tablespoons of uncooked long-grain rice, and with a wooden fork stir it around with the carrots.

Now add the water just to cover, and a very little salt. Simmer, uncovered, for about 25 minutes until both carrots and rice are quite tender and most of the liquid absorbed.

Stir in a tablespoon or two of dried mint (a typical Levantine flavouring) or finely chopped fresh parsley and a squeeze of lemon juice.

This dish is equally good hot or cold.

The quantities will serve two or three people as a first course for a simple midday meal.

TOMATOES WITH TARRAGON BUTTER

1 lb. of firm ripe tomatoes, 1 oz. of butter, seasonings of salt and sugar, 2 teaspoons of tarragon butter.*

Pour boiling water over the tomatoes, skin them and keep them whole.

Melt the butter in a heavy frying pan or in an earthenware poëlon (a shallow casserole with a handle). Put in the skinned tomatoes, sprinkle them with salt and a pinch of caster sugar. Cook over low heat for about 10 minutes, turning them once or twice, very gently.

When the tomatoes are soft and the juice running a little, add the tarragon butter and turn up the heat for a few seconds.

Serve quickly before the tomatoes lose their shapes and begin to turn to sauce.

A delicious and delicate vegetable dish to serve with white fish or a roast of veal.

AUBERGINES À LA TUNISIENNE

2 aubergines weighing approximately 6 oz. each, ¾ lb. tomatoes, 1 medium-sized onion, 1 clove of garlic, ½ teaspoon of ground allspice, a teaspoon of dried basil or mint, a table-

*See p. 87.

spoon of chopped parsley, a tablespoon of currants, cayenne, salt, pepper, 4 tablespoons of olive oil.

Cut the unpeeled aubergines lengthwise into 4 pieces and then into cubes. Put them in a colander, sprinkle them with salt, put a plate and a weight on top and leave them to drain for an hour or so.

Heat the oil in a heavy frying pan, put in the sliced onion, and cook gently until pale yellow and transparent. Now put in the aubergines, shaken dry in a cloth. Let them brown a little on each side; put in the garlic, crushed and broken into three or four pieces. Cover the pan and cook gently about 15 minutes. Now add the skinned and chopped tomatoes, the allspice, the dried basil, a scrap of cayenne and a little freshly ground black pepper, and cook until the moisture from the tomatoes has almost evaporated. Stir in the currants, which should have been previously soaked in a cup of water for a few minutes, and the parsley. The whole cooking time, after the aubergines are put in the pan, is from 25 to 30 minutes, and all the vegetables should be well amalgamated without being in a purée; and there should be a small amount of sauce.

Turn into a shallow bowl or serving dish. This dish is equally good hot or cold, and there should be enough for 3 or 4 people.

SWEET PEPPERS AND TOMATOES STUFFED WITH RICE

Ingredients for the stuffing for 4 fairly large sweet red, yellow or green peppers and 2 or 3 large tomatoes are ¼ lb. rice, 1 onion, a clove or two of garlic, 6 coriander seeds, a teaspoon of dried basil, a tablespoon of parsley, a tablespoon each of currants and pine nuts, or 2 of currants if no pine nuts are available, 2 or 3 tablespoons of olive oil.

Boil the rice in plenty of salted water for about 10 to 12 minutes, so that it remains somewhat underdone. Drain it.

While the rice is cooking fry the sliced onion gently in the oil, add the crushed garlic cloves, coriander seeds, seasonings, and basil. Simmer gently with the pan covered for about 15 minutes. Add the currants, pine nuts and parsley. Mix with the drained rice.

Cut the peppers in half lengthways, remove the core and seeds, rinse them in running cold water and make sure that no seeds remain.

Cut the tomatoes in half, scoop out the flesh and add it to the rice mixture. Fill both peppers and tomatoes with the rice, piling it up very lightly. Put the peppers in an oven dish, pour a tablespoon of stock or olive oil over each, cover the dish closely, and cook in a very slow oven, gas No. 1, 290°F., for 1½ hours. Now put in the tomatoes and cook for a further ½ hour. These peppers and tomatoes can be eaten hot or cold, and are best on their own as a first dish, although the tomatoes make a good accompaniment to lamb or veal or chicken.

Enough for 4 to 6 people.

In Cairo the Sudanese cooks used to prepare huge quantities of these stuffed vegetables for parties and picnics. Courgettes, aubergines, and vine leaves were usually included as well as the peppers and tomatoes, and all were served together in immense shallow copper dishes. I have not included the aubergines and courgettes in this recipe because they seem to me to demand rather more time and finicking work than they are worth – that is when one has to do everything oneself – whereas the peppers and tomatoes are perfectly easy and straightforward.

CABBAGE STEWED IN BUTTER WITH CREAM

The sketchy outlines of this excellent little dish are given in the *Dudley Book*, a collection of recipes put together by Georgiana, Countess of Dudley, and published in 1909.

Ingredients are 1 small very fresh crinkly green cabbage, 1½ to 2 oz. of butter, seasonings of salt, vinegar, pepper and nut-meg, 2 tablespoons of cream.

Trim off the outside leaves of the cabbage, slice the rest, fairly thinly, discarding the hard centre stalk. Put the sliced leaves in a colander and rinse in cold water.

Heat the butter in a saucepan, put in the cabbage, stir it round, add a little salt, let it stew gently for about 5 minutes, stirring most of that time.

Now add the cream and cook for another 2 to 3 minutes. Sprinkle in a few drops of wine vinegar, then light seasonings of nutmeg and freshly milled pepper. Serve very hot while the cabbage is still crisp.

With baked gammon rashers or a few sausages this makes a good, quickly cooked lunch dish.

It is instructive to compare Lady Dudley's recipe with the two following methods, quoted from the admirable book on Chinese cooking for Westerners, of which I have written at length on pages 198 to 201.

STIRRED CABBAGE

'This method is usually for new cabbage.

2 lb. new cabbage, 2 heaped tb/sp. lard or the same amount of vegetable oil, 1½ t/sp. salt, ½ cup water.

Wash the cabbage and cut it into strips of about ¼ inch wide.

'Heat oil or lard in skillet till hot, put the cabbage in and stir for 1 min. Then add salt and water. Keep on stirring for 3 min. more.'

How to Cook and Eat in Chinese, Buwei Yang Chao, 1956

SWEET/SOUR CABBAGE

'This method is for either new or old cabbage. The special name for this dish is 'Sweet and Sour Cabbage'.

2 lb. cabbage, 2 heaped tb/sp. lard or the same amount of vegetable oil, 1½ t/sp. salt, 1½ cup water, 3 tb/sp. sugar, 3 t/sp. vinegar, 1 tb/sp. cornflour.

'Do everything same as in Recipe for Stirred Cabbage, except that you cut the cabbage leaves into 1/square/inch pieces instead of into strips.

'Mix the vinegar, sugar, and cornflour together with an

additional cup of water. When the cabbage is done according to this recipe, put the mixture in and stir. It is done when the juice becomes translucent.'

How to Cook and Eat in Chinese, Buwei Yang Chao, 1956

PAPRIKA CABBAGE

Paprikakraut

'1 white cabbage, 1 onion, 3 oz. butter or lard, 1 large green pepper, caraway seed, salt, black pepper, paprika.

'Cut the cabbage into strips and leave it for 12 hours in a marinade of the vinegar, caraway seed, salt and black pepper.

'Then slice and fry the onion, add the marinated cabbage, sprinkle with paprika and stew for 1 hour or until soft. When ready, mix into it the raw green pepper, thinly sliced.'

'Serves 4.

'Source: Frau Frischmuth, Hotel am See, Alt-Aussee, Styria, Austria.'

The Tenth Muse, Sir Harry Luke, 1962

ROAST ONIONS

This is one of the most primitive but at the same time most appreciated of onion dishes.

Choose medium to large onions, but not monsters, and see that the ones you buy are clean, without grit showing through the skins. Do not peel them.

Put them on a baking sheet or in a tin and let them cook for 2 to 3 hours (according to whether they are in the centre or on a lower shelf) in a very moderate oven, gas No. 3, 330°F.

Serve them hot, exactly as you would baked potatoes, with butter, or cinnamon butter,* and salt.

Allow 2 onions per person.

*See p. 86.

POTATOES COOKED IN MILK

This recipe demonstrates a method which turns old potatoes into something special, and makes new ones, as the French say, *extra*.

For each pound of peeled and thickly sliced old potatoes or of small whole new ones, allow 1 pint of milk. Pour the cold uncooked milk over the potatoes in a saucepan, add a very little salt, *simmer* (if you let them gallop, the milk will boil over and the potatoes will stick, so look out), until the potatoes are just tender but not breaking up. Strain off the milk – it makes good vegetable soup stock – transfer the potatoes to a shallow fireproof dish, sprinkle them very lightly with grated nutmeg and a little dried thyme or basil, add 3 or 4 tablespoons of the milk, and leave them uncovered in a low or moderate oven for about 15 minutes.

Delicious with a plain roast, with steak, chicken, or just by themselves.

Meat dishes

MEAT AND VEGETABLE DISHES

BAKED HARICOTS BEANS AND OX KIDNEY

AN excellent cheap dish, ideal for those who have solid fuel cookers with a slow oven in which a stew-pot can be left for hours without coming to harm.

Ingredients are 1 lb. of good quality white haricot beans; 1 to 1½ lb. of ox kidney; 4 tablespoons of olive oil; 2 medium-sized onions; 2 large carrots; seasonings of salt, freshly milled pepper and, optionally, ground allspice; a bunch of parsley stalks, bayleaves and sprigs of thyme; 2 teaspoons of strong made mustard. Optionally, beef stock, garlic.

To cook the beans and kidneys you need a heavy oven-pot of 4 to 6 pint capacity, and with a well-fitting lid. The shape is not important; sometimes I use a tall, old-fashioned, English straight-sided earthenware jar, sometimes a round, fat-bellied stew-pot, sometimes a deep, oval, enamelled cast-iron casserole. The choice depends mainly upon what other dishes may be cooking in the oven at the same time, and therefore upon which shape may be the most practical for the occasion.

Put the beans to soak overnight in plenty of cold water. Drain them and put them in a big saucepan well covered with fresh cold water. Let them boil for about 20 minutes. Meanwhile skin the kidney, cut it into little chunks, soak it in tepid, salted water while the beans are boiling.

In a frying pan heat the olive oil, in this gently fry the sliced onions and sliced carrots, adding a sliced clove or two of garlic if you like. Put in the drained kidney. Stir all round together for a minute or two; add seasonings of salt, freshly milled pepper and, if you have it, a sprinkling of ground allspice. Put a layer of the strained beans into your oven-pot. Then the kidney and onion mixture. Then a big bunch of parsley stalks, bayleaves and sprigs of thyme tied together. Then the rest of the beans. Then about 1½ pints of hot water, or beef stock should you have it, and salt in moderation. Cover the pot with greaseproof paper or foil, and the lid. Cook in a very slow oven, gas No. 1, 290°F., for 5 to 6 hours. By this time both kidneys and beans should be as soft as butter and the liquid most richly flavoured. Before serving stir in the mustard. You can go on reheating the dish, very slowly of course, almost indefinitely. And there ought to be enough for six very large helpings.

N.B. It would be wrong to suppose that by spending more money on delicate lamb or veal kidneys this dish would be improved. It is the ox kidney which gives the flavour.

BEANS IN THE OVEN

A Piedmontese peasant dish, for those who have a taste for rough country food. Although the spices are very typical of Piedmontese cooking, there seems every reason for us to adopt this dish, and make it our own. It is cheap, the ingredients are readily available, and it is easy to cook.

When you have a piece of pork rind, removed from a 2 lb. piece of belly, spare rib or other cut of pork, sprinkle plenty of coarse salt over it and it will then keep in the refrigerator or a cold larder for two or three days. Rinse it, cut into strips 2 inches wide and 4 to 6 inches long.

Have a big bunch of parsley finely chopped with 2 or 3 cloves of garlic. Add a quantity, about a teaspoon each, of ground cinnamon, cloves, mace and pepper. The dish should be highly spiced, but go easy on the cloves. Spread the strips of rind with this mixture, roll them up, arrange them at the bottom of a deep earthen pot. On top put 1 lb. of red or white haricot beans, soaked overnight. Cover with water by 2 inches. Put the lid on the pot and cook in the slowest possible oven (it is a dish admirably suited to those solid-fuel cookers in which the oven is always heated) all night and serve next day for the midday meal.

COURGETTE MUSAKA

The more commonly known version of this excellent and useful dish is made with layers of aubergines, minced lamb and tomatoes, all rather highly flavoured with onions and spices and herbs, the whole arranged in layers and baked in a tin to make a rich, colourful and rather filling kind of pie. Sometimes courgettes or even potatoes are substituted for the aubergines, and the courgette version is particularly good.

Ingredients are 1 lb. of small courgettes, 1 lb. of finely chopped or minced meat which can be lamb or beef, cooked or uncooked, 1½ lb. tomatoes, a large onion, a clove of garlic, 2 eggs, 4 tablespoons of olive oil, seasonings of salt, pepper, a teaspoon each of freshly ground allspice and dried or fresh mint, 2 or 3 tablespoons each of stock and bread-crumbs.

Wash the courgettes but do not peel them. Cut each one lengthways into slices about one-eighth of an inch thick. Salt them slightly and leave them to drain for an hour or so. Shake them dry in a tea towel, fry them gently in olive oil until they are tender. When all are done put more oil into the pan and in this fry the finely sliced or chopped onion until it is pale yellow. Put in the meat. If it is already cooked just stir it round until it is amalgamated with the onion. If it is raw meat let it cook gently about 10 minutes until it is nicely browned. Add seasonings and herbs and, off the fire, stir in the beaten eggs.

In a separate pan put the skinned and chopped tomatoes and the crushed garlic clove and simmer until most of the moisture has evaporated. Season with salt and pepper.

Now coat a 2 to 2½ pt. square or round and not too deep cake tin lightly with oil. Put in a layer of courgettes, then one of meat, then one of tomatoes, and so on until all the ingredients are used up, finishing with a rather thick layer of the tomatoes. On top sprinkle breadcrumbs and then moisten with the stock. Cover the tin with a piece of foil. Cook, with the tin standing on a baking sheet, in a low oven, gas No. 3, 330°F., for an hour, but at half-time remove the foil. If the musaka looks dry add a little more stock. Serve hot.

With the layers of pale green courgettes in between the red and brown of the meat and tomatoes, this is a very beautiful looking dish, which, provided it has not been overcooked to start with, can quite successfully be reheated.

For a musaka with aubergines instead of courgettes the proceeding is precisely the same, and you need 2 to 4 aubergines according to size, unpeeled, cut lengthways into thinnish slices and salted before being fried in oil.

FRESH MEAT: KEBAB COOKERY

Based on the craze for the so-called barbecue, which hit the British Isles in the late fifties, a whole new tradition of English grill-cookery is now in the making. Its most elementary – and most delicious – manifestation is kebab cookery. This provides something for everybody. No mystique is attached to it. It is simply spit-roasting in miniature. Tender meat and the correct skewers are the basic essentials. The rest is a question of practice with the grill – electric, gas or charcoal.

Many of today's English barbecue-type recipes tend to be based on what we imagine to be the American tradition. Tomato ketchup, soy, Tabasco and Worcester sauces, mustard, sugar, pineapple chunks and bacon are freely combined with chicken and pork chops, sausages and steaks, sweetcorn, mushrooms, green peppers and bananas. What an American of sense feels about all this can be deduced from a reading of the entertaining chapter on the origins and mythology of barbecue cookery in James Beard's *Delights and Prejudices.** My own skewer-cookery recipes derive, as indeed do those given by James Beard, rather from the Levantine and oriental traditions to which English cookery already owes so much. To me, it is hard to improve on the flavouring of lemon and dried wild marjoram buds which give the lamb kebabs of Greece their sharply aromatic scent. A few slices of onion, salt, and bay-leaves provide the rest of the seasoning. There is fruity olive oil, roughly cut parsley, more lemon, more onion, in the salad eaten with the kebabs. Country bread cut in thick chunks and tumblers of golden-pink wine make the whole combination utterly delicious.

The grill: Starting as the pivot of out-of-door entertainments the barbecue-grill has come back into the house. Given the climatic conditions of these islands the development was, from the start, inevitable. It has received quite a push from the cooker designers and manufacturers who have evolved efficient electrically driven spits, and grills evoking the image of charcoal cooking. Some roasting spits even have a special kebab attachment, an ingenious, though to me unnecessary, complication of the simplest and most basic of all forms of cookery. It is only occasionally that I bring my ancient and primitive charcoal cooker out for an airing. More often, in fact with regularity, for it is one of my favourite dishes, my kebabs are cooked under a gas-fired eye-level grill. This does not, and nothing can, produce the same effect as charcoal. I regard it as a sound second best, involving none of the needless palaver attendant on the setting up of specially designed barbecues, roasting apparatus and kebab gear.

The skewers: For good kebab cookery, correctly shaped skewers as well as tender meat are the real essentials. Thin round pin skewers are useless. The threaded meat slides round as you turn them. On twisted metal skewers the meat sticks. Wooden skewers burn. The ones to go for are steel, carbon or stainless, but always flat-edged, like miniature swords. The points are sharp, making the threading of the meat easy. Once on the

*See p. 252.

skewers the meat stays where you put it until you get it on to your plate and ease it off the skewer with a fork.

The meat for lamb kebabs: The best cut for kebabs comes from the front end of the leg of lamb. Butchers call this the fillet end, and whatever the customers may call it, the butchers do not take kindly to cutting less than a 2 lb. piece ('who's going to take the remains of the joint off my hands?'), which yields enough meat for six well-filled skewers, and is more than ample for four people. At a pinch, ready-cut chump chops will serve, or a piece of boned shoulder. For several years Harrods butchery department has been selling ready-boned lamb steaks for kebabs. Other butchers appear not to have noticed.

GREEK LAMB KEBABS
Arni Souvlakia

For 1½ to 2 lb. of lamb, the rest of the ingredients for *souvlakia* are bayleaves; an onion or two; lemons; olive oil; salt; optionally a half tomato for each skewer; and a sprinkling of the Greek marjoram called *rigani*, with the accent on the first syllable. Bunches of this wild marjoram, dried on the stalk with its potently aromatic flower heads as well as its leaves, are to be found in some of the London Cypriot-Greek stores. At least one provincial delicatessen, Kitchen 46, at Aylesbury, Buckinghamshire, also sells *rigani*.

Armed then with correct skewers, and the ingredients to be cooked on them, proceed as follows:

Trim the skin and most of the fat from the meat, keeping aside the firmest and whitest bits of the fat. Cut the meat into, approximately, ¾-inch cubes. From the fat cut also a few much smaller cubes, allowing four to six per skewer.

Peel the onions. Holding them upright on the board, slice them from the top downwards, turning them before each cut. Finally, only the inner core of each onion is left, and the slices to be impaled are thickish and will not break.

Now strew a little salt, and – if you like – freshly milled

pepper over the meat. Then a generous sprinkling of *rigani* or thyme, then the juice of a lemon and about four tablespoons of olive oil to the meat for every four skewers. At this point, the seasoned meat, onion slices and all, can be left in a covered dish until it is convenient to thread the skewers.

When the time comes for this stage of preparation, rub the skewers with a little piece of fat. Thread on a half (transversely sliced) tomato with cut side to face the point of the skewer. From then on thread alternately two or three cubes of meat, one of fat, a small bayleaf, and a piece of onion, until the skewer is not more than half full. (It is a mistake to overload the skewers. There must be space at each end and most particularly at the handle end so that you can turn them easily while they are cooking.)

Push all the contents of the skewer close together, so that meat, onions, bayleaves and fat are closely packed in the centre or towards the end of the skewer. Kebabs should never be cooked with the ingredients loosely strung out. The cubes of meat grill unevenly or get overcooked. The idea is to get the outside edges nicely browned, even slightly charred, while the inside of each cube remains a little pink and retains the juices. The little pieces of fat between the meat cubes lubricate the meat while it is grilling, and when you come to eat the kebabs they are unnoticeable. Little thick squares of bacon fat can be substituted by those who don't like the idea of mutton or lamb fat.

To cook, the kebabs will take 10 to 15 minutes under, and not too close to, a gas grill. Over charcoal about seven minutes is usually enough, depending on the fire, the thickness of the meat cubes, and the distance of the skewers from the heat. In either case, the skewers should be turned two or three times during the cooking. It is at this stage that you appreciate the point of leaving the top end of the skewer empty and clear of the grill. If the meat begins to look dry sprinkle it with a little more olive oil, or keep at hand a pastry brush, a feather or a branch of rosemary, to be dipped in oil for brushing and lubricating the meat.

Bring the kebabs to table complete and intact on their skewers. The visual charm of the dish is wrecked if the meat is pushed off the skewers and on to a dish or plate in the way ordained by the more refined and less comprehending of restaurant proprietors.

In Greece, Crete and Cyprus, lemons, bread and boiled greenstuff (of the spinach or mustard family), seasoned with oil and lemon, are served with the kebabs. Sometimes a separate salad of tomatoes, cucumber and raw onion rings is also offered. Bread, and plenty of it, cut thick, is essential.

Pilau rice as served with kebabs in London Cypriot or Greek restaurants does not appear in the tavernas of Greece, nor so far as I remember in the Greek or Arab restaurants of Alexandria and Cairo. Rice as an accompaniment to grilled meat seems to be rather more of an international hotel cookery notion than a Balkan or Levantine tradition. Still, rice does make a good filler for the hungry, and if rice is to be offered with your kebabs, have it dry, as in the pilaus given on pp. 116 and 117, or plain boiled, rather than moistened with tomato sauce or other fancy additions.

MOROCCAN KEBABS
Brochettes

For this version of kebabs, the meat is seasoned chiefly with cumin seeds, which look something like caraway and smell invitingly of all the spice bazaars of North Africa and Egypt. Ingredients are lamb, beef, veal or kid prepared as for the Greek kebabs, but cut into rather smaller pieces. For the spice mixture a tablespoon of cumin seeds (called, or pronounced, *kaimoon* in Moroccan Arabic) or ground cumin and about one teaspoon each of turmeric, freshly grated dry ginger root, and freshly milled or crushed peppercorns, plus a finely chopped shallot or small onion, a very little garlic, a tablespoon of chopped parsley and a sprinkling of salt.

All the spices are easy to come by in England – easier than the correct herb for the Greek kebabs. Super-bazaars and self-service stores provide good-quality spices well packed and clearly labelled. Indian and Chinese shops offer spices in wondrous profusion. For addresses see list at end of volume.

Heat the cumin seeds or ground cumin for a few minutes in the oven or on a griddle. (This process is the vital one omitted from all written recipes I have seen. The heat releases the aromas.) Pound them to as near powder as you can manage. Mix them with all the other spices. By rights the whole lot should now be sieved and then mixed with the parsley, onion and garlic. The sieving process can however be bypassed, and the mixed powdered spices, parsley and onion mixed directly with the prepared meat, which should be thoroughly turned in them, and left in a covered bowl for a couple of hours before cooking.

Thread and grill the brochettes as for Greek kebabs.

To remove the meat from the brochettes, grilled over charcoal on a little rough earthenware stove known as a *kanoon*, the Moroccans tear open one of their soft flat galettes of bread (called *ksra*) and wrap it round the sizzling meat. This is then easily slid off into the centre of the bread flap, making a primitive sandwich which is marvellously good open-air food. For indoor eating keep the accompaniments as simple as possible. Whatever you have with it the spiced meat comes off best.

First dishes could be fish or chicken-based egg-and-lemon soup, or a courgette and tomato dish. For pudding, baked apricots or a cream cheese and honey pie.

SASSATIES

Originally a Malay dish which became naturalized by Cape settlers, the following recipe for Sassaties is given in an interesting little book of South African cookery, called *Hilda's Where is it?* by Hildagonda Duckitt, first published in 1891.

'Take the thick part of a leg of mutton, cut into small square bits, and fat in between; put into a large earthenware bowl. Mince a raw onion and some lemon leaves, a tablespoon of brown sugar, half a cup of milk, mix all well together and pour over the meat. Now take three or four onions cut small, fry in a pan with a spoonful of butter or fat to a nice brown. Take an ounce of tamarinds (if not to be had use vinegar or lemon juice) pour on it a cup of boiling water; when all the strength has gone out of it, strain, and mix with the onions and let it *boil*; then add two spoonfuls of good curry powder or Indian curry paste (a clove of garlic if liked) chopped up, some salt; mix well together and pour over the meat. The next morning put the meat on skewers, fat and lean alternatively. Carefully take all the sauce, put it into a saucepan, and boil up with a pat of butter. Roast the skewered meat on a gridiron heated on wood coals, and serve with the sauce. Add chutney if liked.'

This kebab dish can be made using lamb in the quantities given for the Greek and Moroccan kebabs. Tamarind pulp is to be bought in Indian stores, and as for the lemon leaves, there is nothing much we can do about them in England. I doubt if they would be greatly missed in the general seasoning of curry and tamarind.

For the reduced quantity of meat, halve the amount of milk and curry powder or paste (the latter is preferable). After it has been stirred into the onion mixture let it cook for at least 5 minutes.

I find this form of kebab rather attractive; the curry flavouring is mild and does not overwhelm the meat.

PORK FILLETS GRILLED ON THE SKEWER

This is an ingenious little recipe adapted from one well known in Italian household cookery.

Apart from a pork tenderloin weighing just about 1 lb. you need 4 to 6 oz. of a cheap piece of flank bacon, white bread, seasonings, herbs, and olive oil.

Cut the pork into inch pieces; prepare the same number of cubes of bread, crustless, and quite a bit smaller than the meat; and double the number of little slivers of bacon. Sprinkle the whole lot with a generous amount of olive oil, freshly ground pepper, marjoram or thyme (the Italians use sage), and a little salt.

Thread the ingredients on to long skewers, in the following order: bread, bacon, pork, bacon, bread and so on, until each skewer is about three-quarters full. These quantities will fill five or six 9 inch skewers.

Grill gently, for about 15 to 20 minutes, not too close to the heat, and turning the skewers from time to time.

The simplicity of the ingredients makes the charm of this little dish, as indeed it does of most skewer-grilled food, and the mixture of the two different varieties of the same basic ingredients – the fresh and the cured pork – is typical of Italian cooking.

The pork fillets can be served on a bed of finely shredded lettuce previously dressed with a little oil, sugar, salt and lemon juice – and lemon quarters all round. If you want something more substantial then have a dish of rice as well.

Enough for three or four, depending on what other courses you've planned for the meal.

FRESH MEAT: LAMB, BEEF, PORK

A Persian Dish

'Take the fleshly part of a Leg of Mutton stript from the fat and sinews, beat that well in a Morter with Pepper and Salt, and a little Onyon or Garlick water by itselfe, or with Herbs according to your taste, then make it up in flat cakes and let them be kept twelve houres betweene two Dishes before you use them, then fry them with butter in a frying Pan and serve them with the same butter, and you will find it a dish of savory meat.'

The Compleat Cook, printed by E. B. for Nath. Brook,
at the Angel in Cornhill, 1658

LAMB AND AUBERGINE STEW

When there are aubergines on the market, this dish is worth trying. It can be cooked in a frying pan or sauté pan, or any wide and shallow utensil of rather large capacity.

One and a half to 2 lb. shoulder or middle neck of lamb, 2 small aubergines, 1 large onion, ½ lb. of tomatoes, fresh or dried mint or basil, salt, pepper, a clove of garlic, 4 tablespoons of oil, and 2 heaped teaspoons of cumin seeds or ground cumin if you prefer.

Have the lamb boned and cut into inch cubes.

Slice the unpeeled aubergines into quarters and then into half-inch cubes, put them in a colander, sprinkle them with a tablespoon of salt, put a plate and a weight on the top and leave them for at least an hour so that the excess moisture drains out. Before cooking them press them as dry as you can.

Heat the oil in a heavy 10 to 12 inch frying or sauté pan and put in the thinly sliced onion. When it has just begun to take colour put in the meat, plentifully sprinkled with the herbs, salt and pepper. Turn the meat cubes over and over until they are nicely browned. (If this operation is neglected the dish will be pallid and sad-looking.) Remove the meat and onions to a dish with a draining spoon and into the same oil put the aubergine cubes. Cover the pan and let them cook gently for 10 minutes, giving a stir from time to time.

Now return the meat and onions to the pan, add the skinned and roughly chopped tomatoes, the crushed garlic and the heated and pounded cumin seeds. Cover the pan again, let it simmer very gently for 1 hour. Or if it is more convenient cook it only for 45 minutes and then heat it up very slowly for half an hour next day. Strew with more mint or basil before serving. Plain boiled rice or pilau rice goes with this dish.

Ample for four.

In countries where aubergines flourish and are cheap, and where meat is scarce and expensive, a dish such as this one

143

would be made with more aubergines and less meat, and the rice would be the really filling element of the meal.

Should you have a little mutton or lamb stock available – about half a pint – omit the tomatoes and use the stock instead, adding it at the same stage of the cooking. This system makes a dish which has more distinction than the tomato-enriched version.

SUSSEX STEWED STEAK

This is one of the excellent old English dishes in which mushroom ketchup and ale or stout make a rich-looking and interesting gravy.

Ingredients are 2½ lb. of a cheap cut such as chuck* steak, top rump or thick flank cut in one piece, an onion, a tablespoon or two of flour, 2½ fl. oz. (5 to 6 tablespoons) each of port and stout, 2 tablespoons of mushroom ketchup or wine vinegar, salt and pepper.

The whole dish takes scarcely five minutes to prepare for cooking.

Season the meat, rub flour on both sides. Put it flat in a shallow baking dish in which it just fits. Over it slice a large onion. Pour in the wine, stout, and ketchup or vinegar. Cover with a double sheet of greaseproof paper, and the lid of the dish. Put it in a very low oven, gas No. 1, 290°F., and leave it for about 3 hours – a little less or longer won't matter. The toughest piece of meat emerges beautifully tender, and the gravy rich, bright brown, excellently flavoured.

Creamy mashed potatoes and perhaps a few fried or grilled mushrooms – if you can get large flat ones – go well with this casserole of steak.

*In the Midlands I have seen this cut labelled 'chine'.

To make a Steake Pye, with a French Pudding in the Pye

'Season your Steaks with Pepper & Nutmegs, and let it stand an hour in a Tray then take a piece of the leanest of a Legg of Mutton and mince it small with Suet and a few sweet herbs, tops of young Time, a branch of Penny-royal, two or three of red Sage, grated bread, yolks of Eggs, sweet Cream, Raisins of the Sun; work altogether like a Pudding, with your hand stiff, and roul them round like Bals, and put them into the Steaks in a deep Coffin,* with a piece of sweet Butter; sprinkle a little Verjuyce on it, bake it, then cut it up and roul Sage leaves and fry them, and stick them upright in the wals, and serve your Pye without a Cover, with the juyce of an Orange or Lemon.'

The Compleat Cook, 1658

BEEF MARINATED AND BRAISED IN RED WINE
Bœuf Mariné en Estouffade

A cheap cut of meat, a generous glass of red wine, aromatic flavourings and herbs, and slow cooking are the basic ingred-ients of any number of the excellent daubes and estaouffats of the old-fashioned French household kitchen. In recent years these splendid dishes have become very much a part also of the English cookery scene.

Ingredients are 2 lb. approximately of chuck† (or shoulder) steak, 1 medium-sized onion, 6 large cloves of garlic, a half-dozen bayleaves, a teaspoon each of dried marjoram, ground cloves, and whole black peppercorns, a tumbler (approximately 6 oz.) of rough red wine, a tablespoon of flour, 2 tablespoons each of olive oil and pure pork lard or 4 tablespoons of olive oil, salt. Optional additions are 6 oz. of stoned olives (black or green) or a *persillade* which is a mixture of freshly chopped parsley, garlic and capers.

*Pastry case.   † See footnote p. 144.

145

Chuck steak is cut from the neck or shoulder of beef. It is excellent moist meat, neither too fat nor too dry. Two pounds of chuck will probably be cut by the butcher into two pieces shaped rather like large, elongated rump steaks. For this dish, the meat should be sub-divided into seven or eight pieces, each one of about the size of a small steak. Cut the pieces according to the natural divisions of the meat and trim off skin and excess fat.

Rub each piece of meat with a little salt, coarsely crushed peppercorns, ground cloves. Put all the meat in a fairly deep, glazed earthenware or china bowl. Add the onion, peeled and sliced into rings, three of the garlic cloves, peeled and crushed with the point of a knife, three of the bayleaves, and the marjo-ram. Now pour in the wine, cover the bowl and leave the meat to marinate for a minimum of six hours, and preferably over-night. About eighteen hours is the longest time which should be allowed for the marinading process.

When it comes to cooking the beef, take the slices from the marinade, shake from them any pieces of onion or herb adhering to them, put them on a board or dish; over them, on to both sides, shake the flour. In a 3 to 4 pint cocotte or cassadou* (this pan with its domed lid is particularly appro-priate for dishes of this kind in which the amount of liquid is small in proportion to the quantity of solids), heat, very gently, the olive oil and the pork lard. In this fry the pieces of meat, three or four at a time. Turn them so that they brown nicely on both sides. Put them to one side of the pan to make room for more slices to be fried. At this stage, turn up the heat slightly, so that the fat, cooled down by the first batch of meat, regains its original temperature, otherwise the second and third batches of meat will start to stew and will not brown.

Meanwhile, pour the marinade with all the onion, herbs, etc., into a saucepan and let it heat to boiling point, then reduce the heat so that the wine simmers until all the meat is browned. Now pour this marinade through a strainer on to the meat. While the wine bubbles, put in the three cloves of garlic

*Made by the French factory of Le Creuset.

and bayleaves set aside when the marinade was prepared. (If you like make up a bouquet of these three bayleaves with a sprig or two of dried wild thyme on the stalk, and a strip of orange peel.) Reduce the heat, cover the pot, place it over a heat-diffuser mat and cook over a very low flame for just about 3 hours. From time to time, move the top layer of meat to the bottom of the pot and vice versa, so that all pieces cook evenly.

About half an hour before serving time add the stoned olives. If the *persillade* mixture (2 tablespoons of chopped parsley, a clove of garlic, about 2 teaspoons of capers) is to be used instead, it should be added only a few minutes before the meat is to be transferred from its cooking pot to the heated serving dish.

Potatoes boiled in their skins, or plain boiled rice, or new carrots are the best accompaniment to beef stews of this family.

Quantities given should provide ample helpings for four people.

BŒUF MIROTON

Miroton is a dish primarily designed for using up beef boiled for a consommé or in the pot-au-feu, from which you take some of the broth to complete the dish.

Suppose you have about 1 lb. upwards of cold cooked beef. Then peel 1 lb. of onions and slice them as thinly as possible.

Put them to melt very gently in 1½ oz. butter, or clear beef dripping, in a fairly large saucepan or a flame-proof stew-pot. When they are soft and creamy – they must not be frizzled – stir in a scant tablespoon of flour. Then add, slowly, about ½ pint of warmed clear beef stock.

Simmer gently for about 10 minutes, stirring from time to time. Now taste for seasoning, and stir in a teaspoon of yellow Dijon mustard. Add a little more stock if the sauce is too thick.

Finally, add your meat, cut into fine, neat slices. Cover the pan, continue cooking just until the meat is hot. Sprinkle plenty of parsley over it and have some plain boiled potatoes with it.

The *miroton* takes altogether about 45 minutes to prepare and cook. It is a good and comforting dish – provided that you like onions – and it shows how much more satisfactory and eco⁄nomical is the system of gently re⁄heating cooked meat in a sauce rather than frying it in fat. In fact it is quite worth boiling a cheap cut of beef – brisket or ox⁄cheek for example – for the express purpose of making this dish.

SPICED BEEF LOAF

Ingredients are 3½ lb. of fairly finely minced beef bought from a reliable butcher, 4 oz. of fat mild bacon, 1 teaspoon each of dried basil and ground allspice, 2 heaped teaspoons of salt, 1 dozen peppercorns, 1 very small clove of garlic, 4 tablespoons of port, sherry or red wine, 1 tablespoon of wine vinegar.

Put the beef into a big china bowl, add the roughly chopped bacon, all the seasonings crushed together, the wine, and the vinegar. Mix very thoroughly, and if possible leave for a couple of hours so that all the flavours have a chance to penetrate the meat.

Turn the whole mixture into a 2½ to 3 pint loaf tin, or two smaller tins. The mixture will shrink during the cooking, so that, initially, the containers should be packed full to the brim. Stand the tins in a shallow baking tin filled with water and cook uncovered in the centre of a slow oven, gas No. 3, 330°F., for 1½ hours.

If the top of the loaf looks like getting too brown, cover with buttered foil or greaseproof paper.

Leave to cool, then store in the refrigerator or a cool larder.

To turn the loaf out of its tin simply run a knife round the edges and ease the loaf out on to a dish. Carve it in rather thin slices, and serve with a salad and/or sweet⁄sour pickled fruits, mild fruit chutney, or a mustardy sauce.

FRESH BRISKET OF BEEF IN JELLY

Brisket is one of the very finest flavoured as well as one of the cheapest cuts of beef which you can buy. Its disadvantage to modern tastes is that it is on the fat side, and this applies especially if you buy a small piece, because you take the risk of getting the fattest end and it will be wasteful. If, however, you buy a sufficiently large joint you find that the fat is evenly proportioned and you will have a beautiful piece of meat at a very economical price, and enough for three or four meals for a household of four people.

For this dish buy a minimum of 5 to 6 lb. of fresh brisket, boned, rolled and tied. Other ingredients are 2 calf's feet or 3 pig's feet, half a bottle of sweetish white or other dessert wine, about 1½ pints of water, 3 or 4 sprigs of parsley, a couple of bayleaves, a sprig or two of thyme and a crushed clove of garlic tied in a bunch, 3 tablespoons of beef or pork lard, and salt.

To cook the beef, choose a heavy iron or earthenware pot in which the meat will fit with just room to spare for the calf's feet and the liquid. Heat the fat and let the meat just gently take colour all round. Add the split calf's feet. Pour in the wine and the water and add the bunch of herbs and a dessertspoon of salt. The liquid should reach just about level with the meat. Cover the pot with foil or greaseproof paper and the lid, transfer it to a very moderate oven, gas No. 3, 330°F., and let it cook for about 5 hours.

Take out the meat, strain the liquid into a bowl. Leave it until next day to set. Take off the fat. There will be a beautiful brown jelly underneath. When you have carved the meat and arranged it on a big round flat dish, chop up the jelly and put it in a mound in the centre.

The meat from the calf's feet can be dressed with a vinaigrette and used as an hors-d'oeuvre for another meal, or they can be cooked again with vegetables and water to make a second stock.

This is an adapted version of a dish called *Beef à la Royal* which is given by W. A. Henderson in his *Housekeeper's Instructor or Universal Family Cook*, published about 1800. In his recipe the brisket is studded with parsley, little pieces of bacon and oysters – a method of introducing salt into the meat.

I have two or three times cooked the dish according to Henderson's recipe and the bacon and oysters give it a very delicious but somewhat odd flavour which perhaps would be thought too eccentric by most people. But if you want to try it, tinned oysters will do as well as, if not rather better than, fresh ones. (American or Chinese tinned clams also serve the purpose very well.) At the period when the book was written, preserved or pickled oysters would almost certainly have been used.

Remember that in warm weather natural aspic jelly goes sour rather quickly, so if it is not all eaten at one meal, melt it down again, let it boil, pour it into a clean bowl and when it has cooled cover it and store it in the refrigerator.

PIÈCE DE BŒUF À LA GLASS
Piece of Beef with Jelly

'Take a prime piece of the buttock or rump of beef, let it hang some time that it may be the more tender, rub it well with saltpetre and some salt, let it lay four or five days, and water it a little that it may not make your jelly too salt, put it into a pot as nigh as you can, and cover it with water, season with some carrots, onions, herbs, whole pepper and spice, take care to skim it well, and let it simmer very gently till it is very tender; when it is cool take it out, strain your liquor through a lawn sieve, take the fat clean off, and boil it to as much as will cover your meat, beat up to a froth the whites of two or three eggs mixt with it, and pass it through a bag or napkin; the next day it will be a clear jelly; and when you serve the beef to table spread it over it; you may cut it in slices for four or five days afterwards, and it will be sweet and good for any use you may have for it, and garnish always with parsley.'

The *Cook's Paradise*, William Verral, Master of the White-Hart Inn in Lewes, Sussex. First published 1759

PEPPER STEAKS

Steak au Poivre

Allow a half teaspoon each of whole black and whole white peppercorns (black for aroma, white for strength) for each fillet or entrecôte steak. Other ingredients are garlic, olive oil, salt, parsley or tarragon butter.

Crush the peppercorns, not too finely, in a mortar. Rub each steak with a cut clove of garlic and about one tablespoon of olive oil. Coat each steak with its portion of crushed pepper-corns. Leave the meat for an hour or two – or overnight – to imbibe the flavours.

Immediately before cooking, sprinkle with coarse salt.

The steaks can be dry-fried in a flat cast-iron pancake pan or on a top-of-the-stove grilling device such as the ridged cast iron Monogrill or the Tostador. In either case no extra fat is needed, and the pan or grill should be made very hot before the steaks are put on to cook. Once the meat is seared on both sides, decrease the heat rapidly. A thick fillet of approximately 7 oz. weight will take about 7 minutes to cook for the medium rare stage, and should be turned frequently, with tongs, *not with a fork*, during cooking.

Have ready a hot serving dish, the parsley or tarragon butter, and whatever vegetable or salad is to accompany the steak. Serve immediately. A grilled steak should no more be kept waiting than should a soufflé or an omelette.

The quantity of pepper suggested in this recipe is ample for most people, but can be increased or decreased according to taste. French restaurant cooks tend to overdo the pepper on *steak au poivre* to the point where their victims choke on the very first mouthful.

SPICED COLD PORK

Provided that you can rely upon a friendly butcher who will bone and tie a cheap joint without fuss and without over-charging for the service, a hand of pork (the trotter and fore-end of the shoulder) makes a buy of wonderful value.

The hand of pork will weigh between 5 and 6 lb. before boning, about 4 lb. when boned and separated from the trotter. The rind should also be removed and be sure that with the trotter, the bones and trimmings, it is included in the parcel.

Ingredients for the spicing are 10 to 12 juniper berries, 1 tablespoon of *gros sel* (unrefined sea or rock salt), 1 teaspoon of whole black peppercorns, 3 or 4 whole white peppercorns, a clove of garlic if you like. For cooking the pork you need bay-leaves, dry fennel stalks, a slice or two of lemon, a large glass (6 oz.) of white wine, water. For flavouring the jellied stock at a later stage, a few drops of Madeira or very good sherry will make all the difference.

Crush the juniper berries, peppercorns and salt in a mortar. If you are using the garlic cut it into tiny slivers and mix it with the spices. Rub this mixture into the meat, pressing it well down so that it penetrates as much as possible.

Put the meat into the pot in which it is to be cooked (you will need a large casserole, preferably oval of about 8 pint capacity), with the trotter, with the bones and trimmings under-neath the joint. Add several bayleaves and dried fennel stalks, and the slices of lemon with their rind.

Leave for a minimum of 2 hours, preferably longer, even overnight. (Pork is a meat which is always at its best when salted and seasoned before it is cooked.)

Pour in the wine, add water to just cover the meat. Put the lid on the pot.

Cook the meat (skin side down) on the lowest shelf of a very slow oven, gas No. 2, 290°F., for about 3 hours. When the time is up prod the thickest part of the meat with a skewer. If it penetrates easily, remove the joint to a dish and leave it to cool.

The bones, trimmings and trotter should be left to cook for another hour or even longer, so that the stock which finally emerges will set to a light jelly. When it is ready, pour the stock through a sieve, decant it into a bowl (there should be about 3 pints), leave it to cool, then put it in the refrigerator until next day.

If you want to serve some of this clear jellied stock with the cold pork, take off the fat, measure out about ¾ pint of the jelly, reduce it by steady simmering in a wide pan to a little under ½ pint. Turn off the flame, add 1 teaspoon of Madeira or failing that good sherry, and a squeeze of lemon juice. Pour into a small bowl and leave to set.

Sauces which go well with the spiced pork are a mustardy vinaigrette, a cherry sauce (page 72) or sweet-sour pickled melon (page 239), but if you decide upon one of these, keep the jellied stock to serve as a consommé. With the potent flavours of the pickle or sauces the delicate jelly will be lost. And if you think you are going to need a more firmly set jelly, then ask your butcher for an extra pig's trotter to put in the pot with the meat.

When carving the cold pork, cut slices from both the lean and the fat end of the roll. There will be enough for at least twelve ample helpings.

BAKED PORK WITH WINE AND ORANGES

A joint or loin of pork, weighing about 4 lb. boned, skinned and tied in a sausage shape; ¼ pint of clear meat or chicken stock; herbs (parsley, dried marjoram, dried rosemary), salt and pepper; 4 tablespoons of madeira, white wine or dry vermouth; breadcrumbs; 3 oranges; a little olive oil; 1 or 2 cloves of garlic.

Chop a clove or two of garlic with a little parsley, marjoram, a scrap of rosemary, and salt and pepper. Rub this all over the meat, pressing it well in along the lean side of the joint. Pour a tablespoon of olive oil into a baking dish, put in the meat and all the bones and skin which have been removed. Let it cook for 10 to 15 minutes in a fairly hot oven at gas No. 6, 400°F., before adding the hot stock. Then cook uncovered in a very slow oven at No. 2, 310°F., for 2½ to 3 hours.

From time to time baste it with a little of its own liquid. A quarter of an hour before the end of cooking, take out the bones and skin, squeeze the juice of half an orange over the meat and add the wine. Strew the breadcrumbs on the fat side of the joint and return it to the oven.

Slice the remaining 2½ oranges into thin rounds, and blanch them for about 3 minutes in boiling water. Drain carefully, and put them in the sauce round the meat for the last 5 minutes of cooking time.

Serve with sliced oranges all round the meat, and the sauce separately. This dish is even better cold than hot, and if this is how you intend to serve it, cook the sauce for an extra half-hour or so after the meat has been removed, strain it into a bowl, chill it and remove the fat before serving it.

Those who like a rather more fat joint could economize by using boned and rolled fore-end of pork, which is appreciably cheaper than leg and loin.

PORK CHOPS BAKED WITH AROMATIC HERBS

This dish is a good example of one in which the scent of aromatic herbs makes the whole difference; it should provide ideas for many others of the same sort.

For two people buy a couple of nice thick chops without rind. Score the meat lightly on each side. Cut a peeled clove of garlic in half and rub the meat with the cut surface. Press in salt and a little freshly milled black pepper. Coat each side of both chops with olive oil. In a baking dish arrange half a dozen twigs of wild thyme, several whole bayleaves and a dozen fennel stalks. On top put the chops. If you have time, make these preparations an hour or so in advance, or in the morning for the evening, so that the herbs and seasonings have already scented the meat before cooking starts. Put the dish under the grill, and let the chops brown lightly on each side. Now cover the dish with oiled paper or foil and transfer it to a low oven, gas No. 3, 330°F., and leave for 40 to 50 minutes.

Finally, pour off into a bowl any excess fat which has come from the meat during cooking. Serve the chops as they are, in their cooking dish, herbs and all.

A simple enough dish, deliciously flavoured; and needing no accompaniment other than a green salad, or a few sliced tomatoes dressed with oil and sprinkled with onion and parsley.

Dried Herbs, Aromatics and Condiments, Elizabeth David, 1967.

CYPRUS SAUSAGES

'Take 8–10 lb. young pork, preferably leg. Separate the lard and pass the lean through the mincing machine. Chop the lard up small, to about the size of peas, and mix together with the minced meat, adding pepper and salt. Add pounded coriander seeds and herbs to taste. Place the whole paste in an earthenware casserole, cover with red wine and soak for 48 hours.

'Clean the gut well and soak in vinegar for 2–4 hours, then fill, tying at intervals of 2½–3 inches. Wrap in a muslin bag and hang out to drain for 4–5 days after puncturing the casings with a pin. The sausages may be eaten after 7–10 days, fried or grilled.

'If boiled in lard for 10 minutes after draining and then allowed to cool and remain in the lard, the sausages will keep from 3 to 4 months.

'*Source*: A village Recipe from Paphos, of which beautiful and romantic mountain District of Cyprus H.C.L. was once the Commissioner.'

The Tenth Muse, Sir Harry Luke, 1954

TO MAKE BRAWN OF A HOG'S HEAD

'Lay the hogs head in cold water all night to soke out the blood the next morning put it in a Kettle and boil it pretty fast till the bones will come out (it should be boiled on a fish plate) put it out as whole as you can, and rake the bones clean out, then cut and mash it with a Knife, strew in some salt to your tast and when cut enough, put it in a cloth and lay it in a cheese press; let lie all night and the next morning put it in pickle to cover it, made as follows – boil salt and water with a little vinegar and put it in when cold.'

The Receipt Book of Elizabeth Raper, written 1756–1770, 1924

TO GARNISH BRAWN OR PIG BRAWN

Brawn, like boar's head (see the Soyer description on page 184) was one of the dishes which seems always to have called for ceremonial decoration, garlands of bayleaves, gilded rosemary and aspic jelly. Robert May's description below makes the presentation sound rather like some beautiful and fantastic Christmas centrepiece.

'Leach* your brawn, and dish it on a plate in a fair clean dish, then put a rosemary branch on the top being first dipped in the white of an egg well beaten to froth ... or a sprig of rosemary gilt with gold; the brawn spotted also with gold and silver leaves, or let your sprig be of a straight sprig of yew tree, or a straight furze bush, and put about the brawn stuck round with bay leaves three ranks round, and spotted with red and yellow jelly about the dish sides, also the same jelly and some of the brawn leached, jagged, or cut with tin moulds, and carved lemons, oranges and barberries, bay-leaves gilt, red beets, pickled barberries, pickled gooseberries, or pickled grapes.'

The Accomplisht Cook, Robert May, 1687 edition

PORK OR PIG'S-HEAD CHEESE

Pig's-head cheese or so-called brawns and galantines are always best when the pork meat has been lightly brined. The salting gives it a better flavour and the saltpetre in the brine a good

*Slice it.

pink colour, without which the finished product tends to look a bit grey and unappetizing.

Get the butcher to put a half pig's head – with the ear and tongue but minus the brains – and a long-cut pig's foot in brine for a couple of days.

Other ingredients are approximately 1 lb. of a cheap and gelatinous cut of beef such as ox cheek or shin, a large onion, 4 large carrots, a bunch of parsley, 2 bayleaves, 8 to 10 whole peppercorns, 1 large leek or a couple of sticks of celery, 2 small cloves of garlic, lemon juice.

Soak the salted pig's head and foot in cold water to cover for a couple of hours.

Put them in a very large saucepan with all the other ingredients except the lemon juice and simmer them very very gently for a minimum of four hours. The slower they are cooked the better the result will be, for if they are boiled too fast both beef and pig's head will be ragged and stringy.

When the head and foot are cooked – the meat should come away from the bones at a touch – remove them, with the beef, to a bowl. As soon as they are cool enough to handle, skin the tongue and also the rough parts of the head round the ear and snout where the skin is coarse. Remove all gristle. (What you leave out of a brawn is as important as what you put in.)

Chop all the pig meat and the skin which is left on it, the foot, and the beef. Cut the tongue into neat little slices. Taste to see if extra salt is needed. A brawn should always be fairly highly seasoned or it will be insipid and cloying, so it will probably need extra pepper, freshly milled, possibly salt, and the strained juice of a whole small lemon. This last ingredient is a highly important one in cold dishes made of fat meat; the point is seldom sufficiently appreciated by English cooks.

Now mix the sliced tongue with all the other chopped meat. There will be enough to fill a 3 to 4 pint mould, basin, terrine, or cake tin, or, if you prefer, two smaller ones.

Add about three soup ladles – approximately three-quarters of a pint – of the hot stock and leave the whole thing to cool. Then cover with a piece of greaseproof paper, a plate which just fits *inside** the tin or bowl, and a weight. Leave until next day. It can be stored in the refrigerator for several days.

Before turning it out, stand the tin or mould in a bowl of hot water for a few minutes.

With a salad, the pork cheese does very well as a main dish for a cold lunch or supper. Served simply with toast or bread and a mustardy sauce it makes an excellent first course to precede a light hot dish.

Pig's head cheese made in this fashion is often called brawn or mock brawn. Properly speaking it is a variation of the latter. Brawn, as understood from the fifteenth century – and possibly earlier – to the beginning of the nineteenth century consisted of a whole pig carcase with the *exception* of the head and feet.

The word cheese in connection with the type of brawn described in the above recipe must have derived from the old system of pressing the mixture in a cheese press.†

FRESH MEAT: ANGLO-INDIAN COOKERY

OFFICER OF THE KITCHEN

Writing in the British India of the nineties, under the pen name of Wyvern, Colonel Kenney-Herbert's cookery books were directed at the bewildered mem-sahibs who often found themselves transported from cosy suburban or small country houses into an uncomfortable situation as ruler of a whole hierarchy of Indian servants, incomprehensible in their ways and highly erratic in the performance of their duties.

Several good cookery books have been written by professional soldiers, and this is perhaps no coincidence. On the whole the most successful books of technical instruction, and this applies as much to cookery as to other subjects, are those in

*For this purpose the base of a small removable-base flan, tart, or cake tin is most practical.

†See the recipe quoted on p. 155.

which the author expresses his views with soldierly precision and authority and is prepared to go to some lengths to defend them.

Colonel Kenney-Herbert's parade-ground voice is lowered in his books to lecture-room pitch, but commands no less attention for that. Copies of *Culinary Jottings, Fifty Breakfasts, Fifty Luncheons, Fifty Dinners, Vegetarian and simple Diet,* are not uncommon in secondhand bookshops and I should recommend anyone with a taste for Victorian gastronomic literature to snap them up. His menu planning, modest though it was for his own times, is over elaborate for ours, and many of his dishes now appear fussy and over-sauced; and, in the style of the period, his pages are peppered with italicized kitchen French. All the same his recipes for such things as consommés, omelettes, vegetables, curries, cold pies and pickled beef and tongues are so meticulous and clear, that the absolute beginner could follow them, yet at the same time he has much to teach even an experienced cook. His remarks about the conduct of the kitchen, the relationship between master and servant, his analysis of the shortcomings of Ramasamy, the Indian cook, compared and contrasted with those of Martha, his English counterpart, and his examination of the kitchen and its equipment provide illuminating and sometimes scarifying sidelights on domestic life in British India, where, wherever the mem-sahib's place may have been, it was certainly not in the kitchen.

The kitchen, in fact, was no part of the house proper, being 'part and parcel of a block of godowns (sheds) not unfrequently within easy access of the stables ... the room is generally constructed with as little ventilation and light as possible, its position with regard to the sun is never thought of, and arrangements for its proper drainage are rare. There is no scullery or place for washing up ... the consequence is that hard by many a cook-room in this Presidency, there is a noisome cesspool. ... In the room itself there is no chimney you see, so the wall, up which the smoke is creeping towards an opening in the roof, is lined by an ancient coating of soot – the floor is of mother earth, greasy black and cruelly uneven in its surface.' 'How comes it to pass,' thunders the Colonel, 'that in India we continue year after year to be fully aware that the chamber set apart for the preparation of our food is, in ninety cases out of a hundred, the foulest in our premises – and are not ashamed? Why are so many of us satisfied with an equipment regarding the miserable inadequacy of which it would be as well to keep silence?' No question of the Colonel being one to keep silence. Not he. 'It is no exaggeration to say that not one Indian kitchen in twenty possesses a proper equipment ... the batterie de cuisine of people with incomes of two thousand rupees a month, and more, is frequently inferior to that of a humble cottager in Britain.'

In Madras in the eighteen-seventies: 'there were many ladies who, when giving out stores for a dinner party, have no hesitation in using tins to the value of many rupees, but if asked for extra cream, butter, eggs and gravy meat begin to consider themselves imposed upon.' It is the familiar trouble, that of the woman – there can be very few left today – who does not care to face the fact that the details of a meal may cost as much and need as much attention as its main features; in our idiom, the Colonel could simply have said that she had her priorities wrong. There must have been some pink faces in the Presidency in 1878 when *Culinary Jottings* appeared. The book was written, it must be remembered, at a period of change in the ways of living of British residents in India. Hitherto there had been little attempt to introduce a European atmos-phere or European food into the houses of British officials. Curry and rice had been the accepted, routine food, and the cooks had been left to their own devices. When accelerated transport brought India nearer home the attempt to instil into wayward Indian servants the principles and virtues of English Victorian housekeepers focused attention upon the primitive conditions under which elaborate cookery was supposed to be carried out. 'Our dinners of today would indeed astonish our Anglo-Indian forefathers,' declares the Colonel. 'Quality has superseded quantity, and the molten curries and florid oriental compositions of the olden times –

so fearfully and wonderfully made – have been gradually
banished from our tables ... men of moderate means have
become hypercritical in the matter of their food, and demand
a class of cooking which was not even attempted in the
houses of the richest twenty years ago ... dinners of sixteen
or twenty, thoughtfully composed, are *de rigueur*; our menu
cards discourse of dainty fare in its native French.'

No wonder that those squalid holes in the ground which
passed for kitchens proved inadequate to the task. It is regret-
table therefore, to have to record that seventy years later, as
British rule in India was at its last gasp, the Colonel's reforming
crusade had had sadly little effect. The kitchens which I
myself had the opportinity of observing in New Delhi were
still unbelievably primitive, and the food which came out of
them an astonishing mixture of English nannies' puddings,
cakes festooned in spectacular spun-sugar work, attempts at
French dishes savagely flavoured with hot green chillies ('I
make a French a-stew as good as you,' one of my Indian cooks
remarked defiantly, and untruthfully), and, oddest of all,
Edwardian fantasies of the school which liked to present food in
any form but its own (mashed potatoes got up to resemble a
roast chicken, mushrooms made out of meringue and the like).

This was just the sort of thing with which Colonel Kenney-
Herbert had no patience whatever. When after thirty-two
years' service in India, he returned to England, he wrote
practical articles on the Arts of Dining, Cooking, and
Management, which were published by the *Nineteenth
Century*, and caused quite a stir. This unusual cavalry officer
then proceeded to found a Commonsense Cookery Association, and eventually a school attached to this Association, with
premises in Sloane Street. The Colonel's aims, as described to
an interviewer from the *Epicure* magazine are worth quoting in
full. They were so admirably put. Did anyone pay attention to
them? Will they now, those cookery advisers whose faith is
so firmly rooted in worked-over, worried, teased-up food?

'Briefly sketched the principles we advocate are economy in
conjunction with thoroughly good cooking, no waste, and the

production of good effects without the employment of ready-made sauces and flavourings. We are strongly opposed to over-ornamentation, the use of fancy colours in savoury cooking, and "poaching" on the confectioner's "preserves" by using forcing bags with pipe, etc., etc., in this branch. Finikin decoration – the making of "pretty-pretty" dishes at the cost of flavour and much valuable time – is a mistake in private houses where the kitchen staff consists of two or three persons. Besides, people of taste have declared against the practice. Simplicity in cooking, simplicity in materials, and simplicity in dishing up are consequently a feature in my teaching.'

The very thoroughness of Colonel Kenney-Herbert's instructions makes quotation of his recipes difficult. Just one of the shorter recipes from the chapter in *Culinary Jottings* entitled 'Our Curries' follows.

QUOORMA CURRY

'The "Quoorma", if well made, is undoubtedly an excellent curry. It used, I believe, to be one of the best at the Madras Club, in days when curries commanded closer attention than they do now.

'Cut up about a pound of very tender mutton without any bone, and stir the pieces about in a big bowl with a dessert-spoonful of pounded green ginger, and a sprinkling of salt. Melt a quarter of a pound of butter in a stew-pan, and throw into it a couple of white onions cut into rings, and a couple of cloves of garlic finely minced. Fry for about five minutes, and then add a teaspoonful of pounded coriander seed, one of pounded black pepper, half one of pounded cardamoms, and half one of pounded cloves. Cook this for five minutes, then put in the meat, and stir over a moderate fire until the pieces seem tender and have browned nicely. Now, take the pan from the fire, and work into it a strong infusion obtained from four ounces of well-pounded almonds, and a breakfast cupful of cream. Mix thoroughly, adding a dessert-spoonful of turmeric powder, and a tea-spoonful of sugar. Put the pan over a very low fire, and let the curry simmer as gently as possible for a quarter of an hour, finishing off with the juice of a couple of limes. This, it will be perceived, is another curry of a rich yet mild description. The total absence of chilli, indeed, constitutes, in the opinion of many, its chief attraction.'

> *Culinary Jottings for Madras*, 'Wyvern' (Colonel Kenney-Herbert)
> 5th edition, 1885

PORTUGUESE CURRY

Vindaloo or Bindaloo

'This well-known Portuguese curry can be made properly of beef, pork or duck. The following is a recipe of the vindaloo in general use:

'Six ounces of ghee or lard, one tablespoonful of bruised garlic, one tablespoonful of ground garlic, one tablespoonful of ground ginger, two teaspoonfuls of ground chillies, one tea-spoonful of roasted and ground coriander-seed, two or three bay-leaves, a few peppercorns, four or five cloves roasted and ground, four or five cardamoms roasted and ground, six small sticks of cinnamon roasted and ground, with half a cup of good vinegar, to two pounds of pork or beef or a duck.

'N.B. The best vindaloo is that prepared with mustard oil.'

BEEF VINDALOO

'Cut up two pounds of fat beef into large squares, and steep them in the vinegar, together with half a teaspoonful of salt and all the ground condiments, from eighteen to twenty-four hours. Then warm the ghee or lard and throw in the meat, together with the condiments and vinegar in which it had been steeped, adding a few peppercorns and bay-leaves, and allow to simmer gently over a slow fire for two hours, or until the meat is perfectly tender, and serve up hot.'

> *The Indian Cookery Book* by A Thirty-five Years' Resident,
> Calcutta, 1944. First edition 1869.

The anonymous author of the above little book (it was most helpful when in 1946 I found myself in New Delhi – and when I had a chance to get in to my own kitchen; mem-sahibs who penetrated their kitchens to the extent of actually putting saucepan to stove were not popular with their cooks) appends to his or her Vindaloo recipes a further note to the effect that a form of this curry made from fat pork, packed in stoneware jars, well covered with mustard oil and made air-tight with a screw-on cover and 'a good sound bladder' could be kept sufficiently long 'to be sent Home round the Cape.' When required for use 'take out only as much as will suffice and simply warm it in a little of its own gravy.' A Portuguese-Indian version of the French *confit de porc* or pork preserved in its own fat. . . .

From the same author comes the following recipe for curry paste, illuminating for the ingredients and the proportions in which they are used. (A mild curry paste exported from Bangalore by the famous firm of Bolst lists as its ingredients sesame oil, ginger, garlic, turmeric, chillies, coriander, acetic acid, poppy seed, curry leaves. Well, it depends what you infer by 'mild'.)

CURRY PASTE

'Is likewise adapted for sending as a present to friends at Home. It is made in the following manner:

'Eight ounces of dhunnia, or coriander-seed, roasted; one ounce of jeerah, or cumin-seed, roasted; two ounces of huldee, or dry turmeric; two ounces of lal mirritch, dry chillies; two ounces of kala mirritch, black pepper, roasted; two ounces of rai, or mustard-seed; one ounce of soat, or dry ginger; one ounce of lussan, or garlic; four ounces of nimmuck, salt; four ounces of cheenee, or sugar; four ounces of chunna or gram dal without husk, and roasted. The above ingredients, in the proportions given, to be carefully pounded and ground down with the best English white wine vinegar to the consistency of a thick jelly; then warm some good sweet oil, and while bubbl-

ing, fry in it the mixture until it is reduced to a paste; let it
cool, then bottle it.

'N.B. Great care must be taken not to use any water in the
preparation, and mustard oil is better adapted than sweet oil
for frying the mixture in.'

CURED AND BRINED MEAT

ENGLISH CURED AND COLD MEAT DISHES

English food, so extravagantly overpraised by its advocates and
so bitterly, and so often rightly, reviled by those who have
suffered from British hotel and restaurant catering, is never seen
to greater advantage than when it is presented in perfect
simplicity, unadorned, and on rather a large scale. In other
words, English party food tends to be very much more acceptable than English everyday cooking. We can make tremendous
efforts for an occasional feast whereas we fall down badly when
it comes to maintaining a regular day-to-day standard of good
cookery.

Observing the frenzied shopping and cooking which goes
on at Christmas-time one cannot help wondering if these
prodigious efforts could not be spread out a little over the rest
of the year. I do not mean, heaven forbid, that we should be
forever cooking mammoth roasts, gigantic sirloins, whole
sides of lamb, and turkeys immense and bulging like captive
balloons. It is not groaning boards we need so much as an
orderly method of producing good quality everyday food
without too much fuss or expense.

Let us consider some of our genuine English culinary assets.
Among the best of them are our cured and salted meats. Hams,
gammons, salt silversides and briskets of beef are not, like the
smoked salmon, oysters and grouse which are triumphantly
trotted out every time someone wants to boost British cooking,
so preposterously expensive that only about half of one per cent
of the population can ever taste them. In contrast to these

luxuries, salt meats offer excellent value for money. It is here especially that we get back to cooking in a certain quantity, because with the possible exception of bacon rashers the true value of cured meats is not perceptible when they are cooked in dibs and dabs. Small joints are wasteful in the carving, the ratio of fat to lean meat is often disproportionate, and the effort and fuel expended are extravagant. The deterrent here is that although salt meat keeps better than fresh meat, once it is cooked, the problem in a great many households is storage.

Refrigerators do not take the place of a properly planned larder and larders are what most of us lack. A whole gammon for example is far too large an item for the average refrigerator, which in any case is by no means the ideal storage place for it.

When you have no alternative but to keep a large piece of meat in a refrigerator remember to keep it wrapped in grease-proof paper frequently renewed and to take it out of the refrigerator an hour or two before the meal. If a ham, or any other meat, is too cold it will be hard and the flavour will be poor. It is worth noting that meats which have been baked keep better, have more flavour, and carve more economically than those which have been boiled. Should you be cooking boiled meats to serve for a party these points scarcely arise. It is when it comes to saving both money and effort in the planning of family meals lasting over several days that they are important.

PRESERVATIVES

'Today we think of sugar and salt as complementary flavourings for food, and our domestic accounts would show a great predominance of sugar. This was not so in the Middle Ages, and it is easy to under-estimate the quantities of salt required in the medieval household. The emphasis in their diet on salted meat and fish, and also on the use of brine or souse for pickling, called for generous amounts of salt in the kitchen. It was a common necessity, so frequently purchased that price records can be kept with almost the same regularity as those for grain.'

A Baronial Household of the Thirteenth Century,
Margaret Wade Labarge, 1965

'All the *manufactured* white edible salts impart a bitter taste to meats and fish cured by them, particularly if the same are to be kept many months. This is the reason why bay salt* is so much used in part, along with the common salt, and if bay salt was less expensive, it would be universally used, and alone. I cannot recommend too strongly the use of the *rock* salt of the Cheshire mines; it acts similarly to the bay salt, and is by no means expensive.

'FOOTS OF SUGAR† can be got from the wholesale grocers, and is much preferable to the common sorts sold. It is nearly double the strength, and is not so rank and mawkish in the flavour it gives. There is a quantity of it at the bottom of every cask of the West India sugar when first opened. It is preferable to treacle in many respects.'

The Art and Mystery of Curing, Preserving, and Potting all kinds of Meats, Game and Fish, by a Wholesale Curer of Comestibles, 1864

PRESERVATIVE PICKLE

'This is proper for cured meats in general, and is recommended for imparting a mild and excellent flavour.

'Rock or common salt	1 lb.
Bay salt	1 lb.
Coarse sugar	1 lb.
Saltpetre‡	¼ lb.
Water	1 gall.'

The Art and Mystery of Curing, Preserving, and Potting all kinds of Meats, Game, and Fish, by a Wholesale Curer of Comestibles, 1864

*See p. 51. †What is now called soft brown sugar.
‡ '*Saltpetre,* also known as *Nitre, Nitrate of Potash,* etc., is a natural product occurring on the surface of the soil in certain hot and dry countries. It is also prepared artificially in France, Germany and other places. The British supply comes chiefly from the East Indies. Besides being the chief ingredient in gunpowder, it is largely used in chemistry, medicine, pickling, and the arts.'

Law's Grocer's Manual, 2nd edition, *circa* 1892

PICKLE OR BRINE FOR MEAT

This is Florence Jack's* recipe for a brine for beef or pork.

'1½ lb. of bay salt (sea salt) or common kitchen salt, 6 to 8 oz. of brown sugar, 1 oz. of saltpetre, 1 gallon of water.

'Put all the ingredients into a large clean saucepan, bring them to the boil and boil from 15 to 20 minutes, skimming carefully.

'Strain and use when cold.'

Miss Jack gives the following instructions for the brining of meat:

'In the wet method the meat is simply put into the pickle and allowed to remain the required time. It must either be completely immersed or turned every day, and must be well covered.

'Pickling is best when done in cool weather. If it is only done on a small scale a large earthenware basin or crock will serve the purpose, but it should have a cover or board to fit it closely. If much pickling is done a wooden trough is better, as it is lighter for handling. Whatever the receptacle, care must be taken to keep it scrupulously clean; it ought to be well scalded and dried in the open air after use.'

COLD BAKED SILVERSIDE OF BEEF

Salt silverside is a true English speciality often overlooked when it comes to home entertaining. A pity, for it can be delicious and, especially when cooked to be eaten cold, is economical and presents the minimum of cooking and serving problems.

5 to 6 lb. of salt silverside of beef, onions, carrots, garlic, bayleaves, peppercorns. Optional: a tumbler of red wine or cider.

Give your butcher due warning that you will be needing a handsome piece of salt beef, otherwise he may not have any which has been long enough in the pickle.

Before cooking it, soak it in cold water for a couple of hours.

Put the beef in a deep oven-proof pot in which there is not too much room to spare. Surround it with a couple of large

* *Cookery for Every Household*, 1914

carrots and onions sliced, a crushed clove of garlic, 2 bayleaves, a half dozen peppercorns and if you are using it, the
wine or cider (all these extra flavourings not only improve the
taste of the meat but help to produce a stock which, next day,
will make the basis of a beautiful beetroot or onion soup), and
fill up the pot with water. Cover the pot closely.

Place low down in a very moderate oven, gas No. 2 or 3,
310° to 330°F., and leave untouched for 3 to 4 hours. Test to
see if the meat is tender. Don't let it overcook, or it will crumble
when carved. Take the joint from the liquid, wrap it in
greaseproof paper, put it in a deep bowl, on top of it put a tea
plate or small board, and a 2 lb. weight. Leave until next day.

With the beef have tomato and cucumber salads, and a
mild fruit chutney.

ENGLISH PICNIC MEATS

English military gentlemen are traditionally fond of their wine
and food, and often uncommonly well informed about
cookery and the management of the kitchen. Several regular
army officers have written successful cookery books. Among
the better known are Colonel Kenney-Herbert's *Culinary
Jottings for Madras* (1886) – an indispensable book for curry
addicts – and his *Commonsense Cookery*, written after his retire-
ment, when he opened a cookery school in Sloane Street,
London. On pages 158-63 Colonel Kenney-Herbert's work is
described in more detail.

The late Sir Francis Colchester-Wemyss, in common with
Colonel Kenney-Herbert, had served in India (indeed it would
have been difficult in those days for a professional soldier to
avoid doing so) and in *The Pleasures of the Table* (1931, reprinted 1962*) hints that his interest in cookery was a by-
product of army life in British India. An early necessity to come
to grips with the recipes which as mess secretary he attempted
to transmit to his regiment's Hindustani cooks fostered an
innate interest in food and wine.

*James Nisbet and Co., Digswell Place, Welwyn, Herts.

Similar unexpected beginnings may well have been responsible for a whole school of cookery writers whose books would make an entertaining and uniquely English collection (in France it is doctors and engineers who are the great amateurs of cookery writing), in which would certainly figure the works of a Major L— author of *The Pytchley Cookery Book* (1886), and *Breakfasts, Luncheons and Ball Suppers* (1887). Both these books contain diverting dissertations on racing, shooting, and travelling luncheons.

Major L's luncheon basket, which he himself designed with the assistance of Messrs Farrow & Jackson, the firm still famous for the supply of wine bins and cellar fitments, played an important part in the major's life. Among other sensible innovations the basket was designed to hold a pint bottle of champagne or claret, and one of sherry or Salutaris water. As he observes 'in the summer the dust and heat make one thirsty, hot and uncomfortable. A good lunch and a glass of good champagne assist to while away the tediousness of the journey, oil the wheels of life, and improve the temper.'

Whether, in the dust and heat, the major contrived to get his champagne and his Salutaris water cooled to a suitable temperature he does not relate (our grandfathers, forever on the march with their champagne and travelling provisions, would have appreciated today's insulated picnic bags), but goes into some detail as to the solid content of the luncheon basket. It was to include, among other trifles, beefsteak or chicken pie, fillets of chicken, grouse or pheasant, cold stewed beef, lamb cutlets in aspic, slices of galantine, lemon biscuits, cakes of all sorts, mince pies and plum pudding. Inclusion of that last item betrays Major L's Indian service days. Colonel Kenney-Herbert also recommended that 'a nice piece of brisket of beef trimmed into a neat shape ... is a very handy thing for the tiffin basket – and a really good cold plum pudding in which a glass of brandy has been included.'

They were right about the plum pudding, those Victorian officers. It does make a marvellous travelling and picnic dish, and, to me, is rather more welcome in the open air than ever it is on the Christmas table. As for the pressed brisket of beef, one of the best of English cold dishes whether for indoors or out, the simple recipe follows.

BAKED SALT BRISKET OF BEEF

Brisket can be baked in exactly the same way as the silverside above. It is plentifully interlarded with its own fat, and is a cheaper cut than silverside, but if cooked in a reasonably large piece, not less than 5 or 6 lb., it is, I think, even better. In small pieces, however, you seldom get the correct proportion of lean to fat, in which case it is no economy and gives little pleasure.

When you get towards the end of these beef joints and they can no longer be properly carved, the rest can be cut in small pieces and with a vinaigrette dressing containing chopped shallots, plenty of parsley, and perhaps a few capers and little bits of pickled cucumber, will make an excellent beef salad.

An avocado salad, advised by Sir Francis Colchester-Wemyss as being the best accompaniment for cold salt silverside, is given on page 96.

MELTON HUNT BEEF

'Choose a round of prime ox beef, about thirty pounds weight, the butcher removing the bone; examine the flap and take out the kernels and skins, and hang it up in a dry air, where let it remain as long as the weather will permit. Then take

'Juniper berries, bruised	2 oz.
Ten shalots, minced	
Allspice, ground	2 oz.
Black pepper, ground	3 oz.
Dried bay leaves	3 oz.
Coarse sugar	2 lb.
Bay salt	2 lb.

'Mix them well, and rub all parts well, particularly the flap and the void left by the bone, every day for a week, and turning it every other day. Then add

Rock salt or common salt	1 lb.
Saltpetre	1½ oz.
Garlic, minced	2 heads

and never omit rubbing well with the pickle every day for ten days. After this turn it daily for ten days more, then take it up, look well to the centre and fat, and setting it up in proper shape, and skewer and bind it firmly. Wipe it dry, and if not immediately wanted, coat it well over with dry bran or pollard, and smoke it a week with

'Beech chips	3 parts
Oak lops	1 part
Fern or grass turfs	2 parts

'Otherwise bake it, and when it has cooled forty-eight hours, not less, it will cut firm and obtain for you high commendation.'

The Art and Mystery of Curing, Preserving, and Potting all kinds of Meats, Game and Fish, by a Wholesale Curer of Comestibles, 1864.

SPICED BEEF FOR CHRISTMAS

Dry-pickled or spiced beef is very different in flavour from the brine-pickled or salt beef sold by the butchers. It used to be a regular Christmas dish in a great many English country houses and farms. 'This is more a Christmas dish than any other time of the year,' says John Simpson, cook to the Marquis of Buckingham, in his *Complete System of Cookery* (1806), 'not but it may be done any time, and is equally good.' He calls it rather grandly *Bœuf de Chasse* but under the names of Hunting Beef, or Beef à l'Écarlate, or simply Spiced Beef, various forms of the recipe have certainly been known for at least three hundred years.

In former times huge rounds of beef weighing upwards of 20 lb. (see the Melton Hunt recipe above) were required to lie in pickle for 3 to 4 weeks. A 5 to 12 lb. piece will however be ready for cooking after 10 to 14 days.

Here are two prescriptions for the spices worked out for varying quantities of meat. The presence of juniper berries among the pickling spices makes the recipe somewhat un-usual. They appear in old recipes from Yorkshire, Cumber-land, Wales, Sussex – those areas, in fact, where the juniper shrub grows wild on the hills. The dried berries can be bought from grocers who specialize in spices, and from any of the small kitchen shops which now sell herbs and spices.

For a 10 to 12 lb. joint		*For a 5 to 6 lb. joint*
5 to 6 oz.	light brown Barbados or other brown cane sugar	3 oz.
1 oz.	saltpetre (to be bought from chemists)	½ oz.
6 oz.	sea or rock salt	4 oz.
2 oz.	black peppercorns	1 oz.
1 oz.	allspice berries (also known as pimento and Jamaica pepper. To be bought from the same shops as the juniper berries).	½ oz.
2 oz.	juniper berries	1 oz.
	For cooking the beef you will need only water, greaseproof paper or foil, and a big heavy cast-iron oven pot.	

Ask the butcher for the best quality round or silverside beef and explain to him what it is for. He will probably be incredul-ous but will know how to cut and skewer it.

First rub the beef all over with the brown sugar and leave it for two days in a glazed stoneware crock or bowl. Crush all the spices, with the salt and saltpetre in a mortar. They should be well broken up but need not be reduced to a powder. With this mixture you rub the beef thoroughly each day for 9 to 14 days according to the size. Gradually, with the salt and sugar, the beef produces a certain amount of its own liquid, and it smells most appetizing. But keep it covered, and in a cool airy place, not in a stuffy kitchen.

When the time comes to cook the beef, take it from the crock, rinse off any of the spices which are adhering to it, but without sousing the meat in cold water.

Put it in a big deep cast-iron pot preferably oval, in which it fits with very little space to spare. Pour in about ½ pint of water. In the old days the meat would now have been covered with shredded suet to keep in the moisture, then with a thick crust made from a pound of flour and 2 oz. of lard, but the suet and the sealing crust can both be dispensed with, two or three layers of greaseproof paper or foil being used instead, to make sure there is no evaporation of juices. Put the lid on the pot. Bake in a very low oven, gas No. 1, 290°F., for 5 hours for a 5 to 6 lb. joint. Take it from the oven carefully, for there will be a certain amount of liquid round the beef. Leave it to cool for 2 to 3 hours. But before the fat sets, pour off all the liquid and remove the beef to a board. Wrap it in foil or greaseproof paper and put another board or a plate on top, and a 2 to 4 lb. weight. Leave it until next day.

The beef will carve thinly and evenly, and has a rich, mellow, spicy flavour which does seem to convey to us some sort of idea of the food eaten by our forbears. Once cooked the beef will keep fresh for several days, in an ordinary larder *provided* it is kept wrapped in clean greaseproof paper frequently renewed. It can also be stored in a refrigerator so long as it is taken out and kept at room temperature for a couple of hours or so before it is to be eaten.

Silverside of beef dry-spiced according to the above recipe is prepared and sold ready for cooking at Harrods' meat counter. Produced on a large scale, and from expertly cut and very high quality Aberdeen Angus meat, Harrods' spiced beef used to be a better product than most of us could achieve at home.

It was thanks to the initiative of Mr Ducat, master-butcher and creator of the famous French *boucherie* at Harrods, that this marvellous dish has been rescued from neglect. In 1958, when I told Mr Ducat that I was going to publish my own version of the ancient Sussex recipe for spiced beef in the Christmas number of *Vogue* magazine, he suggested that he might try preparing the beef and offering it for sale ready for cooking. Since those days Harrods have been selling something like 2½ to 3 tons a year of their dry-spiced beef. It is, however, important to order in advance and to stipulate that the meat spends the requisite time in the spicing mixture. If the spices and salt have not penetrated the meat it will be tough and uninteresting.

On no account should anyone allow themselves to be persuaded that dry-spiced beef should be boiled or simmered on top of the stove.

PICKLED OX-TONGUE

A brined or smoked ox-tongue is nothing if not typical of the survival of the ancient ways of spicing and salting meat which had to be preserved throughout the winter.

Few people nowadays would wish to pickle tongues at home, but for the record, the following Scottish household recipe entitled 'To cure a tongue' tells us how it can be done. The saltpetre is the ingredient which gives the tongue – and other cured meats – its fine red colour and without which it would be a rather unprepossessing grey. Too much saltpetre hardens and dries the meat, so that a half ounce, plus the half ounce of saltprunel* which is only a concentrated form of saltpetre would be a rather over-generous allowance for a large ox-tongue. The next recipe allows only half an ounce of salt-petre or sal prunelle (there are several alternative spellings) and very much more salt.

To Cure a Tongue. 'Wipe the tongue exceedingly well but do not allow it to be touched with water. To one tongue take the following ingredients:

'½ oz. saltpetre, ½ oz. saltprunel, ½ lb. common salt, ¼ lb. sugar, a few cloves.

'Rub these well into the tongue. Lay tongue on a tin sheet or dish and cover well with common salt. Turn and rub well every day for fortnight, when it will be ready for use. It can stand another week.'

Wishful Cooking, Emily Lina Mirrlees and
Margaret Rosalys Coker, 1949

*See p. 49.

NEAT'S* TONGUES, VERY HIGH FLAVOUR

'Having cut away the useless parts at the roots, and removed the gullets, rub the tongues all over with coarse sugar or real West Indian molasses, and let them lie twenty-four hours; then take

Juniper berries	1 oz.
Black pepper, ground	½ oz.
Sal prunelle†	½ oz.
Treacle	1 lb.

mix, and rub with it three days, turning them daily; then add

Bay salt	9 oz.
Common or rock salt	12 oz.

rub three days, and turn the meat daily for a week, when you may dry it and smoke with beech and fern or grass turfs. The above proportions are for one fine tongue of eight or nine pounds.'

The Art and Mystery of Curing, Preserving, and Potting all kinds of Meat, Game, and Fish, by a Wholesale Curer of Comestibles, 1864

ROLLED AND GLAZED OX-TONGUE

Ask your butcher for a brined ox-tongue, and whatever he may instruct you to the contrary, soak it for a minimum of twelve to eighteen hours prior to cooking, in a big basin of cold water changed at least once.

Rinse the tongue, put it in a large pan and cover it copiously with cold water. In this case there is not much point in putting vegetables with the tongue; they will make no difference to its taste, and the cooking liquid is usually too salt to use for stock.

Bring the water very slowly to simmering point. Skim several times, then cover the pot and simmer steadily but not too

*Neat is the old word for an ox. †See p. 49.

fast for about 3½ hours for a tongue weighing approximately 5 lb.

While the tongue is still hot, remove all the little bones, trim off the gristly bits at the root end, and peel off the skin. This has to be done very carefully in order not to damage the tongue itself.

Curl the tongue round in a meat press or a cake tin in which it will just fit. (A tin with a removable base makes the eventual turning out of the tongue much easier.) Press it down. On top put a plate which should fit just inside the tin. Weight it well and leave until the next day.

When you turn it out you can, if you happen to have some meat glaze or jelly from another dish, glaze the tongue. To do this put about a quarter of a cupful in a small pot in a bain-marie, let it melt, and when it has cooled again, but before it sets, paint the tongue with a pastry brush dipped in the jelly. Repeat this three or four times, as each coating sets. Failing home-made meat glaze or jelly, few people nowadays would have any hesitation about using packet aspic.

SMOKED OX-TONGUE

A smoked ox-tongue is drier, harder and more compact than a straightforward brined one. It will need 48 hours steeping in cold water, changed at least twice. Bring it, very slowly, to simmering point and thereafter allow one hour to each pound. The average weight of a smoked tongue is 3 to 3½ lb. It is cooked when a skewer will pierce the thickest part quite easily.

A curious method of keeping cooked tongues in a marinade is given by Robert May in his *Accomplisht Cook* first published in 1660. The tongues are boiled, skinned, larded or not as you please, and packed in a barrel. Spices ('whole pepper, slic't ginger, whole cloves, slic't nutmegs and large mace'), sweet herbs (thyme, rosemary, bay leaves, sage leaves, winter savory, sweet marjoram and parsley) tied up in bundles, 'every sort by itself and then all into one', are boiled in 'as much wine vinegar and white wine as will fill the vessel where the tongues are, and put some salt and slic'd lemons to them, close them up being cold, and keep them for your use upon any occasion; serve them with some of the spices, liquor, sweet herbs, sallet oyl, and slic't lemon or lemon peel.'

LEICESTERSHIRE SPICED BACON

'Many persons are prejudiced against spiced bacon, *generally* because they may have been deceived in the quality of that purchased at the shops; too often indeed is the spicing resorted to that it may cover defects which would have been too glaring if merely salted. Take a middle of well-fed large pork, and divide it into pieces that will suit your salting tub; rub them well over, both sides, with warmed treacle, and let them lie for a week, being rubbed and turned every day; then take a mixture of

'Bay salt, beaten fine	3 lb.
Saltpetre, beaten fine	¼ lb.
Allspice, ground	2 oz.
Black pepper	1 oz.

and rub the meat well with this on the fleshy side only, for a week, after which turn the pieces every other day for a fortnight longer. You may then dry it with cloths, and suspend the meat in a current of air, being turned end for end every third day; and when ready, lay on a nice coat of bran or pollard, and smoke with oak and beech for a fortnight, and finish it by adding peat to your smoking fuel for a week longer. This will be superior bacon.'

The Art and Mystery of Curing, Preserving, and Potting all kinds of Meats, Game, and Fish, by a Wholesale Curer of Comestibles, 1864

THE COOKING OF GAMMON JOINTS

One of the very nicest of all cold meat dishes is a piece of Wiltshire-cured, home-cooked gammon on the bone. It has so much more flavour and character than the steamed, boned, defatted product of the cooked-meat shop.

For a special occasion, or to last a small household for several days, the best cut is a piece of middle leg or a corner. These are lean joints, and easy to carve.

Many provision merchants and grocers nowadays tell you not to soak gammon before cooking it, but in my own mind there is no doubt that it is necessary to do so. Not only is there a risk of its being too salt if this preliminary is omitted, but it should be remembered that all curing processes imply a certain amount of hardening and drying out of the meat, especially when it is also smoked, as most of our gammon is. The steeping in water allows it once more to swell and soften.

BAKED MIDDLE GAMMON

Suppose you have a 5 lb. piece of middle leg, soak it for a minimum of twenty-four hours, and preferably for thirty-six, in cold water to cover (and also keep a cloth or dish over the basin). Change the water two or three times.

When the time comes to cook the gammon wrap it in two sheets of aluminium cooking foil, twisting the edges together so that the joint is completely enclosed.

Stand this parcel on a grid placed in a baking tin. Half fill the tin with water – the steam coming from it during cooking helps to keep the gammon moist.

Place low down in a very moderate oven, gas No. 3, 330°F., and allow approximately 50 minutes to the pound. The only attention you have to give it is simply to turn the parcel over at half-time.

When the cooking time is up, remove the gammon, still in its tin, from the oven, and leave it for about 40 minutes before unwrapping the parcel and carefully removing the rind, which peels away very easily in one piece without damage to the fat so long as the gammon is still warm. Press home-made golden breadcrumbs into the exposed fat surface. Wrap up the joint again, put it in a bowl or dish and if practicable put a board or plate on the top, weight it, and leave until next day.

This compressing of the joint is not vital, but does make carving easier.

Accompaniments. American-style sweet and spiced fruit garnishes and sauces – pineapple, peach, cranberry and the like – are acceptable with a dry gamey-flavoured and highly cured meat such as a genuine Virginia ham,* but mild, moist, English-cured gammons and bacon are best, I think, accompanied by simple lettuce, potato, or other vegetable salads with a straightforward French dressing of olive oil and wine vinegar.

Whether you keep your cooked gammon or bacon in a refrigerator or a larder do keep it wrapped in clean greaseproof paper, constantly renewed. In this way it will keep sweet and moist down to the last slice.

BARBADOS BAKED AND GLAZED GAMMON

Cook a 4 to 5 lb. piece of corner or middle gammon as described above, allowing 45 minutes instead of 50 to the pound.

Remove from the oven, unwrap the foil, and peel off the rind – this is very easily done while the gammon is still hot – and score the fat in diamond shapes. Replace the gammon in the rinsed-out baking tin.

Have ready the following mixture: 2 heaped tablespoons of soft brown sugar, 1 teaspoon of made mustard and 4 tablespoons of milk, all stirred together. Pour this mixture over the gammon, pressing some of it well down into the fat. If you feel you must, stud the fat with whole cloves.

Place the tin near the top of the oven – still at the same temperature – and cook the gammon for another 20 to 35 minutes, basting frequently with the milk and sugar mixture, which will eventually turn into a beautiful dark golden shining glaze.

*The cooked gammon hams sold in English delicatessen and provision shops under the name 'Virginia' bear no resemblance to the true Virginia ham of the United States.

Serve hot with creamed spinach and jacket potatoes or a purée of red lentils, or cold with a salad of cubed honeydew melon seasoned with lemon juice and a pinch of powdered ginger.

N.B. The sugar, mustard and milk-glaze mixture is by far the most effective, as well as the cheapest and most simple, of any I have ever tried. There really is no need for fanciful additions of rum, orange juice, pineapple chunks and all the rest of the fruit cocktail so often nowadays advocated in the colour-cookery pages of magazines.

A SPICED HERB MIXTURE TO SPREAD ON BAKED GAMMON

This mixture is derived from the old recipes for the stuffing to go in a whole chine or back of bacon boiled in the Lincoln-shire manner. This was a dish for harvest suppers.

I sometimes use the spice and herb mixture instead of ordinary breadcrumbs, or in place of a sugar glaze, to spread on the fat side of a piece of baked corner or middle gammon when the skin has been peeled off. A few minutes in the oven will set the mixture, and the joint will not dry out or become overcooked.

For a piece of gammon or bacon of approximately 3 lb. weight, a breakfast-cupful of stuffing should be made up of the following ingredients:

Fresh parsley, fresh or dried marjoram, fresh or dried mint, lemon thyme, chives when in season, the grated peel of one lemon and of half an orange, 1 teaspoon of crushed coriander seeds, approximately a half teaspoon of coarsely crushed black pepper, 3 tablespoons of dry breadcrumbs, 1 whole egg.

The proportions of the fresh and dried herbs can be improv-ised according to fancy and depending upon which are most plentiful. The fresh parsley is important, the mint gives a peculiarly English flavour to the mixture, the lemon peel and the spicy coriander make up for such seventeenth-century flavourings as the violet and marigold leaves which in country districts were still used in the stuffings for boiled bacon chines until well on in the nineteenth century.

This mixture is delicious also as a stuffing for fresh baked pork.

BOILED COLLAR BACON

Collar bacon is one of the best of the cheaper cuts; it can be baked in the same way as the gammon, but for those who prefer the boiling method, the system is as follows: soak a 3 to $3\frac{1}{2}$ lb. piece of collar for about 6 hours – as it is going to be cooked in plenty of water it needs less soaking than if it were to be baked.

Put it into fresh cold water to cover in a capacious pan. Bring it slowly to simmering point, and thereafter keep it cooking, uncovered, with the water just barely moving – on no account boiling – for 30 minutes to the pound. You have to watch it and regulate the heat from time to time. Fast boiling toughens and coarsens the bacon, makes it stringy, dry, and wasteful in the carving.

When the bacon is cooked, turn off the heat, leave the joint to cool a little before taking it out of the pan and peeling off the rind. Then spread with breadcrumbs (or the spiced mixture described above) and leave until next day.

HAND OF SALT OR PICKLED PORK

Brined, salted or pickled pork is one of the ancient and traditional cured meats of the English kitchen. Prepared by a pork butcher who understands the art of brining meat, and cooked by those who appreciate the virtues of slow-baking or simmering, pickled pork has great potentialities. Since the meat is lightly cured and neither dried nor smoked, a leg of salt pork tends to be much more delicate in flavour than a bacon gammon and far cheaper than a good ham.

A hand of salt pork, which corresponds to the forehock in bacon, is a joint which represents first-class value for money, is easy to cook, and for small households makes an economical alternative to a ham, gammon of bacon, or other large joint.

Any self-respecting butcher will brine the joint required; but he will require four or five days' notice. In the case of a hand of pork, ask him also to bone, roll and tie the meat into a long thick sausage shape.

The prepared joint will weigh approximately 6 lb. Soak it for six to twelve hours, then put it in a deep baking tin or earthenware pot with a couple of onions and carrots, a piece of celery, a bayleaf or two, some sprigs of thyme, 4 or 5 peppercorns, a clove of garlic, and water just to cover. Cover the pot, cook in a moderate oven, gas No. 3, 330°F., for three hours. If the pan is not big enough for the joint to be quite covered with water, turn it over at half-time.

When cooked, leave to cool in its liquid for about an hour, then transfer it to a bowl, put a piece of greaseproof paper over it, and a plate or board and a weight on top. Leave until next day before cutting. There is no necessity to remove the rind – not being smoked it is soft and perfectly easy to carve through. The cooking liquid makes the basis of an excellent beetroot consommé or thick lentil or split pea soup.

A 5 to 6 lb. piece of leg of pickled pork, which is a leaner and more expensive cut, the equivalent of a middle or corner piece in gammon, can be cooked in just the same way.

BOILED SALT PORK

A piece of cold boiled salt pork makes a useful addition when you come to eat the rest of your Christmas turkey or chicken cold.

Buy a 2 lb. piece of brined belly of pork, soak it in cold water for half a day, put it in fresh cold water to cover, with 2 carrots, an onion, a bayleaf, a half dozen peppercorns, a few parsley stalks, 2 tablespoons of wine vinegar. Bring to simmering point, skim, cover, simmer gently for 1½ to 2 hours, until the bones can be slipped out of the meat.

Wrap in oiled paper and press until cold.

Carve in thin slices.

Slices of this pork are also good mixed with shredded lettuce as a sandwich filling, or diced and added to potato dishes and omelettes, or sliced, crumbed, and then grilled or fried and served with spinach or sweetcorn – in short, a useful piece of meat for the weekend larder.

BOAR'S HEAD

Nowadays there is no such thing in English cooking as a wild boar. The boars' heads presented on buffet tables during the Christmas festivities, at ceremonial functions, or made for competition display by ambitious apprentice cooks, are concocted out of the perfectly ordinary pig's head which anyone can buy from the butcher. Anyone, however, would scarcely attempt to perform all the rites connected with the confection and trimming of the traditional boar's head.

*

Here is part of Alexis Soyer's formula for what he calls Boar's Head à l'Antique. The description appeared in his *Gastronomic Regenerator* (4th edition) 1847. It makes remarkable reading, in more ways than one.

Apart from the boned and salted head and neck of the beast, you will be requiring a stuffing of 10 lb. of forcemeat made from the flesh of the common pig (boars' heads, but not the rest of the animals, were evidently imported from Germany in Soyer's day) plus the fillets of meat from the neck, squares of fat bacon, a pound each of 'the best preserved truffles' and 'very green pistachios blanched and skinned'.

The boar's head, stuffed, sewn up with packthread and tied in two cloths, was put into a braise or stock made with half a pound of butter, 15 lb. of trimmings of pork or knuckles of veal, 8 onions, 2 carrots, 4 turnips, 8 bayleaves, 1 tablespoon of peppercorns, 12 cloves, 10 sprigs each of thyme and marjoram, 4 blades of mace, 4 calves' feet, a bottle of Bucellas (a Portuguese dessert wine) plus 6 gallons of water and a pound of salt.

After 7 to 8 hours of simmering in this rich stock, the boar's head was left to get half cold in the liquor, then taken out, the wrappings partially undone and then tightly re-bound before the head was set on a baking sheet with a board standing up-right and weighted at each end (like bookends) and another, more heavily weighted, on the top of the head between the ears.

After being pressed all night, the head was unwrapped, a piece an inch in thickness cut from behind the ears (from which part it is carved in as thin slices as possible, the meat having a marbled appearance), the head was then trimmed a little, the ears set in a proper position, the whole glazed with a 'brownish glaze', eyes formed from round pieces of truffle and a little lard and tusks from *pâté d'office* (confectioner's paste made from flour, sugar and eggs).

For the final touches Soyer directs us to 'have some very fresh tulips and roses, which stick tastefully in the ears, and some around, but leaving space to carve, garnish boldly with croûtons of aspic made from the clarified stock.'

SCOTTISH SPICED AND SALTED MEATS

Christina Jane Johnstone, whose *Cook and Housewife's Manual* was published in 1826 under the pseudonym of Mistress Margaret Dods, was the wife of John Johnstone, a Dunferm-line schoolmaster who became editor and proprietor of the *Inverness Courier* and subsequently joint editor with his wife of the *Edinburgh Weekly Chronicle*.

Mrs Johnstone took her pen-name from Meg Dods, land-lady of the Cleikum Inn in Auldtown of St Ronan's, a character created by Sir Walter Scott in *St Ronan's Well*. There were indeed rumours, presumably not discouraged by Mrs Johnstone's publishers, to the effect that the conversational footnotes to many of the recipes were contributed by Sir Walter himself. Nowadays these wordy notes make heavy reading. It is the recipes proper which interest us, so much so that a century and a half after its original publication the book is still a source of reference for cooks in search of traditional Scottish recipes for salmon, game birds and venison, and for the old national dishes such as haggis, cock-a-leekie, sheep's-head broth, Friar's chicken, oat cakes and cream cheeses.

On the salting, curing and smoking of meat and fish as practised in Scotland, Mrs Johnstone is particularly interesting. Notes on salted mutton and goose as well as on hams, beef, sausages and a 'Yule Mart or whole Bullock', figure in the *Cook and Housewife's Manual*. 'Mutton, either ribs or breast, may be salted and served boiled with roots, making at the same time potato soup, seasoned with parsley or celery.' A dish called 'Colliers roast' was a leg of mutton salted for a week, roasted and served with mashed turnip or browned potatoes; in Caithness 'geese are cured and smoked and are highly relishing. Smoked Solan geese are well known as contributing to the abundance of the Scottish breakfast.'

The *Manual* includes no detailed prescription for the mutton hams or the salted and smoked goose. The following recipes will throw some light on the matter of the mutton hams, and on page 205 are some old recipes for salt goose.

SPICED MUTTON

'A boned leg or shoulder of mutton, 8 oz. common salt, 1 oz. bay salt, ¾ oz. saltpetre, 4 oz. moist sugar, 1 teaspoonful pepper, 1 dessertspoonful finely chopped shallot or onion, 1 saltspoonful powdered allspice, 1 saltspoonful powdered cloves.

'Mix the ingredients together, rub the preparation well into the meat, and repeat daily for a fortnight. When ready rinse in warm water and bind into a good shape with strong tape. Cook very gently for 5 or 6 hours in good stock, or water flavoured with vegetables, press between two dishes until cold, glaze, and use as required.

'Time to cook 5–6 hours.'

Mrs Beeton's Book of Household Management, 1906 edition
edited by J. Herman Senn

TO CURE MUTTON HAM

'Cut a hind quarter of good mutton into the shape of a ham; pound one ounce of saltpetre, with one pound of coarse salt and a quarter of a pound of brown sugar; rub the ham well with this mixture, taking care to stuff the whole of the shank well with salt and sugar, and let it lie a fortnight, rubbing it well with the pickle every two or three days; then take it out and press it with a weight for one day; smoke it with saw-dust for ten or fifteen days, or hang it to dry in the kitchen. If the ham is to be boiled soon after it has been smoked, soak it one hour; and if it has been smoked any length of time, it will require to be soaked several hours. Put it on in cold water and boil it gently two hours. It is eaten cold at breakfast, luncheon or supper. A mutton ham is sometimes cured with the above quantity of salt and sugar, with the addition of half an ounce of pepper, a quarter of an ounce of cloves, and one nutmeg.'

The Indian Cookery Book, by a Thirty-five Year's Resident, Calcutta, 1944

WELSH MUTTON HAMS

'Take a couple of legs of prime Welsh mutton, rub them well with treacle made hot, and put them away in a deep pan until the next day. Make a pickle of

'Thyme	1 handful
Marjoram	1 handful
Bay leaves	1 handful
Saltpetre	1 oz.
Black pepper	2 oz.
Bay salt	2 lb.
Water	5 pints

boiled an hour and well skimmed, and when cold to be poured over the meat, and to be rubbed every day, and turned for three weeks. Then take them out of pickle, rub them well in all parts with strong vinegar for one hour, when wipe them dry, and hang them up in a current of air until well dry. Then give them a thorough coat of bran or of oatmeal, and smoke them with

Oak sawdust	2 parts
Peat	1 part
Beech	2 parts
Turfs or fern	1 part

for three weeks or more. Store them in malt cooms and pulverised charcoal, and in three months they will be very good.'

The Art and Mystery of Curing, Preserving and Potting all kinds of Meats, Game, and Fish, by a Wholesale Curer of Comestibles, 1864

Chicken, Turkey, Duck and Goose

CHELSEA SPICE MILE

IT is now (1970) nearly ten years since the huge supermarket in the King's Road, Chelsea, opened its doors. At the time this great food bazaar seemed sufficiently novel to merit a published description. The paragraphs I wrote appeared in the *Spectator* in November 1961. Just for the record, it is reprinted on pp. 190-91 as I wrote it at the time, under the title *Bazaar Smells*.

It was I think the curious juxtaposition of ancient spices which might have been delivered by camel train, but packed so that the customers could not smell them, with the equally ancient sight of spit-impaled chickens, the smell of cooking very far from ancient and by far too apparent, that conveyed to me the impression that some spirit in England was once again, as so frequently in the past, yearning for the orient, that we would soon be up to our ears again in our perennial obsession with far Arabia. It has turned out to be rather a Rosita Forbes, Rudolph Valentino kind of charade, the romance which broke loose on England in the nineteen-sixties, a dressing up in kaftans and beads and brass bracelets, comings and goings to Marrakech and Fez, Mogador and the Barbary Coast – and every week London sports a new oriental restaurant, Persian, Levantine, Pakistani, Turkish, Cingalese, Balinese, Siamese; and this year we learn that the Sahara has replaced Greece as the 'new place'. We shall soon be back to where we came in, dyed blue like the men of the Atlas Mountains – or ancient Britons, take it which way you like.

Back in the King's Road, the Chelsea souk has changed hands, the smelly chickens have gone, and the spices have found their way into the proliferating health-food stores and kitchen-utensil shops, somebody is selling a 'curry kit', and one day soon we may even learn to appreciate kebabs in their plain primitive simplicity without accompanying soggy rice and dishes of inappropriate vegetables.

*

'The reek of fat dripping from the serried ranks of spit-revolving chickens – if chickens they can be called, these grisly little creatures – in the new supermarket in the King's Road, Chelsea, is indescribably revolting. Maybe that's why a stall devoted entirely to the display of spices has been placed in a clearing, easily spotted, of the detergent and cornflake jungle. Not that you can actually sniff at delicious things like cardamom and coriander, mace and cinnamon bark and allspice berries; they're all done up in packets, but packets with a little transparent window, so that you can at least see what's inside. The idea of legging it for home with some of those spices and cooking something with a powerfully aromatic scent which will banish the terrible smell of dirty basting fat (if that's how it stinks after the shop has been open three days, what's it going to be like in a year's time?) from your nostrils is perfectly irresistible. Clever, one must admit. I fell for it. Shovelling half a dozen ounce packets of whole spices which I didn't need into the wire carrier provided by the management I made for the pay-counter. After a ten-minute wait while the customer in front of me had her purchases checked – orange by orange, almost sprout by sprout – I was allowed through the receipt of custom and out into the steady, welcome, refreshing downpour of November's wettest day to date. And home to pound up ginger and cumin seeds, coriander and garlic and peppercorns. It wasn't long before the clean wholesome smells of an ancient Levantine bazaar were edging away the fumes of London's brandest-new supermarket.'

*

'If any readers interested in the intricacies of spice cookery should ever come across an old book called *Indian Domestic Economy and Receipt Book*, published in Madras in 1850, and acknowledged simply to the author of *Manual of Gardening for Western India* without further clue to his identity, they should snap it up. I bought my copy in the early nineteen-fifties and I see that it cost only ten shillings. Among the mass of directions for the English mem-sahibs' dishes of the period the book contains a unique section of Eastern recipes, mostly of Moslem origin, recipes such as I have never seen in any other book, in or out of print, on oriental cookery. The dishes have wild and beautiful names like *Ash Lingra Jagurath* and *Zarebrian Mahee Baykhar* and *Korekah Kubab*. A typical list of ingredients, given in Bombay weights and measures, reads 'mutton, wheat flour, ghee, Kabellie hennah, white chennah, or dhall, chukundar, carrots, paluk, native greens, saffron, onions, sugar, green ginger, cloves, cardamoms, capsicums, cinnamon, lime juice, salt'. Among the author's explanations and general directions is the information that 'the native method of roasting is generally over charcoal, or in a closed vessel, with a portion of melted butter, onions, spices, etc., with which the meat or fowl becomes flavoured; and I may here remark on the subject of roasting in this way; it is by far the cleanest especially out in camp or marching, where the wind and dust cannot be other-wise kept off.' Copy, perhaps, to the open-spit-roasting merchants?'

KUBAB CHICKEN

This is the pot-roasted chicken eventually evolved from one of the recipes given in the Indian cookery book - it is described above - which I ran home to consult the day I bought the spices in that Chelsea bazaar.

For a 2 to 2½ lb. roasting chicken, dressed and drawn weight, prepare the following spice mixture: 2 teaspoons of coriander seeds, 12 black peppercorns, the seeds from 6 cardamom pods, ½ teaspoon of ground cloves, 1 teaspoon of salt, ½ oz. of sliced green ginger (gross weight – there is a good deal of waste when you have peeled the root). Pound all these ingredients together until they are a paste, then work them with about ½ oz. of butter, preferably clarified.

Draw back the skin of the chicken and with a small knife make incisions in the legs and breast. Spread the spice mixture into the incisions and draw the skin back into place. Leave for a couple of hours before cooking.

Put 2 oz. of clarified butter into a deep heavy oven pot and heat it. Put in the chicken, lying on its side. Cover the pot closely. Bake in a moderate oven, gas No. 4, 350°F., for 50 minutes to an hour, turning it over at half-time. Then remove the lid and turn the chicken breast upwards for 10 minutes.

Serve the chicken with the cooking liquid poured over, and lemon quarters round the dish. Boiled rice or saffron rice makes a good accompaniment, although I prefer a salad.

On occasion I have varied the spice mixture, omitting the green ginger and cloves, using cinnamon, saffron, cardamom and a little ground ginger. The salt is important.

CHICKEN POT-ROASTED WITH FENNEL AND HAM

For a 3½ lb. roasting chicken (2¾ lb. dressed and drawn weight) the other ingredients are a half dozen each of dried fennel stalks and whole bayleaves; 4 to 6 oz. mild, cooked ham in one piece; 2 or 3 garlic cloves; a strip of lemon peel; 2 oz. butter; a half dozen whole black peppercorns. Optionally, 4 table-spoons of brandy.

Tie the fennel stalks and bayleaves into a bunch. Put them into an earthenware or cast-iron cocotte or pot. On top put the chicken (lying on its side) stuffed with the peeled garlic cloves, the strip of lemon peel and the ham cut into finger-thick strips and liberally sprinkled with coarsely crushed black pepper-corns (no salt). Add the butter in small pieces. Cover the pot, put it low down into a medium-hot oven, gas No. 5, 400°F. Leave for 45 minutes. Now turn the chicken, basting it with the butter, and return it to the oven. Cook for another 45 to 50 minutes.

Now uncover the pot, turn the chicken breast upwards and leave it to brown in the oven for 10 to 15 minutes.

To give the dish a spectacular finish, and to bring out to their full extent the scents and flavours of the aromatic herbs, transfer the pot to mild heat on top of the stove. Pour the brandy into a ladle, warm it, ignite it, pour it flaming over the chicken, rotate the pan so that the flames spread. After they have died down transfer the chicken to an ovenproof serving dish but leave the juices in the casserole to cook and mature for another 3 or 4 minutes. Pour them off into a sauceboat.

For serving, arrange the fennel stalks and bayleaves on the dish with the chicken.

Make sure, when the chicken is carved, that everybody has a share of the little strips of ham from the inside of the bird.

Basically, this is a dish of the old-fashioned country cooking of Tuscany. The final blaze of brandy is a modern flourish.

PARSLEY AND LEMON STUFFING FOR A CHRISTMAS TURKEY OR CAPON*

For a 10 to 12 lb. turkey stuffing: ½ lb. dried breadcrumbs, 2 large lemons, 6 tablespoonsful of finely chopped parsley, one teaspoonful of dried marjoram, the same of lemon thyme when available; ½ lb. unsalted butter, 3 whole eggs, salt, freshly milled pepper.

To prepare the breadcrumbs for the stuffing, cut the crusts from a sliced white loaf, dry the slices on a baking sheet in a low oven until they are quite brittle, but not coloured. Pound them to crumbs with a rolling pin, or in the electric blender.

To make the stuffing, mix the breadcrumbs with the parsley (be sure to wash it before chopping it), add the marjoram, the grated peel of the two lemons and the strained juice of one.

---

*This recipe, derived originally from one given by Colonel Kenney-Herbert (his work is described on pp. 158–63), makes by far the best stuffing I know for a turkey or a large roasting chicken. Together with the recipes for cooking the turkey and for the giblet gravy to go with it, it is reprinted from *Dried Herbs, Aromatics and Condiments,* published in 1967.

Beat in the eggs, then the softened butter. Season very lightly. Stuff the bird (body and crop) and secure the flaps with small metal skewers, so that the stuffing will not burst out during cooking.

For a 6 to 7 lb. capon, reduce the quantities by one third.

TO COOK THE TURKEY

Rub the bird with $\frac{1}{4}$ lb. of butter, putting lumps between the thighs and body. Wrap the bird in cooking foil, also lavishly buttered. Stand the parcel, the turkey lying on its side, on a rack in a baking tin, and place it low down in the oven pre-heated to very moderate (gas No. 3, 330°F.). A 10–12 lb. bird takes $2\frac{3}{4}$ to 3 hours to cook.

At half time turn the bird over, and 30 minutes before time is up, take away the foil and turn the bird breast upwards so that it will brown. Over it pour a little glass of white wine or vermouth. Mingling with the buttery juices in the pan, this will produce a most delicious little extra sauce.

A capon can be cooked in exactly the same way, allowing approximately 2 hours' cooking time.

GIBLET GRAVY

The giblet gravy is best started off a day ahead of time. Put the giblets (keep the liver for another dish) with 2 carrots, one onion, a small glass of white wine or vermouth, a bouquet of herbs, $\frac{1}{2}$ lb. of stewing veal, and two halved and grilled tomatoes into a small soup pot. Set over a low flame without other liquid. Let the wine cook and all the ingredients take colour before adding salt and enough water to cover. Transfer the pot, covered, to a very low oven (perhaps at the same time as the bread for the stuffing is drying) for about 2 hours. Return it to the oven again, if there is room, while the turkey is cooking. At about the same time as you open the oven to take the foil off the turkey, remove the giblet stock, strain it, transfer it to a sauce-

194

pan and keep it ready on the top of the stove for the final heating up.

A lovely little book of Moroccan cookery, beautifully written and illustrated, is the fourth Marquis of Bute's *Moorish Recipes*, published in 1956 by Oliver and Boyd. Maybe one would not want to cook many of the recipes, but they give a vivid idea of how spices, condiments and herbs are used in North African cookery; and the illustrations show in precise detail the elegant shapes of Moroccan cooking pots and serving dishes.

Altogether this little volume is a particularly interesting manifestation of the Englishman's interest in the cooking traditions of Arab countries. Unhappily the book is now out of print, but below are two of Lord Bute's recipes. In both, the use of spices is restrained, and the flavours very subtle.

MAKALLI

'This is a Fez dish.
  Ingredients:

Chicken	1
Leek	1
Citron	1, preserved
Saffron	½ teaspoonful
Salt	½ "
Ginger	1 "
Olive oil	little more than ½ pint/300 gr.
Olives	half handful, stoned (say 6)

'Clean chicken and put it with neck and liver into an earthenware dish.

Pound together in a mortar the leek and the peel of half a citron.

Mix this well with a tablespoonful of water and the saffron and salt.

Spread this over the chicken.

Add one teaspoonful of ginger, the olive oil and 1 pint (500 grammes) of water.

Boil for an hour, or until chicken is nearly tender, basting it occasionally with the sauce round it.

Then put in half handful of olives ready stoned and ½ table-spoonful of chopped citron peel and

Cook again for a few minutes before serving.'

*

By preserved citron I think that the author means a lemon preserved in salt, one of the specialities of Morocco, to be seen in the food markets in Marrakesh. It is difficult to find a substitute for these lemons so characteristic of Moroccan cooking. One day no doubt somebody will find a way of importing them. Meanwhile, the recipe on p. 242 will provide an approximation to the real thing.

The old English recipe for a 'Capon larded with Lemons,' dated 1658 and quoted on page 197, makes almost as beautiful reading as Lord Bute's description of Moroccan dishes.

DEJAJ MAHAMMARA
Roast chicken

'Ingredients:

'Chicken	1, cleaned
Chervil	½ tablespoonful
Leek	½ ,,
Butter	2 tablespoonfuls
Cummin	1 teaspoonful
Red pepper	1 ,,

'Pound the chervil and leek together in a mortar.

Mix this well with the butter.

Mix this again with the cummin and red pepper until the whole is in a paste.

Roast the chicken on a skewer over the fire, turning it and putting the paste over it with a knife.

As the chicken gets nearly cooked make some cuts in the
breast and put in more of the paste.
Cooking will take about half an hour.
Can be served hot or cold.'

To boyle a Capon larded with Lemons

'Take a fair Capon and truss him, boyl him by himselfe in
faire water with a little small Oat-meal, then take Mutton
Broath, and half a pint of White-wine, a bundle of herbs,
whole Mace, season it with Verjuyce,* put Marrow, Dates,
season it with Sugar, then take preserved Lemons and cut
them like Lard, and with a larding pin, lard it in, then put the
capon in a deep dish, thicken your broth with Almonds, and
poure it on the Capon.'

The Compleat Cook, 1658

CHICKEN ON THE ROCKS

From the *Observer* of 9 July 1967, I quote this recipe given
from a book called '*A Snob in the Kitchen*' by one Simonetta. No
further details were given, except that the columnist told her
readers that 'A friend in Paris swears by this easy way with a
battery bird.'

I have not tried the recipe because I do not willingly buy
battery birds. Perhaps extra money spent on a free-range,
properly fed chicken would save the cost of the salt – (true,
gros sel is a lot cheaper in France than in England). But this is
not the first time I have read about salt-baked chickens, a
survival, I rather fancy, of primitive gipsy or 'robber' cooking.

'14 cups of coarse salt, 1 broiler. Spread four cups of rock
salt at the bottom of a roasting pan with lid. Put the chicken on
this bed of salt and pour six cups of salt around it on all sides.
Put the remaining salt on top of the chicken, close the pan, and
place in a hot oven (gas no. 6, 400°F.) for one and a half hours.
When the cooking time is up remove the pan, break the salt

*See p. 34.

which will have formed around the chicken, and serve. Save the salt, it will serve again and again.'

SALT AND THE DUCK

'I want everything Chinese tonight,' the girl used to say in the restaurant advertisement in the West End theatre programmes; if you study one of the cheapest and most informative of the current books on Chinese food,* you could almost have it – and without going to a restaurant.

What you will have done is to spend your day cutting, chopping, slicing, shredding, opening tins, soaking dried squid, mushrooms and prawns, washing your rice. You will have a chicken cut up in about forty-eight pieces, each the identical size and all laid out in neat rows on a scrubbed board. Your vegetables, sliced on the bias (there is a sketch in the book to show you how) will look like pieces of material cut for dolls' clothes by some great Paris dressmaker and the colours, translucent green of cucumber, orange of carrot, pearly white of spring onion, will be clear and clean as in a new paint-box. The scrubbed order dazzles.

And when you come home from your theatre you take a quick swig of rice wine (or substitute sherry as Mrs Chao advises) and then into the pan with the sesame oil and one after the other of the ingredients, and in a second everything is sizzling and smoking and after five minutes stirring, turning, shaking (no, there is rice to cook, that does take a little longer) your Chinese dinner is laid out in little bowls and dishes all ready to eat.

Alas, that is not the story of my life, and probably not of yours. I enjoy Chinese, or Anglo-Chinese, food in London Chinese restaurants quite enormously (although I wish some of their cooks weren't such duffers at rice; or is it just that the rice they use is of poor quality?), and am convinced that the invasion of the Chinese caterers can eventually have nothing but a beneficial influence upon our own. Already, I fancy, the

* *How to Cook and Eat in Chinese*, Buwei Yang Chao.

Chinese under-cooking of vegetables has made some small, very small, dent in the English conviction that they should all be boiled until limp; the system of making an infinitesimal quantity of chicken, duck, meat, prawns, mushrooms do duty for what in European cooking would be a half pound of each is always a wonderful demonstration of ingenuity; and generally speaking the approach seems to be as described by Mrs Chao in a paragraph on how to get your fishmonger to give you a fish complete with its head and liver; in Chinese cooking everything that can be eaten is eaten, and in American cooking – the book was written for the American market, but the remark applies also to a certain extent here – everything that can be thrown away is thrown away.

Above all, I find the way food is served in Chinese restaurants, each item in its own dish or bowl and all put on table heaters in front of you infinitely alluring. It is this civilized aspect of the service which draws me to Chinese restaurants as much as the food itself; and once experienced, the English system of bringing platefuls of hors-d'oeuvre or meat and v. getables all dished up together seems abrupt and gross in comparison. (The French too have always understood the importance of the visual appeal of food presented in its own serving dish, and of giving the customer the chance of helping himself; in even the scruffiest of bistros and *routier* restaurants the food used to be brought on dishes which were left upon the table, and however cramped the space there was still always room for them. Unhappily the English habit of dabbing the food on the plate and shoving it in front of the customer is spreading to France.)

What I feel about any serious attempt to cook a complete Chinese meal at home – an isolated recipe or two one can always manage – is that while French, Italian and other styles of European cooking may be vastly different from our own, the systems are still Western systems, basically understandable to us. In Chinese cooking there is so much we simply do not apprehend and which we cannot learn from books. Even the handling of a frying pan demands a different technique from the one we know; come to that the frying pan itself is differently shaped (anyone interested to know what some of the traditional Chinese kitchen utensils and serving dishes are like will find informative drawings in Frank Oliver's excellent *Chinese Cooking** and in Gloria Bley Miller's immensely comprehensive *The Thousand Recipe Chinese Cook Book*†). The cutting and chopping and slicing followed by the last-minute frenzy of frying and stirring is daunting; and having to get so many of the ingredients out of tins without knowing how much resemblance, if any, they bear to the fresh product, depresses me. All of which is by no means to say that Mrs Chao's book is not extremely helpful and informative and written with so much common sense, such convincing advice as to the right and wrong ways to adapt Chinese cooking to Western tastes and techniques, that even somebody who has never eaten any kind of Chinese food at all and doesn't intend to start now should still find valuable kitchen sense and recipes which they could use. If as a nation we could appropriate into our cookery no more than just a couple of the simple cabbage recipes, Mrs Chao would not have laboured in vain; and of course it would be very wrong to infer that all Chinese cooking is of the split-second stir-fry variety, although this may seem to be the most characteristic to Westerners. There are just as many different methods in Chinese cookery as in French cooking, and more than in our own; they are very clearly explained and set out in this book; and then there are all the lovely duck recipes, for which Mrs Chao's recipes appear easy and straightforward, worlds away from the honey-bedaubed, sherry-soaked, and pineapple-garnished fancies of magazine Chinese cookery. (When we get to work adapting the recipes of other countries we tend to elaborate rather than simplify them, whereas the reverse would be preferable.)

Curiously, a dish which Mrs Chao calls Salt-water duck, or Nanking fresh-salted duck is almost identical with that salt duck which is a perfectly genuine traditional and most delicious Welsh speciality, except that – and oh the difference – in the

*André Deutsch, 1955   †Paul Hamlyn, 1966

Principality the duck was eaten hot and with an onion sauce, whereas the Chinese serve it, and rightly so, cold. Mrs Chao explains how it should be cut, too – and this is illuminating, for it is both neater and more economical than our system. I may say that to my mind the salting and subsequent water-simmering of the duck produces a far finer dish than roasting. And a dish called Soo Chow duck, which alas Mrs Chao doesn't give, but which may be found at the Good Earth Restaurant* in the King's Road, Chelsea, includes among its ingredients a most extraordinarily good dried mushroom, called in Chinese *dung koo* and in Japan, as I am reliably informed, *cortinellus shiitake*. Never mind, the dish is worth trying if you go to the restaurant, and the mushrooms can be bought from Cheong-Leen's Chinese supermarket, 4-10 Tower Street, London W.C.2.

WELSH SALT DUCK

This method of salting and cooking a duck is adapted from a Welsh recipe dating back at least a century. (So far as I know, the first time it appeared in print was in Lady Llanover's *Good Cookery* published in 1867.) In the original, the duck was eaten hot, with an onion sauce, which would have been rather heavy, but both the preliminary salting and the slow-cooking methods are worth reviving; they produce a deliciously fla-voured and tender duck; and the melon goes to perfection with cold duck. It goes without saying that, if you prefer, the salad of sliced oranges more usual with duck can be substituted.

1 large duck (about 6 lb. gross weight), $\frac{1}{4}$ lb. of sea or rock salt or coarse kitchen salt, 1 honeydew melon, lemon juice.

Buy your duck three days in advance. Place it in a deep dish. Rub it all over with salt. Repeat this process twice a day for three days. Keep the duck covered, and in a cool place, (use the giblets at once for stock, and the liver for an omelette) ideally in a larder rather than the refrigerator.

*This restaurant closed in 1974.

In the morning for the evening cook the duck as follows: first rinse off excess salt; then place the bird in a deep oven-dish. (I use a large oval enamelled casserole, which will stand inside a baking tin.) Cover the duck with cold water, put water also in the outer tin. Transfer the whole contraption to the centre of a very low oven, gas No.2, 310°F., and cook, uncovered, for just 2 hours. Remove the duck from its liquid (which will probably be rather too salt to use for stock) and leave it to cool.

Serve the duck quite plain and cold, its sole accompaniment the flesh of a honeydew melon cut into small cubes and seasoned only with lemon juice. Jacket potatoes could also be served with the duck, but are hardly necessary, and do nothing to help the appreciation of this very delicately flavoured bird.

SALT-WATER DUCK

It is interesting to compare the following Chinese method with Lady Llanover's Welsh recipe.

'Salt-Water Duck' is not a kind of sea-gull, but a land-based duck. It is simply the Nanking name for fresh-salted duck, which is one of the good things of Nanking. It is a cold dish and different from heavily long-salted duck.

'One 5–7 lb. duck, 3–4 tablespoons salt, 1 teaspoon Szech-wan pepper (get it in Chinatown under the name of *chu'untsiu* or *fa-tsui*, or substitute with cinnamon), 8 cups* water.

'Mix pepper with salt. Rub it on the duck all over, neck and all, both inside and outside. If it is winter, you can simply put the duck in a pan and keep it in an unheated room. If it is summer, put it in the icebox. Let it stand for 1 to 2 days. Then rinse off slightly with cold water the salt on the surface of the duck.

'Put the duck in a pot with the water and heat with big fire; when it boils, turn to medium fire and boil for 1 hour. If the duck is bought tender, boil only 40 minutes, as this kind of duck is good when it is not too soft. After cooking, cool or chill before serving.

*3¼ English pints.

'*Method of serving*: Chop each leg, including upper leg, into 6 pieces. Pull off each wing and chop into 3 sections. Separate chest from the back. Chop back into small pieces. Then comes the best part of the duck, the white meat, which is now reddish. First cut lengthwise in two. Then chop sidewise into ½-inch-wide pieces.

'Now, lay the back bones, wings and neck on the plate as foundation, then the leg pieces all round, finally the 2 rows of white meat on the top. Now is the time for rice wine (but substitute sherry).

'The bones, however, are far from being the worst part of the duck because the most savourous part is in the bones. Very often, we enjoy sucking the bones more than eating the meat.

'*Warning*: This dish will keep for only 3 days – if it goes that far.'

How to Cook and Eat in Chinese, Buwei Yang Chao, 1956

DUCK AND BROWN LENTIL BROTH

The stock from a salted duck carcase is rather strong to be used as a basis for most vegetable soups. Two for which it is successful are mushroom and beetroot. A third solution, simple and cheap, is this most interestingly flavoured clear broth.

For 2 pints of strained duck stock (all fat removed) you need 2 tablespoons of brown lentils, also called whole or German lentils.

Wash the lentils, put them with the stock in a saucepan, bring to simmering point, skim, cover the pot, cook extremely gently until the lentils are absolutely soft, which will take about 1½ to 2 hours. The soup should not boil nor even simmer, it must cook with scarcely a murmur.

Strain without pressing the lentils.

The broth will be a most appetizing clear dark brown, and the only additions it will need are a squeeze of lemon juice and possibly a little extra salt.

FEZANJAN

'1 duck, ½ lb. shelled dry walnuts, rice, 1 pint pomegranate juice, butter (or margarine), 2 teaspoons ground cinnamon, 1 teaspoon gravy browning, 1 pinch powdered nutmeg.

'Fry the duck whole until golden brown. Then add a cup of water and simmer; as it simmers dry, add more water.

'Meantime mince the walnuts in a mincer, fry in a little butter and add to the pomegranate juice, which will draw the oil from the nuts. (If pomegranate juice is not available, lemon or red-currant juice may be substituted provided they are sweetened to taste and are sufficiently diluted to be drinkable while still retaining their tartness.)

'Now drain the duck, adding all its juice to the nut-and-pomegranate sauce.

'Carve the duck into pieces of a reasonable size, place in the pot, which is nearly full of the sauce, and add 2 cups of water and the spices. Boil slowly with the lid on. When the duck is tender and the sauce thick and brown, turn out and serve with plain boiled rice.

'*Source*: Mrs Arthur Kellas, British Embassy, Teheran. A well-known Persian delicacy.'

The Tenth Muse, Sir Harry Luke, 1954

SMOKED GOOSE

'In some places, particularly Caithness, geese are cured and smoked, and are highly relishing. Smoked Solan geese are well known as contributing to the abundance of a Scottish breakfast, though too rank and fishy-flavoured for unpractised palates. They are ate as whets or relishes.'

From *The Cook and Housewife's Manual*, Mistress Margaret Dods (Christina Jane Johnstone), 4th edition, 1829

To Dry a Goose

'Take the fairest and fattest goose you can gett dry him well within take out the soule* then take some bay salt and beat it well and lett him lye a fortnight in salt then tye him up in paper and hang him up in Chimney where they burn woode or coale let him hang a fortnight or 3 weekes in that time he will be readye to boyle you may keep him longer if you please before you boyle him.'

> *Dorset Dishes of the 18th Century,*
> compiled and edited by J. Stevens Cox, F.S.A., Dorchester, 1961

To Salt a Goose

'Take a fat Goose, and bone him, but leave the breast bone, wipe him with a clean cloath, then salt him one fortnight, then hang him up for one fortnight or three weeks, then boyl him in running water very tender, and serve him with Bay-leaves.'

> *The Compleat Cook, 1658*

An excellent Meat of Goose or Turkey

'Take a fat Goose, and Powder† it with Salt eight or ten days; then boil it tender, and put it into pickle, like Sturgeon-pickle. You may do the like with a very fat Turkey; but the best pickle of that is, the Italian Marinating, boiling Mace, Nutmeg, &c. in it. You may boil Garlick in the belly of the fouls, if you like it, or in the pickle.'

> *The Closet of the Eminently Learned Sir Kenelm Digby Knight Opened, 1669*

SALTED GOOSE

'A Goose, 2 oz. saltpetre, 7 oz. sugar, 3 lb. salt.
  'Boil up 5 quarts of water with the saltpetre, sugar and salt,

*The black spongy part adhering to the back of the goose.
† To powder meat meant to salt it.

and pour hot over the goose, which has been cleaned and trussed. Leave the goose lying in this decoction for three days, then boil slowly until tender. The goose should be served cold with a sauce made of lightly whipped cream in which are mixed white vinegar, grated horseradish and a pinch of sugar. The sauce should be frozen in the refrigerator before serving. A Scanian speciality.

'Recipe given to H.C.L. while on a visit to Malmo, capital of the South Swedish Province of Scania, by the British Vice-Consul, Mr Hans Ekman, M.B.E.'

The Tenth Muse, Sir Harry Luke, 1954

* *

Sweet Dishes and Cakes

SPICED fruit cakes, buns and biscuits play so large a part in English cookery that a full description with recipes both ancient and modern demands very much more space than could be accorded the subject in the present volume. A study of the old recipes reveals so much beautiful writing and so many absorbing details that this facet of our cooking tradition will form, together with breads and yeast cakes, a separate little book. With the exception, then, of one good dark ginger cake and an easy recipe for parkins (or perkins as the word was sometimes spelled) no recipes for cakes, biscuits or breads are included in this chapter.

For those readers who are particularly interested in English fruit cakes, spiced breads and the like, reliable recipes are to be found in such books as *Talking about Cakes, with an Irish and Scottish accent*, by Margaret Bates, Vice-Principal of the City of Belfast College of Domestic Science (Pergamon Press, 1964; Penguin Books, 1973); *Home-made Cakes and Biscuits*, and *Home baked: a Little Book of Bread Recipes*, both by Cecilia and George Scurfield, published by Faber in 1963 and 1956 respectively.

Florence White's *Good Things in England* first published by Cape in 1931 and still in print should need no introduction as an authoritative work on traditional English cooking. The book includes a great number of interesting cake recipes, while the little paperback volume called *Farmhouse Fare*, published by Countrywise Books, includes a chapter on cakes, buns and biscuits which provides a good insight into the remarkable variety of our cake recipes, and into our continuing attachment to the art of baking.

THE CHRISTMAS PUDDING IS MEDITERRANEAN FOOD

A white cube of a house, two box-like rooms and a nice large kitchen. No bath. No plumbing. A well and a fig tree outside the front door and five yards away the Aegean. On the horizon a half circle of the islands of Andros, Tinos, Seriphos. In the village, about three dozen houses, two churches (one Orthodox, one Roman Catholic), one provision shop. Down on the shore one shack of a tavern, and in the village street a more important one, stacked with barrels and furnished with stout wooden tables. Christo, the owner of this second tavern, was one of the grandees of the village. He operated, in addition to the tavern, a small market garden, and sold his produce in the island's capital seven miles away. He also had a brother-in-law, called Yannaki. Yannaki was that stock Greek village character, the traveller come home after experiencing glamorous doings and glorious events in far-off places. True to type, he spoke a little Anglo-American and, more uncommonly, a little French; he was always on hand to help out if foreigners came to the village. He seemed a kind and cheerful man, rich too; at any rate, he owned a spare donkey and was prepared to lend me this animal, along with a boy to talk to it, so that I could ride into the town when I needed to stock up with fresh supplies of beans and oil, bottled wine, cheese, dried fruit, and boxes of the delicious Turkish Delight which was – still is – a speciality of the island.

Before long it transpired that the greatest favour I could bestow upon Yannaki in return for the loan of his transport would be some tomato soup in tins and perhaps also a jar or two of English 'picklies'.

Handing over to one of the brothers who owned the hotel and the Turkish Delight factory in the capital a bundle of drachmae which would have kept me in wine and cheese for a month, I got in return four tins, vintage, of the required soup. Of English piccalilli, which I took it was what Yannaki meant by picklies, there was no sign nor sniff, and very relieved I was. Many more such exotic luxuries, and it would be cheaper for me to leave my seashore village for Athens and a suite at the Grande-Bretagne.

The tomato soup gave Yannaki and Christo and their families a great deal of pleasure. It was the real thing, no mistaking it. In return I was offered baskets of eggs, lemons, oranges, freshly dug vegetables and salads, glass after glass of wine in the tavern. And, then, next time the picklies? I *was* English wasn't I? Then I should certainly be able to produce these delicacies.

For days I scanned the horizon for sight of an English yacht. I could, in my turn, have bartered fresh vegetables and fruit for the jars of mustard pickles which I knew must grace the table of any English *lordos* grand enough to be roaming the Aegean seas. It was late in the season. That way no yacht came.

Anybody who has experience of the stubborn determination, courteous but quite unrelenting, of an Aegean islander when he has made up his mind about something will understand why, in the end, I was obliged to set to and make those confounded pickles myself.

Into the town then for mustard, vinegar, spices. Long mornings I spent cutting up cauliflower and onions, carrots and cucumbers. Afternoons, I squatted in my kitchen fanning the charcoal fires into a blaze brisk enough to boil the brew. The jars, the only ones I could find, which I had bought to pack the stuff in were of one oke capacity, three pounds, near enough. Also they were of rough earthenware, unglazed, and exceptionally porous. Before I could even give the filled jars away they were half empty again, the liquid all soaked up by that sponge-like clay. Every one had to be replenished with a fresh batch of pickle. To me the mixture seemed fairly odd, but with my village friends it was successful enough. In fact, on the barter system, I could have lived for nothing so long as I was prepared to dedicate my life to pickle-making. Before long, though, it was getting on for December, and references to 'Xmas pudding' began to crop up in the tavern talk. By now I had learned a little more about these kindly village tyrants. If Christmas pudding they wanted, Christmas pudding I should have to give them. But not, so help me, made on the improvized happy-go-lucky system I'd used for the mustard pickles. Once more then into the town (I never could stay five seconds on a horse or a mule or even a bicycle, but by that time I had at least found out how to sit on a donkey and get the animal moving over stony paths and up and down steep hills) to telegraph home for a recipe. When it arrived, it turned out to be one of those which calls for a pound of almost everything you can think of, which was lucky. Simply by multiplying each by three it was all turned into okes. A large-scale Christmas party was now simmering, so there wouldn't, I thought, be an oke too much.

Now, all those with their fine talk of the glories of Old English fare, have they ever actually made Christmas pudding, in large quantities, by Old English methods? Have they for instance ever tried cleaning and skinning, flouring, shredding, chopping beef kidney suet straight off the hoof? Have they ever stoned bunch after bunch of raisins hardly yet dry on the stalk and each one as sticky as a piece of warm toffee? And how long do they think it takes to bash up three pounds of bread-crumbs without an oven in which they could first dry the loaves? Come to that, what would they make of an attempt to boil, and to keep on the boil for nine to ten hours on two charcoal fires let into holes in the wall, some dozen large puddings? Well, I had nothing much else to do in those days and quite enjoyed all the work, but I'd certainly never let myself in for such an undertaking again. Nor, indeed, would I again attempt to explain the principles of a hay-box and the reasons for making one to peasants of whose language I had such a scanty knowledge and who are in any case notoriously unreceptive to the idea of having hot food, or for that matter hot water or hot coffee, hotter than tepid.

All things considered, my puddings turned out quite nicely. The ones which emerged from the hay-box were at just about the right temperature – luke-warm. They were sweet and dark and rich. My village friends were not as enthusiastic as they had been about the mustard pickles. What with so many of the company having participated in the construction of the hay-box, my assurances that the raisins and the currants grown and dried there on the spot in the Greek sun were richer and more juicy than the artificially dried, hygienically treated and much-travelled variety we got at home, my observations on the incomparable island-made candied citron and orange peel (that was fun to cut up too) given me by the neighbours, and the memorable scent of violets and brilliantine given to the puddings by Athenian brandy, a certain amount of the English mystery had disappeared from our great national festive dish.

That *le plum-pudding n'est pas Anglais* was a startling discovery made by a French chef, Philéas Gilbert, round about the turn of the century. No, not English indeed. In this case le plum-pudding had been almost Greek. What I wish I'd known at the time was the rest of Gilbert's story. It seems that with a passing nod to a Breton concoction called *le far* 'obviously the ancestor of the English pudding', an earlier French historian, Bourdeau by name, unable or perhaps unwilling to claim plum pudding for France, says that it is precisely described by Athenaeus in a report of the wedding feast of Caranus, an Argive prince, The pudding was called *strepte*, and in origin was entirely Greek.

CHRISTMAS PLUM PUDDING

I still have noted on a torn envelope the outlines of that recipe, in Greek measurements, as I used it thirty years ago on the island of Syros. I have never made the pudding again, and since some relevant details such as the quantity of candied peel and spices appear to be missing, I shall quote another recipe which seems to me to be similar. It comes from one of those collections popular in Edwardian days, made by the lady of the household in collaboration with her cook and friends. The author, Miss Eleanor Jenkinson, kept house for her father, the Rev. John Jenkinson, at Ocklye, Crowborough. Most of her recipes are on a fairly modest scale. The lavishness of the Christmas pudding simply indicates that housekeepers in those pre-1914 days would not bother to make festive puddings in niggling quantities – but note that no sugar is required. (The recipe for Brandy Butter is on p. 88.)

'Two pounds and a quarter of stoned raisins, two pounds and a quarter of currants, six ounces of finely-chopped candied peel, thirteen eggs, one pint and a half of milk, one teacupful and a half of breadcrumbs, one pound and a half of flour, one pound and a half of finely chopped suet, three wineglasses of brandy, two wineglasses of rum.

'Mix these ingredients well together, put into buttered basins, and boil for fourteen hours. This quantity makes two large puddings.'

The Ocklye Cookery Book, Eleanor L. Jenkinson, 1909

MINCEMEAT

Christmas mincemeat and Christmas plum pudding and cake are all such typical examples of the English fondness for spiced fruit mixtures that it seems almost unnecessary to include recipes for them in this little book. It so happens though that I have been asked many times for a good mincemeat recipe, so perhaps an interesting one is not all that common. This is the one I use. The friend who passed it on to me was very insistent that bought shredded suet should not be used. It would prevent the mincemeat from keeping, so she told me. I am afraid that I disobeyed her instructions and used bought packet suet. (Shredding suet is a terrible task. I cannot make myself spend so much time and effort on it.) The first batch of mincemeat I made using ready-prepared suet kept for five years.

The last jar *was* a bit dried out. I added more brandy and it came back to life.

The ingredients are: 1½ lb. sharp apples; ¾ lb. stoneless raisins; ¾ lb. currants; ¼ lb. mixed peel; ¾ lb. suet; ¾ lb. sultanas; 2 oz. skinned and coarsely chopped almonds; ½ teaspoon each of grated nutmeg, cinnamon, mace; ¾ lb. sugar; rind and juice of 1 lemon and 1 orange; ½ gill (2½ oz.) of brandy or rum.

Wash and dry all fruit. Chop the peeled and carefully cored apples. Mix all ingredients well together, adding brandy last.

Fill stoneware jars and tie them down with thick grease-proof paper, or alternatively pack the mincemeat into glass preserving-jars with screw or clip-on tops.

This amount makes approximately 6 lb. of mincemeat.

PARHAM CHEESE-LOAVES

From an unpublished manuscript book of recipes from Parham, the Sussex house which was for long owned by the Curzon family, descendants of Robert Curzon, famous traveller and author of *Monasteries in the Levant**, comes this variation of the cheese-cake, which is original and delicious. It has a warm flavour, and requires no pastry.

In the original wording 'Take Cheese Curds and white bread grated, yolks of Eggs, Clove, Mace, Nutmeg, mix them well together, sweeten it to Yr. taste with fine sugar, then take some stone porringers. Butter 'em and put in the curd. Bake them but not too much. When they're baked, turn them out and cut a little hole on the Tops and draw Butter up thick and put in them. Set them in the oven again a little to rise and colour them. Serve them.'

The proportions I use are as follows: to a pound of sieved curd cheese, 2 oz. of white breadcrumbs, 2 oz. of sugar, 5 or 6 yolks very well beaten, and about half a teaspoon each of nutmeg and mace, rather less of ground cloves, and a teaspoon of salt. As for stone porringers, it is not difficult to devise a

*1839.

substitute – small soufflé or pie dishes, dariole moulds, ramekins, or even one large charlotte tin. Fill the buttered tin or tins by only four-fifths.

For small sizes allow approximately 20 minutes baking, for one large one, 35 to 40 minutes, at gas No. 4, 370°F.

With a modern oven the second cooking is not really necessary as the loaves will be sufficiently risen, but what is important with all cheese-cake recipes is to have very dry cheese, or moisture will come out during cooking and spoil the texture of the finished dish.

N.B. For a smaller quantity proportions are 4 oz. of white cheese, 2 oz. of white bread soaked in 4 tablespoons of milk, 2 oz. of sugar, 2 whole eggs. This amount will fill a half-dozen 2 oz. oval dariole moulds, which are the ones I prefer for these little cheese loaves.

Above all, *forget not the salt.*

Many of the Stuart period cookery books give recipes for cheese loaves similar to that in the Parham Ms. The following one is dated 1658. A porringer seems to have been commonly used as a measuring vessel, particularly for curds.

TO MAKE LOAVES OF CHEESE-CURDS

'Take a Porringer full of Curds, and four Eggs, whites, and yolks, and so much flower as will make it stiff, then take a little Ginger, Nutmeg, & some Salt, make them into loaves and set them into an oven with a quick heat; when they begin to change Colour take them out, and put melted Butter to them, and some Sack, and good store of Sugar, and so serve it.'

The Compleat Cook, 1658

SPICED CREAM CHEESE

The idea for this sweet dish stems from the recipe for Parham cheese-loaves, given on page 213. This version is uncooked and very quickly made.

Ingredients are ½ lb. of cream cheese or of home-made milk cheese (not commercial cottage cheese, and not any of the demi-sel tribe); ¼ teaspoon each of ground mace, cloves and freshly grated nutmeg, and salt; 1 tablespoon of sugar; cream to pour over the sweet just before it is served.

Work the spices, salt and sugar very thoroughly into the cream cheese. If it is very dry, add a little milk or cream.

Wring out a piece of muslin in cold water, put it into a cheese-draining mould (a pierced earthenware, china or metal mould), turn the cream cheese into the lined mould.

Leave the cheese overnight, with the mould standing on a plate.

Next day unmould the cream cheese into a soup plate or dish of similar depth, over it pour just enough cream (¼ pint should be sufficient) to cover the cheese and give it a smooth and completely veiled appearance.

Serve caster sugar separately. This is for the crunchy bite of the sugar which is so attractive in conjunction with the soft cream cheese rather than for extra sweetness.

Enough for three to four people.

An alternative way of presenting this cream cheese is to mould it in individual heart-shaped moulds – also muslin lined. Turn them out, and present them on a big flat dish.

CREAM CHEESE AND HONEY PIE

For the pastry: 4 oz. flour, 2 oz. butter, about 3 tablespoons of very cold water.

Crumble the butter into the flour, make it into a soft light dough with the water. Roll into a ball, then spread it into an 8 inch removable-base flan or tart tin, patting it into place with your fingers.

For the filling: 6 oz. of double cream cheese, ¼ pint of milk or thin cream, 4 tablespoons white sugar, a teaspoon each of grated lemon peel and cinnamon, 4 teaspoons of honey, 2 whole eggs.

Beat the cream cheese until smooth, adding the milk or

cream gradually. Then stir in the sugar, lemon peel, cinnamon, honey (warmed if stiff) and lastly the beaten eggs.

Pour this mixture into the pastry case, stand the flan tin on a baking sheet and cook in the centre of a preheated moderately hot oven, gas No. 5, 375°F, for about 45 minutes. After the first 15 or 20 minutes look to see if the top is browning too fast. If so, cover with a round of buttered greaseproof paper which should be ready prepared.

SNOW CHEESE

All the spiced and salt food described in this book would be very boring, and bad for our stomachs if we made entire meals every day of these dishes. A little relief is provided by sharply aromatic lemon-flavoured dishes such as this one, and the lemon solids which follow.

This lovely sweet dish is not strictly a cream cheese, but the system on which its confection is based is very similar to the French *crémets*. Recipes for snow cheese occur in English cookery books certainly as far back as the mid-seventeenth century, and possibly earlier. My own recipe is based on one from an early Victorian Ms. in my possession.

Three quarters of a pint of double cream, 4 oz. of caster sugar, 1 lemon, 2 egg whites.

Pour the cream into a large bowl; stir in the sugar, the grated peel of the lemon, and its strained juice. Have also ready a round sieve or a cheese mould standing over a plate and lined with a piece of muslin wrung out in cold water.

Whisk the cream mixture until it stands in peaks. Don't overdo it or it will turn to a grainy mess. Fold in the stiffly whipped egg whites. Turn into the lined sieve. Leave to drain overnight. Turn out on to a shallow dish.

Serve the snow cheese with plain wheaten biscuits or crisp ice wafers.

LEMON SOLIDS

These creamless lemon confections are a cross between a lemon curd and lemon jelly. They have a sharp refreshing flavour and served in syllabub, custard or other small glasses they make a pretty and inviting array.

Four sheets of leaf gelatine – or 1 oz. of powdered gelatine – 1 pint of hot water, 3 oz. of caster sugar, 2 large lemons (peel and juice), 4 egg yolks, 4 tablespoons of sherry.

Cut the leaves of gelatine into strips, put them in to a saucepan and pour the hot water over. Leave to soak for 15 minutes at least. For gelatine crystals the soaking process is the same.

Grate the peel from the lemons – for this job there is on the market a special and very effective little knife – add it with the sugar to the water and gelatine. Heat very slowly without allowing it to boil.

Have ready the egg yolks, the lemon juice and the sherry beaten together, in the blender if you have one. Pour a little of the sugar-and-water mixture into the egg yolks and lemon juice. Stir or beat again. Return to the main mixture in the saucepan and stir again over very low heat until the eggs have thickened very slightly.

Strain the whole mixture into a jug. Stir until it has cooled. Pour into jelly glasses or custard cups. There should be enough to fill eight. Leave overnight in a cold larder or in the refrigerator. The little confections should be just set, not rock-like or rubbery.

DEVONSHIRE JUNKET

Why is junket always looked upon as a dish for children? To me, the slippery mass of curdled milk was rather frightening, and the whey underneath positively repellent. Nowadays I find junket rather delicious. The cool, white, shiny curd is soothing, its slipperiness somehow enticing. In fact the very qualities which put me off as a child are the ones which now commend the dish to me.

One thing seems fairly sure, and that is that the following recipe, given by Georgiana, Lady Dudley, in *The Dudley Book*, 1909, was not intended for the nursery. Lady Dudley's lavish hand with the brandy or whiskey (this is how she spells it) gives us a new view of the innocent junket. The finishing touch of grated nutmeg seems to be an essentially English tradition. Brandy butter, rice pudding and milk punch are among dozens of other confections calling for the same ritual sprinkling of spice. In many countries, powdered cinnamon would take the place of the nutmeg.

'A large wineglassful of best pale brandy, or whiskey, in a glass dish. Add a quart of new milk just warm, a little pounded sugar to taste, and one and a half tablespoonsful of rennet (Stone's almond-flavoured is best), stir it altogether and leave it to cool. It must not be moved for twenty minutes. Then fill up the dish with thick cream, and dust a little grated nutmeg over the top. It can be served after it is cool.'

TO MAKE A JUNKET

'Take Ewes or Goats milk, if you have neither of these, then take Cows-milk, and put it over the fire to warm, then put in a little Runnet to it, then pour it out into a dish, and let it cool, then strew on Cinnamon & sugar, then take some of your aforesaid Cream* and lay on it, scrape on sugar and serve it.'

A True Gentlewoman's Delight, The Countess of Kent, 1653

*The 'aforesaid Cream' is a kind of scalded milk, heated in 'a wide earthen pan till it begin to heave in the middle, then take if off, but jog it as little as you can, then put it into a room where it may cool, and no dust fall into it, this Milk or Cream you may keep two or three days.'
The recipe is entitled 'How to scald Milk after the Western fashion'.

ALMOND RICE

'One quart of new milk, four even tablespoonfuls of Carolina rice, lemon rind, essence of almond, two ounces of ground almonds, and fifteen lumps of loaf sugar.

'Put the milk in a double saucepan; add to it the rice, three pieces of very thin lemon rind, the sugar, and half a teaspoonful of essence of almonds. Boil very slowly for four hours, stirring occasionally. Five minutes before removing from the fire add two ounces of ground almonds. Stand for a few minutes in cold water, and when cool pour into a silver dish and sprinkle with powdered cinnamon, and decorate with whole almonds.'

The Gentle Art of Cookery, Mrs C. F. Leyel and
Miss Olga Hartley, 1925

HOW TO MAKE A PIPPIN TART

'Take fair Pippins and pare them, then cut them in quarters and core them, then stew them with Claret-Wine, Cinnamon and Ginger, let them stew half an hour then pour them out into a Cullender, but break them not, when they are cold, lay them one by one into the Tart, then lay on Sugar, bake it, ice it, scrape on sugar, and serve it.'

A True Gentlewoman's Delight, The Countess of Kent, 1653

TO MAKE A CLOSE TARTE OF CHERRIES

This recipe is something of a curiosity. I include it because the mustard, cinnamon and ginger would make a mixture similar to the cherry sauce given on page 72. Muscadine was a sweet wine, probably Cretan, and damask water is rose water.

'Take out the stones, and laye them as whole as you can in a Charger, and put Mustard in Synamon and ginger to them, and lay them in a Tarte whole, and close them and let them stand three quarters of an houre in the Oven, then take a sirrope of Muscadine, and damask water and suger, and serve it.'

The Good Huswife's Jewell, Thomas Dawson, 1585

To make Black Tart Stuff

'To a dozen pound of Prunes take half a dozen of Maligo⁄* Raisins, wash and pick them clean, and put them into a pot of water, set them over the fire till all these are like pulp, and stir them often lest they burn to, then take them off, and let them be rubbed through a hair Sive hard with your hands, by little and little, till all be through, then season them to your taste with searced† Ginger.'

A True Gentlewoman's Delight, The Countess of Kent, 1653

TOMATO COMPOTE

When the potentialities of the tomato were first explored it was often used for sweet dishes as well as for sauces and soups. Italian children used to be given tomato paste, solidified and sun⁄dried to a deep mahogany colour, as a sweetmeat. Late⁄ nineteenth⁄century cookery books nearly all include recipes for a tomato jam. Escoffier gives a couple, and in England an eight⁄volume *Encyclopedia of Practical Cookery*, published in 1899, gives a formula for candied tomatoes, several for jam, and another for green tomatoes to be stewed in a sugar syrup and eaten cold with cream. Evidently, even tomato soups were heavily sweetened. A booklet put out in 1900 by the Franco⁄ American Food Company of Jersey City made the point that its tinned tomato soup was a spiced rather than a sweet soup, 'and our increasing sales of this variety show that it suits the taste of the majority', although sugar could be added 'when desired'.

Although slightly strange, tomato jam is a most delicate and attractive preserve, with the charm of the unfamiliar. Tomato

* Malaga   † literally, sieved: in our terms, powdered.

compote, evolved (by me) from the *Practical Cookery* recipe is also, admittedly, odd, and I think very good. A trial costs little. It is made with whole tinned tomatoes, preferably the very small round variety from Bulgaria, sold at about 2s. 6d. for a 32 oz. tin. There are also excellent and cheap Roumanian tinned tomatoes.

Put the contents of the tin into a colander, strain off most of the juice and keep it for soup or sauce (from a 32 oz. tin there will be a good half pint). Weigh the tomatoes and an equal quantity of caster sugar.

Make a syrup by boiling the sugar with ¼ pint of water to the pound for a minute or two. Tip in the tomatoes. Simmer them gently in the syrup for about 30 minutes. They should remain whole and identifiable. Skim, add the juice of half a lemon. Serve very cold, with thin pouring cream. In a plain white china or clear glass bowl the tomato compote looks irresistible. It has something oriental about its appearance and flavour, and goes well after a curry or spiced kebabs. It is very sweet, so a little goes a long way.

HOT CHESTNUTS AND PRUNES

'Peel, blanch and boil till tender a pint of chestnuts. In another saucepan stew one pound of prunes (which have been soaked overnight) with enough water to cover them. Drain the prunes, reserving the juice. Mix the prunes and the chestnuts, adding a little powdered cinnamon, sugar and lemon juice. Moisten with the prune juice, add a wineglassful of sherry, and serve hot in a silver dish.'

The Gentle Art of Cookery, Mrs C. F. Leyel and Miss Olga Hartley, 1925

APPLE GRASMERE

I don't know if this is, properly speaking, a traditional English dish, but Grasmere Gingerbread, on which the crust is based, is a variety of shortbread rather than real gingerbread which is certainly well known in the Lake District, and the friend who gave me this recipe was brought up in that part of England. Anyhow the combination of the soft apple purée with the light crisp crust is excellent; it is known in my household, I am sorry to say, as Lady Windermere's Flan.

First core, peel and slice 3 lb. of cooking apples, and stew them almost to a purée with 6 oz. of white sugar and a quarter pint of water. Leave them to cool.

Put the apples in a fairly deep pie dish, or a round or oval earthenware or fireproof glass dish which can be brought to table. Capacity should be 2½ to 3 pints.

Prepare the following mixture: crumble 4 to 5 oz. of softened butter with 8 oz. of sieved flour; add 2 oz. each of soft light brown Barbados sugar (not Demerara) and white caster sugar, a pinch of bicarbonate of soda, and a teaspoon of powdered ginger. Cover the apples lightly with this mixture, levelling it out with a palette knife but without pressing it down. Bake in the centre of a moderate oven, gas No. 4, 350 to 355°F., for 30 minutes. The crust should be the palest biscuit colour, and the pudding is served cold.

These quantities make ample helpings for six people.

In the summer this pudding is delicious made with raspberries, which do not however, need pre-cooking. Simply put 1 lb. of the fresh fruit in the dish and sprinkle a little white sugar over it before spreading the shortbread mixture on the top.

CINNAMON ICE CREAM

The idea for this rather unexpected recipe came from that vast compendium, *Cassell's Dictionary of Cookery, circa* 1880. To judge by the measurements given in the Cassell's volume, the original recipe was of much earlier date.

The cinnamon makes an interesting and attractive flavour for an ice cream.

Put 1 pint of double cream, 4 oz. of white sugar, and ¼ oz. (approximately 3 level teaspoons) of powdered cinnamon in the top half of a double boiler, or in a bowl fitting into a deep saucepan. Heat over gently simmering water. Beat together, preferably in a blender, 4 egg yolks and ½ pint of milk. Amal-gamate the two mixtures, and continue the steady cooking until you have obtained a fairly thick custard. Strain into a deep jug or bowl. Chill in the refrigerator before freezing.

CINNAMON TOAST

This is English buttered toast, crustless, dripping with butter and liberally sprinkled with cinnamon and sugar.

Cinnamon toast used to be a sustaining tea-time treat for hungry Oxford undergraduates. The college scouts were the great experts at preparing the delicacy. As I remember, the toast was cut into fingers, and kept warm in a covered muffin dish.

Owing to a childhood association of cinnamon-flavoured hot drinks administered as cold cures, cinnamon toast was no favourite of mine. Now I find it delicious, and a splendid sustainer of energy when writing or other work makes the cooking of a proper meal impossible.

CHOCOLATE CHINCHILLA

This is a splendid – and cheap – recipe for using up egg whites left from the making of mayonnaise, béarnaise or other egg-yolk based sauces. It is also a dish which demonstrates how excellent is the combination of chocolate with cinnamon. This flavouring stems from the sixteenth century, when the Span-iards first shipped the product of the cocoa bean from South America to Spain. Chocolate, both drinking and eating versions, spiced with cinnamon is still sometimes to be found in Spain, and also I believe in Mexico, although almost everywhere else cinnamon has long been superseded by vanilla as the favourite aromatic for flavouring chocolate.

Ingredients are 5 to 7 egg whites, 2 oz. of unsweetened cocoa powder, 3 oz. of caster sugar, 1 heaped teaspoon of ground cinnamon.

Mix together the cocoa, sugar, and cinnamon. Whip the egg whites to a stiff snow. Tip the cocoa and sugar mixture on to the egg whites. Fold the two together, gently but thoroughly. A large metal spoon or a wide flexible spatula are the best implements to use for this operation.

Have ready a buttered ring mould, kugelhopf, or best of all a steamed pudding mould with a central funnel and clip on lid. Austrian and German cooks use these moulds for all puddings and cakes in which there is a high content of whisked egg white. The central funnel helps enormously in the even distribution of heat throughout the mixture, which in a soufflé dish or plain mould tends to remain moist in the centre for some minutes after the rest of the pudding is cooked. Whatever mould is used for this recipe, the capacity should be approximately 1½ to 2 pints.

Having filled your mould with the prepared mixture, stand it, uncovered (for this particular recipe the lid of the mould is not necessary) in a baking tin with water to reach halfway up the dish or mould.

Cook the chinchilla – which is really a kind of soufflé without egg yolks – in the centre of a moderate oven, gas No.3, 330°F., for about 45 to 50 minutes. It will rise in a spectacular manner. But since it is to be eaten cold, it will sink in an even more spectacular fashion unless, when taken from the oven, it is left to cool in a warm place, protected from draughts and sudden changes of temperature. When cold, the pudding, although shrunk, will have become compact enough to turn out easily. It will have a good texture and a very rich dark colour.

With the chinchilla serve fresh thin pouring cream to which has been added a little sherry, rum or brandy.

*

Cinnamon, by the way, varies a good deal in strength. If it has been kept for a long time in your kitchen cupboard, you may find that one heaped teaspoon is not enough to flavour the chocolate.

FRITTERS OF ELDER-FLOWER

'Take some elder-flowers and pound them in the mortar, mix them with cream cheese and grated Parmesan, fresh eggs, a pinch of cinnamon, a few drops of rose water. Work the lot into a paste and then form little round cakes or balls.'

'Fry in butter, serve hot with sugar sprinkled on the top.

'(Popular in the seventeenth century, and not so bad as it sounds.)'

Venus in the Kitchen, Norman Douglas, 1952

THICK PERKINS

'14 oz. flour, 2 oz. oatmeal, 1 dessertspoonful ground ginger, 1 teaspoonful mixed spice, 1 small teaspoonful carbonate of soda, 4 oz. brown sugar, 4 oz. butter, 8 oz. treacle, 2 eggs, a little milk.

'Mix together the flour, oatmeal, ginger, spice and soda. Then put in a pan the sugar, butter, and treacle, and make these hot. Beat up the eggs in a little milk and mix with the ingredients in the pan. Then add the mixture of dry ingredients, but do not let the final mixture get too soft. Put into a flat tin, filling to the depth of 1 inch only, and bake for $\frac{1}{2}$ hour in a slow oven.'

A Book of Scents and Dishes, Dorothy Allhusen, 1927

DARK GINGER CAKE

This excellent recipe came to me from my partner, Renée Fedden, who tells me that it is one which found uncommon favour with her daughters and their school friends. The recipe is based on one from that delightful book *Au Petit Cordon Bleu* by Dione Lucas and Rosemary Hume, published in 1936.* I have simply added one or two details.

Ingredients are $\frac{1}{2}$ lb. plain flour, $\frac{1}{4}$ lb. each of butter and dark

*J. M. Dent & Sons Ltd.

soft Barbados sugar, 2 whole eggs, 10 oz. of black treacle, 2 oz. each of preserved ginger in syrup and sultanas or stoneless raisins, 1 teaspoon of ground ginger, ½ teaspoon of bicarbonate of soda, 2 tablespoons of milk.

The tin for this cake is an ordinary round English one, 3 inches deep, 6 inches in diameter, and 2 pint capacity.

Set the oven to gas No. 3, 330°F.

Beat the softened butter to a cream. Add the sugar and amalgamate thoroughly. Then beat in the eggs. Now put in the flour, pour in the treacle, then add the sultanas or raisins (dusted with a little flour, so that they are dry), then the preserved ginger removed from its syrup and cut into little slices, then the ground ginger. Finally, the milk should be very slightly warmed, and into this stir the bicarbonate of soda. Add this to the cake mixture.

Have your cake tin ready buttered and floured, turn the mixture into it, put it to cook in the centre of the oven, with a baking sheet on the shelf. Leave for 1 hour. Now turn the oven down a little, to gas No. 2, 310°F., cover the top of the cake with a piece of greaseproof paper (if you use the non-stick kind called Bakewell there is no need to butter it) and leave for another 45 minutes.

When you take the cake from the oven leave it for about 5 minutes before turning it out, upside down, on to a cake rack to cool.

A moist, rich and very dark cake.

N.B. The best way to measure treacle is to coat the pan of your weighing scales with a little flour, then pour in the treacle. This way it will not stick to the pan. If you have to measure the treacle by guess work a little more or less will cause no disaster – and if you buy it in 1 lb. tins, then it is not too difficult to judge when you have poured out about two-thirds of it.

If you like a really squidgy ginger cake then reduce the cooking time by 15 minutes.

* *

Savouries

A FEW months after Norman Douglas died in February 1952
his last work was published. It was a cookery book called
Venus in the Kitchen,* a collection of allegedly aphrodisiac
recipes. I use the word allegedly because, as I knew very well
from the comments he let drop about it during the last few
months of his life, the book was intended more as a spoof or
a send-up than as a serious work on the powers of aphrodisiac
foods. Belief in such things was to Norman just another
example of the boundless extent of human credulity, to be
treated with the joyous tolerance he showed towards nearly
all such foibles.

As far as the recipes in his book were concerned, I
sure that Norman had never cooked
that he often set saucepan to stove
to being a kitchen technician. H
he wanted to go into his saucep
the wines, the herbs, the fr
truffles, white and black, w
of ancient Rome and Gree
was gifted also with a
ordinary capacity for the
cordials and stimulants
rose and cinnamon,
cooked with dried
saffron, cinnamon
and were certainly
to be taken seriou
intend, although

*Heinemann,
Siren Land, 1911
1923.

verse, that they had actually worked, he would have been delighted.

Two of the recipes from *Venus in the Kitchen* are reproduced below and others are on pages 225 and 246.

TONGUE SAVOURY

'Take a piece of boiled smoked tongue. Pound it in the mortar together with a piece or two of preserved ginger and a few leaves of sage; flavour with French mustard. Coat with this paste some slices of toast and serve.'

Venus in the Kitchen, Norman Douglas, 1952

ANCHOVY TOAST

'Cut some slices of bread, toast nicely, trim to any shape required. Have ready a hot-water plate, on which put four ounces of butter; let it melt; add the yolks of four raw eggs, one tablespoonful of anchovy sauce, Nepaul pepper* to taste. Mix all well together, and dip the toast in, both sides; let it well soak into the mixture. Serve very hot, piled on a dish, and garnished with parsley.

'Anchovies have long been famed for their lust-provoking
es.'

Venus in the Kitchen, Norman Douglas, 1952

IS AU PARMESAN
rmesan Cheese

d about the length of an anchovy in good
lf of an anchovy, with the bone upon
them some Parmesan cheese grated
in an oven, or with a salamander,
or lemon, and pile them up in

'This seems to be but a trifling thing, but I never saw it come whole from table.'

The Cook's Paradise, William Verral, Master of the White-Hart Inn in Lewes, Sussex, Sylvan Press, 1948. First published 1759

POTTED CHEESE

Originally regarded as no more than a thrifty way of storing surplus cheese for household use, the old recipes are coming back into use as methods of giving flavour, character and improved texture to the factory cheeses which have so little personality of their own.

Most successful of potted cheeses are the ones made with Roquefort (Boulestin's recipe for Roquefort, worked with butter and a very little Armagnac, is one of the best cheese mixtures ever invented), Stilton, Gorgonzola and other blue cheeses. Proportions of fresh butter to cheese vary according to the fat content of the cheese to be used. As a rough and ready guide, 2 oz. of butter to ½ lb. of cheese is about the right quantity.

For potted Gorgonzola or Stilton simply work the butter and cheese together until the whole mass is smooth and creamy. Add a couple of teaspoonfuls – no more – of brandy or Armagnac and a scrap of cayenne.

Many recipes advocate the addition of Port to potted blue cheeses. In my experience this is a mistake. Port is, as we know, an excellent wine to drink *with* cheese. *In* the cheese it is over-powering – and produces an unappetizing purplish tinge.

For potted cheddar, grate the cheese on a coarse grater before working it with the butter. Flavourings of made mustard, freshly milled pepper, cayenne, mace, or nutmeg, are improve-ments; so are small quantities of grated Parmesan, or, to make a creamier mixture, demi-sel cream cheese. An infinitesimal quantity of Madeira gives a subtle flavour to Cheddar and Cheshire mixtures. This is a hint from the celebrated Hannah Glasse's *Art of Cookery Made Plain and Easy,* 1747. A quarter pint (5 oz.) of Canary* to 3 lb. of cheese, ½ lb. of butter and

½ oz. of powdered mace is Mrs Glasse's formula. She adds that 'a slice of this exceeds all the cream cheeses that can be made.'

Small quantities of potted cheese for current consumption need not be sealed. For long storage, pack potted cheese into wide jars and cover as usual with clarified butter.

THICK PARMESAN BISCUITS

A little-known recipe from *The Cookery Book of Lady Clark of Tillypronie*, compiled from a treasure-house of notebooks left by Lady Clark and published in 1909, nine years after her death. As is inevitable in books compiled from cookery note-books, Lady Clark's recipes are often sketchy. It is for the ideas, the historical aspect and the feeling of authenticity, the certainty that these recipes were actually used and the dishes successful – or they would not have been recorded – that the book is so valuable.

This recipe is an exceptionally good one. With the help of a friend, I once made a huge batch of them for an Anglo-Greek wedding party held in my London house. Smoked salmon and chicken sandwiches made with the home-baked bread of the house, and an immense pyramid of the delicate Greek short-bread cakes called *kourabiedes* made by the bridegroom's mother, Greek sugared almonds, and an English cake (bought) comp-leted a quite notable although extremely simple wedding buffet.

For a dozen biscuits: ¼ lb. plain flour, 2 oz. each of butter and grated Parmesan, the yolk of one egg, salt, cayenne pepper.

Rub the butter into the flour, add the cheese, egg and season-ings. Moisten with a little water if necessary. Roll out the dough to the thickness of half an inch. Cut into 1 inch diameter rounds. Arrange on a baking sheet. Bake in the centre or lower centre of a very moderate oven, gas No. 2, or 310–330°F., for just on 20 minutes. Serve hot.

Lady Clark makes the point that it is the *thickness* of these

*A wine said to have been similar to a dry Madeira.

biscuits that gives them their character. The Parmesan is also essential. English cheese will not do.

The biscuits can be stored in a tin and heated up when wanted.

BREAD AND BUTTER, SALT AND NEW WALNUTS

'Thick slices of a new household bread – the round, flat *pain de ménage*; all the better when a little wood ash from the oven bottom still clung to the underside, were spread thickly with cream butter and studded with halves of fresh walnuts, peeled of their thin bitter skin and sprinkled with freshly ground coarse crystal salt.

'Enough to make a gourmet out of any child.'

The Taste of Madeleines, Eileen Culshaw, 1963

SALTED ALMONDS

With drinks, the cashews and peanuts of commerce make wretched substitutes for salted almonds; and salted almonds, whatever the promises held out by the words vacuum-sealed or oven-fresh on tins and jars are not to be bought. They must be prepared at home, and on the day they are to be eaten. Five or six hours after the almonds come out of the oven they are at their best. Within twenty-four hours they have already lost their pristine freshness. It is, goodness knows, easy to prepare almonds for salting. They cost half the price of salted almonds in jars or tins and taste twice as good.

If blanched whole almonds are not to be found, the skinning process is a matter of minutes. Plunge the almonds into boiling water. When the water has again boiled, turn the almonds out into a colander. While they are still warm, slip off the skins. This part of the operation can be done in advance.

All that is needed apart from the blanched almonds is an oven, a baking tin, kitchen salt and kitchen paper, and, if possible, a tiny phial of sweet almond oil bought from the chemist, and cayenne pepper in a sprinkler. Butter, very highly refined olive oil or deodorized ground-nut oil will pass instead of almond oil. Corn oil, with its detestable taste and greasy cling, will not pass for this, nor so far as I am concerned, for any other purpose whatsoever.

It was a Sudanese cook called Suliman who cooked for me in Egypt who discovered how the best salted almonds are made. Suliman used not more than a teaspoonful of almond oil or butter per half pound of blanched almonds, and it does not matter whether Valencia or Jordan almonds are used. What you do is to put the prepared almonds in a baking tin rubbed with the oil or butter. The tin then goes into the centre of a very slow oven (the oven in my Cairo kitchen was a tin box perched over a primus stove. The magic of this primitive device can be very well reproduced with any gas, solid fuel, or electric oven at a temperature of approximately gas No. 2 or 210°F.) and there leave it for about 45 minutes until the almonds are pale toast colour. Have ready on the table a sheet of greaseproof paper and some perfectly ordinary kitchen block salt (about three tablespoons to the half pound) or if you prefer, *gros sel*. Free-running table salt is to be avoided for this purpose. Empty the toasted almonds on to the paper. Swish them round in the salt. Gather up the corners of the paper and twist them so that you have a tightly fastened little parcel which you put away in a drawer, or in the kitchen cupboard. This part of the ritual is not so much a matter of witchcraft as of plain common sense. In my experience, it is necessary to conceal salted almonds from all eyes until the appropriate time comes for them to be produced. Nothing yet invented so sets the gastric juices to work as the sight of a plateful of freshly toasted and salted almonds. Even to say the words or see them written does the trick. (Whoever thought of calling the cocktail bar at the old Trocadero the *Salted Almond* knew a thing ot two.) Left where anybody can see them, a pound of salted almonds will be devoured within fifteen minutes.

When therefore the moment to set out the almonds arrives, unwrap the parcel, shake the almonds free of excess salt and over them shake an infinitesimal sprinkling of cayenne pepper.

There is very little question of salted almonds left over from one evening being produced again the next. There never are any left over. Should there be, re-toast them in a slow oven – but they will not be the same. Suliman used to put any left over into a rice dish. And he could not be persuaded to make salted almonds in a hurry. He held it essential to give them their few hours in the salt. He was right. The important points about salted almonds are that they must be so dry from the slow toasting in the oven that they squeak as you bite into them; at the same time they must be salty in taste but not to the extent that their own flavour is killed.

Chutneys and Pickles

BOULESTIN FALLS IN LOVE WITH ENGLISH FOOD

'I had meals in all sorts of places, hotels, restaurants, tea shops and taverns. The food struck me as good when English, indifferent when pretending to be French. But I made two discoveries: mint sauce and Indian curry. I think I am one of the very few French people who genuinely likes mint sauce. As for curry I had a beautiful one at Romano's where it was then prepared once a week by a Hindoo. I secured the recipe for both preparations.

'After a perfect fortnight I returned to Paris full of intense and confused memories, a tin of curry powder, hundreds of cigarettes, a marvellous greenish-brown rain-proof, several ties and the feeling that I must learn English and come again every season.'

*

'At St Aulaye in September I tried to make my father appreciate the charms of London and English cooking. Marvellous steaks and chops, I said, and the grill shining, sparkling behind a glass screen.

'"Not better than this bifsteak," said my father, "I am sure . . ."

'I took refuge in my exotic dishes. The curry was on the whole a success because in the south-west spicy cooking is liked, but the mint sauce!

'"Do you mean to say," said my father, "that they really eat mint with lamb?"

'I said they did and that it was delicious. He shook his head thoughtfully.

'"What a funny country!" he said. "Now a little garlic inserted near the bone . . ."

'My trouble was the mint. I had not been told what kind of mint

234

was wanted, so I tried the gardeners; they had never heard of it, mint is not cultivated in French gardens. I tried the country, exploring streams and marshes, found some wild mint and did the best I could. It was not the right flavour. I did not know then that there are many kinds of mints and that the one which is used for the sauce* does not grow wild.'

Myself, My Two Countries, X. M. Boulestin, 1936

PUMPKIN AND TOMATO CHUTNEY

It is not generally known that pumpkin can make an excellent chutney, rich and dark. The recipe below produces a mixture with a taste which is spicy but not too sharp; the pumpkin slices retain something of their shape, and shine translucently through the glass jars.

Greengrocers very often sell pumpkins by the piece at about a shilling a pound. A whole one is of course cheaper, but remember that once it is cut it will not keep longer than about ten days.

Ingredients are a 2½ lb. piece of pumpkin (gross weight), 1 lb. of ripe tomatoes, ½ lb. onions, 2 oz. of sultanas, ¾ lb. each of soft dark brown sugar and white caster sugar, 2 tablespoons of salt, 2 scant teaspoons each of ground ginger, *black* pepper-corns and allspice berries, 2 cloves of garlic, 1¼ pints of white, red or rosé wine vinegar or cider vinegar.

Peel the pumpkin, discard seeds and cottony centre. Slice, then cut into pieces roughly 2 inches wide and long and ½ inch thick. Pour boiling water over the tomatoes, skin and slice them. Peel and slice the onions and the garlic.

Put all solid ingredients, including spices (crush the pepper-corns and allspice berries in a mortar) and sugar, in your preserving pan. (For chutneys, always use heavy aluminium, never untinned copper jam pans.) Add vinegar. Bring gently to the boil, and then cook steadily, but not at a gallop, until the mixture is jammy. Skim from time to time, and

---

* Common spearmint, *mentha spicata*, is the one ordinarily used for mint sauce.

towards the end of the cooking, which will take altogether about 50 minutes, stir very frequently. Chutney can be a disastrous sticker if you don't give it your full attention during the final stages.

This is a long-keeping chutney, but, like most chutneys, it is best if cooked to a moderate set only; in other words it should still be a little bit runny; if too solid it will quickly dry up.

Ladle into pots, which should be filled right to the brim. When cold cover with rounds of waxed paper, and then with Porosan skin or a double layer of thick greaseproof paper. Transparent covers which let in the light are not suitable for chutney.

The yield from these quantities will be approximately $3\frac{1}{2}$ lb.; and although it may be a little more extravagent as regards fuel and materials, I find chutney cooked in small batches more satisfactory than when produced on a large scale.

It is worth noting that should it be more convenient, all ingredients for the chutney can be prepared, mixed with the sugar and vinegar, and left for several hours or overnight (but not longer than 12 hours) in a covered bowl before cooking.

SPICED QUINCES

Peel and core the quinces, cut each into about 8 pieces. Cover them with cold water and add a small handful of coarse salt. Boil quickly for ten minutes and strain. To each pint of this juice add a pound of white sugar, $\frac{1}{4}$ pint of Orleans or wine vinegar, and a teaspoon of whole coriander seeds; bring to the boil, put in the fruit and simmer until the slices are tender. Next day drain off the syrup, bring it to the boil, pour it back over the quinces packed into preserving jars, and screw or clip down the covers while still warm.

These spiced quinces are excellent to eat with boiled bacon, cold or hot, with pork, with mutton, and with cold turkey.

It is worth noting, especially now that quinces have become rather rare and unfamiliar to English cooks, that the fruit is at its best when picked slightly unripe and left to mature in a warm kitchen. When the fruit is yellow and the scent – it is unmistakable – is fully developed, cook the quinces without further delay. If left too long the flesh becomes cottony, does not absorb the sugar, and gives a dry leathery preserve.

Spiced quinces keep a long time.

ESCOFFIER'S PIMENTO CHUTNEY

Unexpected recipes from authors regarded as classic are always interesting, provided one knows and trusts the taste of that author. I have to confess that in this respect I do not invariably feel confidence in Escoffier – I find for example that his fruit and ice cream dishes are unnecessarily recherché and fussy, although it must be allowed that the over-working of food and a professional reluctance to present a peach, a nectarine, a pear or a bunch of muscat grapes as nature made them was the tendency of Escoffier's time. A point about his work which it is more rewarding to remember is that he was a Provençal who was born and spent his early boyhood in Villeneuve-Loubet in the Alpes Maritimes. One has the impression from his post-*Guide Culinaire* books and from articles written for professional publications that he did not ever entirely lose the taste for the village cooking of his very humble childhood and that sometimes he was bored – as who is not by his own public image – with exquisite subtlety and the standards of perfection he had himself created, and had wistful hankerings for the primitive food of his childhood. Today's interest in all regional cooking and in particular in the dishes of his own native Provence would surely have been welcome to him.

I do not know whether Escoffier's sweet pepper and onion mixture, a cross between a chutney and a sauce to be eaten with cold meat, was derived from a Provençal recipe – it is a little reminiscent of the Italian *peperonata* – whether he evolved it from some other source, or invented it entirely. It is an uncommonly interesting and unusual sauce; Escoffier calls it simply *piments pour viandes froides* and the recipe is to be found in his *Ma Cuisine*,* published by Flammarion in 1934, the year before the author's death at the age of eighty-nine. This Escoffier sauce, one which evidently never found its way into the bottles of the Peckham factory he founded in 1898 is one which became a favourite of mine during the years I lived in Egypt. The ingredients were all to hand, cheap and common, and the sauce was a great enlivener for the local meat. My own slightly simplified and reduced version of the recipe is no longer quite that of Escoffier.

You need 2 large, fat, fleshy, sweet and very ripe red peppers (about 1 lb. gross weight), ½ lb. of mild Spanish onions, 1 lb, of ripe tomatoes, 1 clove of garlic, ¼ lb. of raisins, half a tea-spoon each of salt, powdered ginger (or grated dried root-ginger) and mixed spices such as allspice, mace and nutmegt ½ lb. white sugar, 4 tablespoons of olive oil and ¼ pint of fine wine vinegar.

Melt the finely chopped onions in the olive oil, add the chopped peppers (well washed, all core and seeds removed), salt and spices, and after 10 minutes the peeled and chopped tomatoes and the raisins, garlic and sugar; lastly the vinegar. Cook extremely slowly, covered, for at least one hour and a quarter.

A tall marmite-type pot rather than a wide preserving pan should be used for the cooking of this confection. The sauce does not, and I think is not supposed to, turn into a jam-like substance. It is an iridescent bronze dish, *mordoré* to use the marvellous French word.

Bottled in screw-top jars the mixture keeps well for two or three weeks, although I have never made enough at one time to report as to whether it has a more enduring shelf life. It is good with cold lamb and salt beef.

*There is now an English translation. See p. 251.

SWEET-SOUR MELON PICKLE

Made with honeydew melon, this is a most delicious and unusual pickle to serve with all the cold meats and poultry of the Christmas season, and is also excellent with curry.

For an average size honeydew melon weighing about 4 lb. when bought, about 3 lb. when skin and pips have been removed, the other ingredients are ½ pint of mild wine vinegar or Orleans vinegar, 1½ lb. of preserving or other white sugar, a couple of teaspoons of pickling spice tied in a twist of muslin.

Pare the melon thinly. Cut in half, throw away the seeds, slice the fruit, then cut it in cubes roughly 1½ inches wide by ½ an inch thick. Bring a large wide pan of water to the boil, throw in the melon, and as soon as the water comes to a full boil again, remove the fruit with a perforated spoon to a colander to drain, then plunge it all into a bowl of cold water. When it has cooled, bring the vinegar to a full boil. Put in the strained melon, and cook it in the vinegar for 2 minutes after the vinegar has come back to the boil. Then pour all into a large china or glazed stoneware bowl, cover when cold, and leave for 48 hours. At this stage, the melon takes on a somewhat sinister aspect. It looks dull and jammy. During the second cooking it will clear, and all will be well. Strain off the vinegar, bring it to the boil with the sugar and the little bag of spices, and simmer 15 minutes removing the scum as it rises. Put in the melon, boil 3 minutes, and then take out the melon with a perforated spoon and pack it into preserving jars. Extract the bag of spices. Give the syrup a final boil and a skim. When cool pour it over the fruit, filling the jars quite full. Screw or clip down the lids when cold.

Leave for at least a fortnight before broaching the jars. This pickle keeps exceptionally well, even after a jar has been opened.

MILD GREEN TOMATO CHUTNEY

2 lb. green tomatoes, 2 lb. cooking apples, ½ lb. onions, 1¼ lb. brown sugar, 1 lb. stoneless raisins or sultanas, 2 teaspoons each of ground ginger, allspice and crushed black pepper-corns, 2 cloves of garlic, 2 tablespoons of salt, approximately 1½ pints Orleans or white wine vinegar.

Peel the apples and onions and slice them. Put them, with the chopped tomatoes,* raisins, sugar, spices, salt, and garlic into a saucepan. Moisten with a little of the vinegar; cook gently, adding the rest of the vinegar as the chutney boils down, for about an hour. Towards the end, stir constantly, for as they thicken chutneys catch very easily. When the mixture is of a jam-like consistency it is ready.

Pour into warmed jars. When cold cover with thick grease-proof paper so that the light is excluded.

A long-keeping chutney.

PICKLED EGGS

A most useful preparation, particularly in summer when a few hard-boiled eggs come in so handy for a quickly made salad, or as an accompaniment to cold meat. Eggs pickled in vinegar are a familiar sight in English country pubs.

Boil a dozen very fresh eggs quite hard. Shell them. Put them in a large glass or stone jar. Boil just under 2 pints of white or rosé wine vinegar or cider vinegar with 2 tablespoons of mixed pickling spice for 5 minutes. When cold, pour the vinegar, spices included, over the eggs and cover the jar. It is customary to leave the eggs a couple of weeks or so before broaching the jar, but in fact you can eat them as soon as you like.

An outsize glass-stoppered sweet jar is the ideal receptacle

---

*If you have the time, skin the tomatoes. To do this, pour boiling water over them, leave them for a few minutes, and peel them with a sharp knife. This small extra trouble makes a perceptible difference to the finished chutney.

for pickled eggs. Failing this, use a stoneware jar with a lid. Jars with metal screw tops are always to be avoided where vinegary preparations are concerned.

N.B. Duck eggs are not suitable for this recipe.

MANGO CHUTNEY

Although we cannot make mango chutneys in England we consume quantities, most of them imported in bulk and packed for sale under names echoing the days of the British *Raj* – Major Grey, Colonel Skinner, Bengal Club and the like.

According to the old recipes, these chutneys were not cooked. The fruit, onions, salt, spices, sugar and vinegar were mixed in jars, corked down, and left out in the sun until matured. The following recipe from *Indian Domestic Economy* (Madras, 1850) is a typical one:

'Green mangoes peeled and minced fine half a seer,* green ginger two ounces, garlic three ounces, dried chillies ground and mixed with vinegar sufficient to moisten it well, eight ounces; sugar and salt eight ounces of each; mix all well together, put it into a jar or bottle corked close out in the sun for a fortnight, and stir it occasionally. Obs. – Ten good-sized mangoes when peeled and sliced are equal in weight, or nearly so, to an English pound.'

SWEET MANGO CHUTNEE

A more modern method than the one described in the Madras book is given in *The Indian Cookery Book* by 'A Thirty-Five Years' Resident' – published in Calcutta in 1944.

This recipe would produce something much more like the sweet chutney we know in England than the former recipe, which calls for an enormous quantity of hot chillies.

'Ingredients: A hundred mangoes, peeled and sliced, two seers of tamarinds stoned, the syrup of six pounds of sugar

* A seer is the equivalent of a kilo, or approximately 2 lb.

boiled in three quarts of vinegar, one tablespoonful of finely-pounded cinnamon, two pounds of salt, two pounds of sliced ginger, two pounds of cleaned and picked raisins, three quarts of vinegar, and one dessertspoonful of grated nutmeg.

'Peel the mangoes, cut them into fine slices, and steep them in salt for thirty-six hours; drain away the salt water, and boil them in the three quarts of vinegar; when cool, remove them into a preserving pan, mix in all the condiments and other ingredients, and allow the whole to simmer for half an hour, pouring in the syrup gradually and mixing all the time, until the vinegar and syrup have been absorbed, and the chutnee has acquired the desired consistency; bottle and cork when perfectly cold.'

LEMONS PRESERVED IN SALT

Steep four whole large lemons in cold water for three days, changing the water daily. Now cut the lemons in quarters, pack them in a wide glass or stoneware jar – avoid porous earthenware – with a level tablespoon of sea salt or *gros sel* to each lemon. Press a double thickness of greaseproof paper directly over the lemons, and on top put a 2 lb. weight or a smooth clean stone. In warm weather the jar should be kept in the refrigerator.

At the end of a week the salt and the juice drawn from the weighted lemons are on the way to forming a preservative brine. Remove the paper and the weight, cover the jar, keep it in a cool place or, to be on the safe side, in the refrigerator. The lemons should be left for another two to three weeks to mature but if urgently needed, can be used at once.

It is the peel and pith rather than the flesh of salt lemons which give the characteristic pungent and sharp tang to dishes such as the spiced chicken quoted from *Moorish Recipes* on p. 195. Very small slivers of salt lemon, both peel and flesh (remember to remove the pips) make a refreshing addition to a salad of shredded lettuce, diced onion and mint.

* *

Beverages

OFTEN quoted as an example of the quaint and uncertain rules by which our ancestors cooked – a sauce to be stirred 'an Ave Maria while' – a soup to be 'boiled simpringly' – the posthumously published *Closet of the Eminently Learned Sir Kenelm Digby Knight Opened, Published with his Son's Consent 1669*, has been in other respects underestimated. There is no call for condescension where Sir Kenelm Digby's writing is concerned. His book is a beautiful piece of English kitchen literature as well as a collection of recipes set down with considerable accuracy, for Sir Kenelm had a sharp eye for detail. The book is also a document of great historical interest.

It was Sir Kenelm's evident mania for the brewing of mead, metheglin, hydromel and such-like popular drinks of the Stuart period that was the undoing of his reputation as a cookery author. As arranged for publication (possibly by a man who had been his steward), the book opens with upwards of one hundred receipts for Digby's favourite brews, based on honey, home-made ale, highly spiced and flavoured with all the herbs and flowers of seventeenth-century English gardens and hedgerows. The instructions and lists of ingredients are repetitive and few readers persevere beyond the first half-dozen receipts. Were the forbidding blocks of print divided up, as they can be without in the slightest respect altering the punctuation or the flow, into verse form, it would be seen that like all the best recipes, these are runes, litanies, something even of magic spells. They should be read aloud:

To make White Metheglin

'Take Sweet-marjoram, sweet-bryar-buds,
Violet-leaves, Strawberry-leaves,
of each one handful,
and a good handful of Violet flowers
(the dubble ones are the best)
broad Thyme, Borrage, Agrimony,
of each half a handful,
and two or three branches of Rosemary,
the seeds of Carvi,* Coriander, and Fennel,
of each two spoonfuls,
and three or four blades of large-mace.
Boil all these in eight Gallons of running-water,
three quarters of an hour.
Then strain it, and when it is but blood-warm
Put in as much of the best honey
As will make the Liquor
bear an Egg the breadth of six pence above the water.
Then boil it again as long as any scum will rise.
Then set it abroad a cooling;
and when it is almost cold,
Put in half a pint of good Ale-barm†;
And when it hath wrought
till you perceive the barm to fall,
Then Tun it,
and let it work in the barrel, till the barm leaveth rising,
filling it up every day with some of the same Liquor.
When you stop it up, put in a bag
with one Nutmeg sliced,
a little whole Cloves and Mace,
a stick of Cinnamon broken in pieces,
and a grain of good Musk.

*Caraway.   †A form of yeast.

You may make this a little before Michaelmas
and it will be fit to drink
at Lent.

*

'This is Sir Edward Bainton's Receipt
Which my Lord of Portland who gave it me
Saith,
Was the best he ever drunk.'

Appended to another of his extraordinary repertory of
recipes for 'meath', metheglin, and hydromel, Sir Kenelm
Digby gives this explanation of his 'handfuls' of herbs:

*'The handfuls of Herbs, are natural large handfuls (as much as you
can take up in your hand) not Apothecaries handfuls, which are much
less. If a pottle* of Barm do not make it work enough to your mind, you
may put in a little more. Discretion and Experience must regulate
that.'*

SANGAREE

'1 sherry glass Madeira, ½ pint water, 1 lime, a pinch of nutmeg,
sugar to taste, ice.
'Squeeze the juice of the lime into the Madeira and water,
mix in the sugar and nutmeg, add the ice and serve in a long
glass.
'For 1 person.
'*Source*: A traditional eighteenth-century Barbadian middle-
of-the-morning or luncheon drink, as now served at the
Bridgetown Club.
'An eighteenth-century Sangaree glass originally made for
the owner of the Windsor Plantation, Barbados, and inscribed
'Success to Windsor', was the wedding-present of the women
and girls of Barbados to H.M. Queen Elizabeth II.'

The Tenth Muse, Sir Harry Luke, 1962

*A half-gallon measure.

HIPPOCRAS APRHRODISIAC

'Here is the recipe for this unrivalled stimulant:

'Crushed cinnamon	30 grammes
Ginger	30 grammes
Cloves	8 grammes
Vanilla	8 grammes
White sugar	2 pounds
Red Bourgogne wine	1 quart'

Venus in the Kitchen, Norman Douglas, 1952

TEA WITH EGGS

'The Jesuite that came from China, Ann. 1664, told Mr Waller, That there they use sometimes in this manner. To near a pint of the infusion, take two yolks of new laid eggs, and beat them very well with as much fine Sugar as is sufficient for this quantity of Liquor; when they are very well incorporated, pour your Tea upon the Eggs and Sugar, and stir them well together. So drink it hot. This is when you come home from attending business abroad, and are very hungry, and yet have not conveniency to eat presently a competent meal. This presently discusseth and satisfieth all rawness and indigence of the stomack, flyeth suddainly over the whole body and into the veins, and strentheneth exceedingly, and preserves one a good while from necessity of eating. Mr Waller findeth all those effects of it thus with Eggs. In these parts, He saith, we let the hot water remain too long soaking upon the Tea, which makes it extract into it self the earthy parts of the herb. The water is to remain upon it, no longer that whiles you can say the *Miserere* Psalm very leisurely. Then pour it upon the sugar, or sugar and Eggs. Thus you have only the spiritual parts of the Tea, which is much more active, penetrating and friendly to nature. You may from this regard take a little more of the herb; about one dragm of Tea, will serve for a pint of water; which makes three ordinary draughts.'

> *The Closet of The Eminently Learned*
> *Sir Kenelm Digby Knight Opened*, 1669

Angelica: *Yes, I saw you together, through the keyhole of the closet, one night, like Saul and the witch of Endor, turning the sieve and shears, and pricking your thumbs to write poor innocent servants names in blood, about a little nutmeg grater, which she had forgot in the caudle cup . . .'*

> *Love for Love*, William Congreve, 1695

A caudle was a hot drink, usually ale, spiced, thickened with eggs, and with the ritual grating of nutmeg on the top. The Countess of Kent's caudle, spiced with mace instead of nutmeg is as follows:

To make a caudle

'Take Ale the quantity that you mean to make, and set it on the fire, and when it is ready to boil, scum it very well, then cast in a large mace, and take the yolks of 2 eggs, for 1 Mess, or one draught, and beat them well, and take away the skin of the yolks, and then put them into the Ale, when it seetheth, be sure to stir them well till it seeth again for a youngling, then let it boil a while and put in your Sugar, and if it be to eat, cut three or four toasts of bread thin, and toast them dry, but not brown, and put them to the caudle, if to drink put none.'

> *A True Gentlewoman's Delight*, The Countess of Kent, 1653

TURTLE LADY CURZON

Under this notable name, and presumably created in honour of the lady* who was Vicereine of India from 1899 to 1905, a concoction of turtle consommé, curry powder and cream is –

*Both the first and second Lady Curzon were of American birth.

or was – to be found on the menus of British-owned trans-atlantic liners (the Queen Elizabeth for one) and has now, I see, found its way, with full dress treatment, into the pages of the American *Gourmet* magazine. Say what you like, there is something impressive about a recipe entitled Basic Lady Curzon Soup.

Should you really feel a need – a basic one – to throw curry powder into your tinned turtle consommé (called soup on the label) then I suggest that the curry powder, no more than a half teaspoonful to a half pint of consommé, be first warmed on an iron pan or in the oven, stirred into the hot consommé, left there for a minute, and then strained out. As for the cream, unless you like your soup to look like English office tea, add it separately at the table.

I have included this recipe in the beverage section because it seems to me that it is a restorative or a substitute for a hot meal, rather than a consommé or soup for dinner, although I learn from *Gourmet* that at a famous Vienna restaurant called *Am Franziskanerplatz* Lady Curzon soup is always served in thimble-sized cups. At the current price a tin which normally yields two teacups of turtle consommé, thimbles would indeed seem to be indicated.

* *

Bibliography and Reading List

FIFTEENTH CENTURY

Two Fifteenth-century Cookery Books: Harleian MS. 279 (ab. 1430) and Harleian
MS. 4016 (ab. 1450) with extracts from Ashmole MS. 1439, Laud MS.
553, and Douce MS. 55: Edited by Thomas Austin. Published for the
Early English Text Society by the Oxford University Press, London, New
York, Toronto. First published 1888, reprinted 1964

SIXTEENTH AND SEVENTEENTH CENTURY

A compendyous regyment of a dyetary of helth, made in Moñtpylior: compiled by
Andrewe Boorde, of Physicke Doctor, *circa* 1562
The Good Huswife's Jewell: Thomas Dawson, London, 1585
Delightes for Ladies: Sir Hugh Plat, London, printed by Peter Short, 1st edition
circa 1600. Reprinted by Crosby Lockwood and Son Ltd, London, 1948
The English Hus-wife: Gervase Markham, London, 1615
A True Gentlewoman's Delight: Countess of Kent, London, W. G. Gent. 1st
edition 1653 printed by R. Norton
The Compleat Cook: London, Nath. Brook at the Angel. 1st edition 1655
The Queens Closet Opened . . . transcribed by W. M. London. Printed for
Nathaniel Brook at the Angel in Cornhill. 1st edition 1655
The Accomplist Cook: Robert May. 1st edition 1660, London. Printed by R.
W. for Nath. Brook at the sign of the Angel in Cornhill
The Closet of the Eminently Learned Sir Kenelm Digby Knight Opened, London.
1st edition 1669, London, printed by E. C. for H. Brome. Reprinted by
Philip Lee Warner, 1910

EIGHTEENTH CENTURY

The Compleat Housewife: or Accomplish'd Gentlewoman's Companion: E. Smith,
London. Printed for R. Ware, S. Birt, T. Longman, C. Hitch, J. Hodges,
J. & J. Rivington and M. Cooper. 15th edition 1753. 1st edition London
1727
The Modern Cook: Vincent la Chapelle, London, Thomas Osborne, 1733
The Art of Cookery Made Plain and Easy: Mrs Hannah Glasse, London, printed
for the author 1747, 6th edition 1758, 9th edition 1765. London

The Receipt Book of Elizabeth Raper, and a portion of her Cipher Journal. Written 1756–70. First published London, the Nonesuch Press, 1924

The Diary of a Country Parson 1758–1802: James Woodforde, Passages selected and edited by John Beresford, London, O.U.P., World's Classics edition, 1963

The Cook's Paradise: A Complete System of Cookery, William Verral, London, printed for the Author and sold by him: As also by Edward Verral, Book seller, in Lewes; and by John Rivington in St Paul's Church yard, London, 1759. Reprinted by the Sylvan Press, 1948

The London Art of Cookery: John Farley, Principal Cook at the London Tavern, London, 1783, 4th edition 1787.

The Housekeeper's Instructor: or Universal Family Cook: W. A. Henderson, London, J. Stratford. First published *circa* 1795, 12th edition 1805

Dorset Dishes of the 18th Century: Compiled and edited from manuscript receipt books by J. Stevens Cox, F. S. A. Dorchester, The Dorset Natural History and Archaeological Society, 1961

NINETEENTH CENTURY

A Complete System of Cookery: John Simpson, London, W. Stewart, 1806

A New System of Domestic Cookery: Mrs Maria Eliza Rundell, London, printed for John Murray, Fleet St., J. Harding, St James's Street, and A. Constable & Co. Edinburgh, 1806

The Cook and Housewife's Manual: Mistress Margaret Dods (Christina Jane Johnstone). Edinburgh, Oliver & Boyd. London, Simpkin and Marshall, 1826

The Cook's Dictionary: Richard Dolby, late cook at the Thatched House Tavern, St James's St., new edition 1832.

Modern Cookery for Private Families: Eliza Acton, London, Longman, Brown, Green & Longman's, 1st edition 1845

The Best of Eliza Acton: Edited by Elizabeth Ray, with an introduction by Elizabeth David, London, Longman, 1968

Indian Domestic Economy and Receipt Book: By the author of 'Manual of Gardening for Western India'. 1st edition 1849. 2nd edition, revised, 1850

Gastronomic Regenerator: Alexis Soyer, London, Simpkin Marshall & Co., 4th edition 1847. First published 1846

Shilling Cookery for the People, Alexis Soyer, London, Geo. Routledge & Co., 1855

Le Cuisinier Européen: Jules Breteuil, Paris, Garnier Freres, 1860

Mrs Beeton's Book of Household Management: Edited by J. Herman Senn, London, Ward Lock, 1906. First published 1861

Gunter's Modern Confectioner: William Jeanes, Chief Confectioner at Messrs Gunters, Confectioners to her Majesty, Berkeley Square. London, John Camden Hotten. First published 1861

The Art and Mystery of Curing, Preserving, and Potting all Kinds of Meats, Game, and Fish: A Wholesale Curer of Comestibles, J. R., London, Chapman & Hall, 1864

Good Cookery: Lady Llanover, London, Richard Bentley, 1867

The Indian Cookery Book: A Thirty-five Years' Resident. Calcutta, Thacker, Spink & Co., 1944. 1st edition 1869

Le Grand Dictionnaire de Cuisine: Alexandre Dumas, Paris, Alphonse Lemerre, 1873

Culinary Jottings for Madras: 'Wyvern' (Col. Kenney Herbert), Madras, Higginbotham & Co., 5th edition 1885. First published 1878

Cassell's Dictionary of Cookery: London & New York, Cassell, *circa* 1885

The Pytchley Book of Refined Cookery and Bills of Fare: Major L. —., London, Chapman and Hall. 1st edition 1885

Breakfast, Luncheons and Ball Suppers: Major L. —., London, Chapman and Hall, 1887

Law's Grocer's Manual: Compiled and arranged by James T. Law, London. Sold by Gilbert and Rivington Ltd. 2nd edition *circa* 1892

TWENTIETH CENTURY

Hilda's 'Where is it?' of Recipes: Hildagonda J. Duckitt, London, Chapman and Hall. 2nd edition 1903

Potter's New Cyclopaedia of Botanical Drugs and Preparations: R. C. Wren, F.L.S. Re-edited and enlarged by R. W. Wren, M.P.S., F.L.S., F.C.S. London, Sir Isaac Pitman & Sons, for Potter and Clarke, 1956. 1st edition 1907

The Cookery Book of Lady Clark of Tillypronie: London, Constable, 1909

The Ocklye Cookery Book: Eleanor L. Jenkinson, Cassell, London, 1909

The Dudley Book: Georgiana, Lady Dudley, London, Edward Arnold, 1909

The Book of Herbs: Lady Rosalind Northcote, London, The Bodley Head, 1912

Cookery for Every Household: Florence Jack, First published 1914. London, T. C. and E. C. Jack Ltd, 1931

A Garden of Herbs: Eleanour Sinclair Rohde. First published *circa* 1919. Reprinted New York, Dover Publications Inc., 1969

The Gentle Art of Cookery: Mrs C. F. Leyel and Olga Hartley, London, Chatto and Windus, 1925

The Magic of Herbs: Mrs C. F. Leyel, London, Jonathan Cape, 1926

A Book of Scents and Dishes: Collected by Dorothy Allhusen, London, Williams and Norgate. 1st edition 1926

Herbs, Salads and Seasonings: X. M. Boulestin and Jason Hill, London, Heinemann, 1930

The Pleasures of the Table: Sir Francis Colchester-Wemyss, Welwyn, Herts, James Nisbet, 1931. Reprinted 1962

Good Things in England: Edited by Florence White, London, Jonathan Cape, 1951. 1st edition 1932

Good Food: Ambrose Heath, London, Faber & Faber, 1932, reprinted by Neville Spearman, 1965

Ma Cuisine: A. Escoffier, Paris, Ernest Flammarion, 1934, English translation by Vyvyan Holland, London, Paul Hamlyn, 1965

Farmhouse Fare: Countrywise Books, 1st edition 1935, 6th edition 1963

Myself, My Two Countries: X. M. Boulestin, London, Cassell, 1936

Sussex Recipe Book, with a Few Excursions into Kent: M. K. Samuelson, London, Country Life, 1937

The Englishman's Food: a History of Five Centuries of English Diet: J. C. Drummond and Anne Wilbraham, London, Jonathan Cape, 1957. 1st edition 1939

Au Petit Cordon Bleu: Dione Lucas and Rosemary Hume, London, J. M. Dent, 1939

Wishful Cooking: Emily Lina Mirrlees and Margaret Rosalys Coker, London, Faber, 1949

A Book of Mediterranean Food: Elizabeth David, Penguin, 1969. 1st edition London, John Lehmann, 1950

French Country Cooking: Elizabeth David, Penguin, 1969. 1st edition, London, John Lehmann, 1951

Venus in the Kitchen: Norman Douglas, London, Melbourne, Toronto, W. Heinemann, 1952

Italian Food: Elizabeth David, Penguin, 1969. 1st edition London, Macdonald, 1954

Food in England: Dorothy Hartley, London, Macdonald, 1954

The Tenth Muse: Sir Harry Luke, London, Putnam, 1954. 2nd enlarged edition 1962

Summer Cooking: Elizabeth David, Penguin, 1969. 1st edition London, Museum Press, 1955

Chinese Cooking: Frank Oliver, London, André Deutsch, 1955

Moorish Recipes: John, 4th Marquis of Bute, K.T., Edinburgh and London, Oliver and Boyd, 1956

Home Baked: a Little Book of Bread Recipes: Cecilia and George Scurfield, London, Faber, 1956

French Provincial Cooking: Elizabeth David, Penguin, 1968. 1st edition, London, Michael Joseph, 1960

Of Herbs and Spices: Colin Clair, London, Abelard-Schuman, 1961

Indian Cookery: Mrs Balbir Singh, London, Mills and Boon, 1961

An Herb and Spice Cook Book: Craig Claiborne, New York, Evanstown and London, Harper and Row, 1963

Home made Cakes and Biscuits: Cecilia and George Scurfield, London, Faber, 1963

Talking about Cakes, with an Irish and Scottish Accent: Margaret Bates, London, Pergamon Press, 1964

Delights and Prejudices: James Beard, New York, Atheneum, 1964. London, Gollancz, 1964

A Baronial Household of the Thirteenth Century: Margaret Wade Labarge, London, Eyre and Spottiswoode, 1965

Herbs for Health and Cookery: Claire Loewenfeld and Philippa Back, London, Pan Books, 1965

The English Silver Pocket Nutmeg Grater: Elizabeth B. Miles. Cleveland, Ohio, 1966

The Thousand Recipe Chinese Cook Book: Gloria Bley Miller, New York, Atheneum, 1966, London, Paul Hamlyn, 1966

Dried Herbs, Aromatics and Condiments: Elizabeth David. Twenty-page booklet published by the author, 46 Bourne Street, London, S.W.1. 1967

English Potted Meats and Fish Pastes: Elizabeth David. Twenty-page booklet published by the author, 46 Bourne Street, London, S.W.1, 1968

How to Cook and Eat in Chinese: Buwei Yang Chao, London, Faber and Faber, 1956

Charcuterie and French Pork Cookery: Jane Grigson, London, Michael Joseph, 1967. Penguin, 1970. U.S. edition entitled *The Art of Charcuterie*, New York, Alfred A. Knopf, 1968

Herbs and Spices: Rosemary Hemphill, Penguin, 1968

A Book of Middle Eastern Food: Claudia Roden, London, Nelson, 1968. Penguin, 1970

The Cooking of the British Isles: Adrian Bailey, New York, Time-Life Books, 1969

South-East Asian Food: Rosemary Brissenden, Penguin, 1969

The Oxford Book of Food Plants: S. G. Harrison, G. B. Masefield and M. Wallis, London, O.U.P., 1969

Chinese Gastronomy: Hsiang Ju Lin and Tsuifeng Lin, New York, Hastings House, published in association with K. S. Giniger Co. Inc., 1969. London edition Nelson, 1969

The Spice Trade of the Roman Empire, 28 B.C. to A.D. 641: J. Innes Miller, Oxford, Clarendon Press, 1969

Middle Eastern Cooking: Harry G. Nickles, New York, Time-Life Books, 1969

The Cooking of Vienna's Empire: Joseph Wechsberg, New York, Time-Life Books, 1969

Indian Cookery: Dharamjit Singh, Penguin, 1970

The International Wine and Food Society's Guide to Herbs, Spices and Flavourings: Tom Stobart, David and Charles, 1970

Some Shops and Suppliers

BRAND NAMES

Although it is no doubt asking for trouble to single out favourite brands of spices, herbs and grocery products, there are now so many, sold at such bafflingly discrepant prices (in an Oxford Street store for example I have seen display racks of American-packed herbs which included a small jar of bayleaves priced at 45p. while on the shelf below was a range of highly reputable English-grown herbs selling at what appeared in comparison to be derisory prices) that it does seem only fair to mention a few which over the years I have found to be reliable.

Among the spices, then, the Canadian-packed *Schwartz* brand are well packed, many of them in sensibly small quantities. Their cayenne is put up in a good shaker, there are small packets of cardamoms, and saffron in a neat little glass jar. *McCormick* spices are good, and widely distributed through supermarkets. Although this company is American-based many of their spices are bought on the London market and packed in this country, only the more fanciful blends such as barbecue seasoning and the like being imported from the States. This company, together with Schwartz, must be given a good deal of the credit for the current revival of interest in spices for household cooking. With subsidiary companies in France, Germany, Holland, Switzerland and Sweden as well as in England, McCormick appear to be the giants of the retail spice industry. The Venetians and the Genoese of the fifteenth century would have envied them their enterprise, their resources and their influence.

Among English-grown dried herbs, the products of the *Chiltern Herb Farm* are excellent, and their spices retail at fair prices. The best Provence herbs on the stalk are packed in cellophane sachets, and are exported by several different growers. Their dried fennel stalks, wild thyme, and bay leaves are particularly aromatic.

Prices of sea salt and rock salt show the wildest of discrepancies. In a kitchen shop or fancy provision store you may well be charged more for a 3 oz. package or jar of Mediterranean salt than you pay in an ungreedy health food shop for a 3 lb. jar of pure Cheshire rock salt. If you want the best value in pure salt for cooking and for the table, this is the one to go for. The producers are Messrs Ingram Thompson, 113 The Albany, Old Hall Street, Liverpool L3 9EY. They will supply a list of stockists on request. Their salt from the Lion Salt Works near Northwich – the last of its kind in Cheshire – is packed in 6 lb. and 3 lb. clear plastic jars, in 2 lb. bags and 1½ lb. blocks. I use it for all my bread as well as for all cooking.

Among flavouring essences, although vanilla beans give the most delicious scent and flavour to creams, ices, and fruit dishes, they are expensive, so for those who use vanilla essence, the American *McCormick* deserves a mention. It is made from pure vanilla, contains no synthetic, and is the only one of its kind distributed throughout the country. The same company produce a pure almond essence, an extract of bitter almonds, so potent that only two or three drops are needed to scent a cake. *The Culpeper House* shop at 21 Bruton Street, London W.1, also lists pure vanilla and almond essences.

Rice is a commodity still little understood in this country. It is regarded as a background filler, rather than as a delicacy in its own right. For those who appreciate this point, the Piedmontese dwarf Vialone or Arborio rice is indispensable for a risotto. By far the best brand currently available is packed and exported by a firm called *Curti*. The white rice rather than the yellow is the one to choose, the latter being a processed variant. A brand called *Soho*, which also packs white as well as yellow rice is a fair second best. When buying long-grain rice for Indian dishes, ask for Pakistani-grown Basmati. The kind sold loose or packed in plain polythene bags is usually the best quality. The smartly packaged varieties are currently less good but do have the great advantage of availability in chain dairy shops and supermarkets.

Among French mustards the brands to look for are *Bocquet, Grey Poupon, Florida, Maille, Vert Pré*. All these are genuine French mustards, mixed in the Dijon manner, although not all are made in or near Dijon. It should not be difficult to learn to discriminate between the authentic French mustard and the English imitations, if only because the latter are so astonishingly unlike the originals. One of the false French mustards however appears all too plausible; it has a French brand name, is packed in a white jar which looks as if it ought to be French, and is the nastiest of the whole lot. True English mustards are rather too biting for my taste, but when English mustard is needed it seems like sense to buy *Colman's* mustard flour and mix it as it is required. *Savora*, although much admired in France, seems to me too sweet and at the same time rather crude. The current craze for mustards containing a proportion of coarsely crushed seeds was triggered off by the extraordinary success of the Pommery *moutarde de Meaux* when in 1970 the producers redesigned their packaging, covering the corks of the stoneware jars with a layer of scarlet sealing wax. The mustard itself also seems to have undergone a change since the days when it was made only in small quantity. It is now too violent for my taste. Some of its imitators are crude in the extreme.

POIVRE VERT

It was the French who launched what is virtually a new spice. This is called *poivre vert* and is exactly what it says it is: pepper which is green in both senses – green because it is the unripe, fresh peppercorn, and green in colour. Soft as a berry, *poivre vert* can be mashed to a paste in a moment, and so has great potentialities for spicing sauces and butters, and for spreading on meat or chicken to be grilled. In French, German and Swiss restaurants it is making its appearance in a variation of *steak au poivre* and, less successfully, with duckling.

Exported from Madagascar and packed in tins or sealed glass jars, several brands of *poivre vert* have now reached the English market. The best come from the Sagrimant company, who tin the green berries in natural juices without preservative. Once opened, the contents should be transferred to a small glass or stoneware jar with a good stopper. Stored in the coldest part of the refrigerator the green peppercorns will keep for about three weeks. Used in discreet quantities they make a delicious and subtle spicing for pork chops and roasts and for chicken. A spiced butter made with two teaspoons of *poivre vert* mashed to a paste with a couple of ounces of butter and a sprinkling of cinnamon is excellent with grilled salmon as well as with steak. Fresh cream heated with a teaspoon or two of crushed green pepper berries and a little parsley makes a simple and delicious sauce for turbot or for a poached chicken.

With pork dishes to be eaten cold, and in pork terrines, a little spicing of green pepper berries is well worth trying. For example, the pork and spinach terrine on page 99 is improved, I think, by the addition to the seasoning of a scrap of crushed garlic and a half dozen or so whole green pepper berries.

Green peppercorns canned or bottled in vinegar are not suitable for any of the dishes described.

DRIED FRUIT

Health-food and wholefood stores are usually the best places to find good quality dried fruit such as dates, prunes, raisins and apricots. (When buying dried apricots take a good look at the label. If sulphur dioxide has been used in the preservation process this must be stated on the packet. Speaking for myself, I would go without, rather than eat the chemically treated variety. This is not a matter of principle. It is one of taste.) Look out for dried whole wild apricots from Afghanistan. Hardly larger than cherries, these apricots are delicate and delicious. Try them in a pilau instead of raisins.

Plain unflavoured yoghourt is another commodity likely to be found in health-food stores, although the French Danone brand, which is quite good, is now widely distributed to delicatessen and provision stores as well as to health-food shops. Among such shops in London, the best known is *Wholefood*, 112 Baker Street, w.1, who have a price list and a limited delivery service. Also in Baker Street, at No. 78, is a branch of *Health Foods*, who have other shops at 12 Gloucester Road, s.w.7, and 137 Kensington Church Street, w.8. The Aetherius Society, 757 Fulham Road, London s.w.6, has a good shop. Addresses of other branches from them.

Most department stores now have special health-food sections or counters, and all over the country the trend is growing. Such departments and shops no longer cater exclusively for cranks and nut-food addicts. They are frequented by an ever-increasing body of customers who are in full revolt against chemicalized foods and the false flavours, the uniform texture and the lack of savour characteristic of mass-produced foodstuffs, chemically grown vegetables, battery-reared poultry and pre-cooked rice. A comprehensive list of health-food shops can be obtained free from the Vegetarian Society, 53 Marloes Road, London, w.8. Telephone 01-937 7739.

PARMESAN CHEESE

Among all the condiments mentioned in this book, genuine Parmesan cheese in the piece is currently the most elusive. Apart from the Soho shops (*Lina Stores*, 18 Brewer Street, w.1, *Henry Camisa*, *Delmonico*, *Parmigiani*, all in Old Compton Street, w.1) the authentic article, at any rate the authentic article in its finest form, is a rarity. No person who has seen and tasted genuine *grana*, as Parmesan is called in its native provinces of Parma and Emilia, could possibly be fooled by the Argentine and other imitations on the market, but how many among the thousands of English holiday visitors to Italy actually go into the shops to take note of local produce?

The finest Parmesan cheeses are considered to be those produced in the district of Reggio Emilia. These, branded with the words 'Parmigiana Reggiano', are the ones to look for. Unfortunately, other Italian producers do not mark their cheeses, and it is not always easy to distinguish between differing qualities. A pale straw/yellow colour, very fine honeycombing, and a craggy aspect are the signs to look for. A waxy grey look and a soapy pink are signs of poor quality, and while the smell of a good Parmesan is sweet and clean and pungent, poor samples are acrid and prickly, akin almost to inferior pepper.

At *Harrod's* of Knightsbridge and at *Paxton and Whitfield* of Jermyn Street, w.1, Parmesan in the piece is usually of a reliable, although not brilliant, quality. The little sachets of ready/grated Parmesan now sold in nine out of ten English grocers' shops are useful as an emergency store. Although the cheese in these packets conveys little idea of the true flavour of a freshly grated and first/rate Parmesan for pasta and risotto, it does serve as a useful condiment.

* *

Acknowledgements

A SUBSTANTIAL part of the material which now appears in this book was first published in the *Spectator* during the years 1961 to 1964. From the properties of saffron and the ingredients of made mustard to odd tales of plum pudding and salted almonds, from the uses of dried herbs to the origins of Cumberland sauce, from the problems arising out of cookery-book weights and measures to the publication of a new oddity in kitchen literature or the emergence of the super-bazaar in our food-shopping lives, articles on any subject connected with cookery were welcomed by the then editors of the *Spectator*. At a time when it was next to impossible to sell a cookery article not primarily concerned with recipes and techni-calities, the attitude of the *Spectator* was imaginative and, as it proved, far-sighted. It is a pleasure to record my gratitude to the editors for the opportunities they then gave me.

Also included in this book are extracts from articles on English sauces which first appeared in *Nova* during 1965, when the magazine was launched, and some brief notes on English cookery writers and their books which were written for leaflets published by Messrs Christopher & Co., the London wine merchants beloved of so many generations.

Here and there in the book are recipes and extracts from articles which originally appeared in *Vogue, House and Garden*, Harrod's *Food News*, the *Sunday Times*, the *Sunday Dispatch*, the *Daily Telegraph*, and *Wine and Food*.

In addition, I would like to make the following acknowledgements for permission to reproduce material in this book:

For four recipes from *Cookery for every Household* by Florence Jack to Thomas Nelson and Sons Ltd, London.

For three recipes from *The Gentle Art of Cookery* by Mrs C. F. Leyel to Chatto & Windus Ltd, London.

For three recipes from *How To Cook and Eat in Chinese* by Mrs Buwei Yang Chao, copyright © 1945, 1949, 1963, 1970 by Buwei Yang Chao. Reprinted by permission of Faber & Faber Ltd, London, and of Random House Inc., New York.

For an extract from *Indian Cookery* by Mrs Balbir Singh to Mills & Boon Ltd, London.

Acknowledgements

For an extract from *Life in a Baronial Household of the 13th Century* by Margaret Wade Labarge to Eyre & Spottiswoode Ltd, London, and to The Macmillan Co., New York.

For an extract from *The Magic of Herbs* by Mrs C. F. Leyel to the Executors of the late Mrs C. F. Leyel.

For two recipes from *Moorish Recipes* by Lord Bute to the Lord Robert Crichton-Stuart, and to Oliver and Boyd Ltd, Edinburgh.

For an extract from *Myself, My Two Countries* by X. M. Boulestin; reprinted by permission of A. D. Peters & Co., London.

For a recipe from *The Taste of Madeleines* by Eileen Culshaw to the author.

For three recipes and one other extract from *The Tenth Muse* by Sir Harry Luke to the author, and to Putnam & Co., London.

For three recipes from *Venus in the Kitchen* by Pilaff Bey, edited by Norman Douglas, to William Heinemann Ltd, London, and to The Viking Press Inc., New York.

Every effort has been made to trace copyright holders but the publishers would be interested to hear from any copyright holders not here acknowledged.

Index

Entries in bold denote recipes

Index

Index

Index

Index

BY THE SAME AUTHOR

Mediterranean Food

A practical collection of recipes made by the author when she lived in France, Italy, the Greek Islands and Egypt, evoking all the colour of the Mediterranean but making use of ingredients obtainable in England.

French Country Cooking

Some of the splendid regional variations in French cookery are described in this book.

French Provincial Cooking

'It is difficult to think of any home that can do without Elizabeth David's *French Provincial Cooking* . . . One could cook for a lifetime on the book alone' – *Observer*

Italian Food

Exploding once and for all the myth that Italians live entirely on minestrone, spaghetti and veal escalopes, this exciting book demonstrates the enormous and colourful variety of Italy's regional cooking.

Summer Cooking

A selection of summer dishes that are light (not necessarily cold), easy to prepare and based on the food in season.

English Bread and Yeast Cookery

Here are breads of all colours and flavours: wholemeal, white, wheatmeal, barley, rye and oatmeal. There are many of our delicious spiced breads, like bara brith and saffron cake; yeast buns such as Chelsea, Bath and Hot Cross; leavened pancakes, muffins, crumpets, pikelets and oatcakes are all described with Mrs David's usual vigour and originality.

An Omelette and a Glass of Wine

'This compilation of Elizabeth David's short pieces on food and wine written over the past thirty years is irresistible' – *Sunday Times*